CONTEMPORARY TOOLS AND TECHNIQUES FOR STUDYING WRITING

STUDIES IN WRITING

VOLUME 10

Kluwer Academic Publishers continues to publish the international book series Studies in Writing, founded by Amsterdam University Press. The intended readers are all those interested in the foundations of writing and learning and teaching processes in written composition. The series aims at multiple perspectives of writing, education and texts. Therefore authors and readers come from various fields of research, from curriculum development and from teacher training. Fields of research covered are cognitive, socio-cognitive and developmental psychology, psycholinguistics, text linguistics, curriculum development, instructional science. The series aim to cover theoretical issues, supported by empirical research, quantitative as well as qualitative, representing a wide range of nationalities. The series provides a forum with research from established researchers, with contributions of young researchers.

Contemporary Tools and Techniques for Studying Writing

Edited by

Thierry Olive
CNRS & University of Paris VIII, France

and

C. Michael Levy
University of Florida, U.S.A.

SPRINGER-SCIENCE+BUSINESS MEDIA, B.V

A C.I.P. Catalogue record for this book is available from the Library of Congress.

DOI 10.1007/978-94-010-0468-8

Printed on acid-free paper

TABLE OF CONTENTS

PREFACE

With some pride I hereby introduce the 10th volume in the *Studies of Writing* book series. This volume aims to be a tool-book for writing research. In my opinion, the editors and authors of this volume succeeded in this endeavor. Four guiding questions are answered in all chapters on online-techniques.

How to... The key to such a book is providing insight in the decisions researchers make when developing 'tools and techniques'; such information is not found in journal articles and in the best case hidden in technical reports. This book provides readers with detailed information about the ins and outs of various online techniques.

*When to...*Another contribution of this tool-book is to provide insight into when the 'tool' can be used, in other words, to relate the tool or technique to the theoretical claims about the writing process or cognitive processes underlying writing processes. Theory, methodology, tools and techniques, handling data and interpretation form a coherent unit.

When not to ... 'There is no cow without a spot' (Dutch: er is geen koe zonder vlekje) is the literal translation of a Dutch expression. Techniques/tools have their limitations, and their problems: in applying them, and/or handling or interpreting the data they produce. In a book like this, researchers took the opportunity to provide readers with a look behind the curtains, in the process of research. Scientific, critical reflection is one of the strong features of this book.

*What to know...*It is not sufficient to only know how the technique works. It is not sufficient to merely know when to apply the technique. Research questions and techniques originate from 'schools of thought', from specific scientific perspectives. Where necessary, this tool-book provides necessary background information and references to underlying theories.

This 10th volume shows how rapidly the tools for studying writing processes were improved. In the first volume of the series, titled Theories, Models & Methodology (1996), some first accounts on methodology were presented. And now, after five years, a complete book, on a particular set of tools, is available. This is one of the synergetic results of the intensive worldwide collaboration, based in the Special Interest Group on Writing of the European Association on Research of Learning and Instruction (EARLI), where researchers from all around the world and all kinds of disciplines found their counterparts.

Gert Rijlaarsdam
University of Amsterdam

Dear Readers,

We would like to invite you to visit the following website:

http://www.psychologysoftware.com

Here you will find almost all the software mentioned in this book
free of charge.

Best wishes,
Thierry Olive & C. Michael Levy

REAL TIME STUDIES IN WRITING RESEARCH: PROGRESS AND PROSPECTS

C. MICHAEL LEVY* & THIERRY OLIVE**

** University of Florida (USA), ** CNRS & University of Paris VIII (France)*

Abstract. The last half of the 20th century provided an opportunity for the explosive growth and development of research on writing. From a product-oriented to a process-oriented approach, new theoretical models of writing emerged. Following this shift in conceptual frameworks, new methods of investigations were applied in research. However, in the context of this development, careful analyses of the literature demonstrate clearly that systematic, theoretically-driven empirical research focused on writing has been barely measurable compared with research on speech production and language comprehension. Methods presented in this book illustrate how the study of writing processes is becoming ever more tractable with the use of real time methods that take advantage of their unobtrusive recordings of the writing process.
Keywords: real time studies, models of writing, writing processes.

1. INTRODUCTION

In the field of writing studies, no development has been mode influential than the process-oriented approach. A rapid glance through the major journals in the field clearly illustrates the changes that followed the shift between the product-oriented approach to the process-oriented approach. This is indeed obvious when one looks at the kind of studies conducted since the publication of Hayes and Flower's (1980) well-known chapter. The number of studies emphasizing the analysis of written texts to understand the composing process drastically decreased.

The short history of writing research illustrates how changes in conceptual framework have an impact on the methods of investigation that are used. The aim of this introductory chapter is to provide an overview of this history by highlighting the coupling between writing theories and tools and techniques for the study of writing. The chapters that follow will give a snapshot of the real time methods that currently accompany the newest conceptions of the writing process and processes.

This chapter is structured in three parts. First, we surround the strange paradox in which writing studies are embedded. Indeed, although writing is an activity in which we all are frequently engaged during our life, psychological research has paid relatively little to the understanding of the writing process. Next, we briefly describe how

C. M. Levy &T. Olive (2001). Real time studies in writing research: progress and prospects. In: G. Rijlaarsdam (Series ed.) & T. Olive & C. M. Levy (Vol. eds.), Studies in Writing: Volume 10: Contemporary Tools and Techniques for Studying Writing, p. 1-8.

methodological investigations of writing have evolved in parallel with new different theoretical approaches of writing. Finally, we give an overview of the chapters presented in this book.

2. THE PARADOX OF WRITING STUDIES IN PSYCHOLOGY

The last half of the 20th century provided an opportunity for the explosive growth and development of research in human cognition and particularly in writing. However, in the context of this development, careful analyses of the literature demonstrate clearly that systematic, theoretically-driven empirical research focused on writing has been barely measurable (Levy, 1997). Even within the domain of language, research on speech production and language comprehension has dwarfed the scholarly work on written language production. That writing has not been a major subject of research by psychologists, despite the fact that their professional recognition depends heavily upon the quality and quantity of their own writing, creates an interesting paradox.

This paradox can be explained partly because writing is clearly one of the most complex activities that people can accomplish. For instance, writing first involves cognitive processes. It engages not only text-related cognitive processes, but also processes involved in multiple cognitive activities, such retrieval from long-term memory, lexical access, defining goals, and so forth. Further, as Faigley (1986) claimed, writing and especially academic writing, involves collaborative and social acts. From this perspective, writing has been studied by paying attention to how the writer is a constituent of a culture and to how writing is inserted in a social space. But writing is also a *mode of learning*, a *discovery process*, and so on. In fact, writing is clearly a multi-dimensioned activity. This surely explains why writing is inherently difficult to study.

The scarcity of research in writing is well illustrated, as Levy (1977) indicated, in the field of human cognition studies where writing has very few connections with other theories of cognitive activities. Surprisingly, studies conducted on discourse production processes have largely ignored what has been discovered in text production research. The same strange phenomenon is observed in text comprehension studies, although research on revision should highlight what happen when one reads a text. In this sense, writing research seems to have developed almost independently from other fields in cognitive psychology.

Nevertheless, an other reason, and perhaps the principal reason, that explains the current paradox derive from the scarcity of tools and techniques that can be used to investigate writing. Indeed, for a discipline that historically has sought cause-effect relationships, isolating the causes of specific written responses (*i.e.*, effects) has been as elusive as finding the Holy Grail. It has been as difficult for researchers to devise methods to study writing processes in isolation as it has been for them to constrain and to assign quantitative values to writers' responses.

An important step for research tools and methods for investigating writing resulted from the changes in theoretical conceptions on writing that appeared in the mid 1970s. A large body of researchers, teachers and scholars began to be concerned with the cognitive processes underlying writing. This resulted in a parallel change in the methods of investigation. The next section describes this theoretical development and the methodological changes that accompanied it.

3. FROM OFF-LINE TO REAL TIMES STUDIES

Before the end of the 1970s, the goal of writing studies was mainly educational. Psychologists conducted studies about writing and its teaching in the way that scholars and students think about composing issues. The main framework that guided these researches was rhetoric. The writing process was conceived in three main stages: pre-writing (searching information and conceiving meaning), then writing and, finally, re-writing. Writing was investigated by looking at factual descriptions of the composition process (biographic information about the writers, correspondences of established and famous writers, journals, prefaces, etc.). Texts were dissected according to the formal descriptive categories of rhetoric (modes of arguments and of discourses) and with respect to texts considered as good or poor following the grammar and usage conventions.

However, during the 1970s, the focus of attention began to shift. Not only conceptions of basic research on writing, but also those of teachers and of scholars. It began to appear that it was impossible to understand what happen in the writer's mind during a composition by looking only at the texts and documents produced by the writers. Taking into account that limit of past studies, the field of writing studies redefined itself. The major aim was now to find out what actually happens when people write – in other words, to discover the cognitive processes that occur during writing (Emig, 1971; Britton, Burgess, Martin McLeod, & Rosen, 1975). This shift from exclusive written products studies to the examination of the writing processes was accompanied with changes in the methodologies of research. Case studies were one of the tools that researchers began to use in order to investigate the procedure in which writers are engaged during composition. More importantly, during this period, writers' verbalizations began to be intensively used following the principles of thinking-aloud protocol analysis proposed by cognitive theorists (Newell & Simon, 1972).

Thinking-aloud protocol analysis was the first new major technique available for studying the cognitive processes involved in writing in the 1980's. With this technique, while composing, writers simply speak aloud about anything that comes to mind. They are explicitly instructed to avoid introspecting. Using this experimental paradigm, Hayes and Flower (1980; Flower & Hayes, 1980) developed their well-known model of writing.

The seminal work of Hayes and Flower actually initiated the experimental process-oriented approach of writing and definitely broke with the product-oriented one. They identified writing as a problem-solving activity engaging several cognitive processes. The conceptual model of writing they proposed was structured in several structural and functional systems. Three main writing processes (Planning, Translating and Revising) were identified that are managed by a particular processor: the monitor. Further, structural parts representing the task environment and the knowledge involved in writing were added in the model. Their model was therefore directly in the line of the conceptual framework delineated by Newell and Simon for the *General Problem Solver* (1972). Hayes and Flower (1980; Flower & Hayes, 1980) thus related writing research to what was at the time a mainstream theoretical perspective in cognitive psychology. Writing was not only considered as a cognitive situation but also, and perhaps mainly, as a problem-solving activity. As Faigley (1986) indicates, the Flower and Hayes model promoted a 'science consciousness' within the writing community, and especially among teachers and scholars.

As writing was now considered in the light of the information-processing paradigm, methods coming from this paradigm could be integrated in composition studies. However, the studies that examined the process of writing as it unfolded in real time came slowly and infrequently. The technology of 1980's had not developed sufficiently for such studies to be feasible in many laboratories.

A major development in writing process research occurred in the last decade of the 20th century, as the desktop computer became ubiquitous and software development tools came to market, enabling those even with modest budgets and computer skills to push the frontiers of writing research ahead dramatically. Complex experiments can now be created and administered, and copious behavioural data can be collected and analysed in sophisticated new ways. Our understanding of the writing process has grown impressively from new real time methods that have been developed, enabling researchers to take full advantage of their capability to unobtrusively make archival recordings of the writing process.

Currently, the main models of writing (Kellogg, 1996; McCutchen, 1996, Berninger & Swanson, 1994) systematically include general components of human cognition. For instance, all three of these models integrate human processing limits by describing the links with working memory. This is particularly obvious in Kellogg's model (1996) where relations between writing processes and the different systems of working memory are detailed. Consequently, research methods initially developed in the studies of working memory are now applied in writing studies. The chapter of Levy and Ransdell (this volume) is an example of such work. Further, low-level cognitive processes are also taken into account. For instance, graphic transcription processes related to the execution of the written texts are also included and kinematic aspects of handwriting can now be measured with the help of digitiser tablets. The same thing happens for the study of low-level lexical processes in writing that were not studied a few years ago. Priming studies developed for speech production research can now be fruitfully used to understand the characteristic of the processes involved in lexical access and in spelling (see Bonin & Fayol in this volume).

With both these new tools and techniques and the integration of principle of cognitive science in writing research, writing processes are thus studied more easily, experimental paradigms can be shared among multiple laboratories, findings can be replicated (or not), and theories of writing can be extended, modified, abandoned, and created anew. The Internet will certainly help to extend and generalize our knowledge in the near future, as writing researchers reach out to the world community for research participants.

Clearly, the study of writing processes is in flux, but it is becoming ever more tractable. The ensemble of chapters in this volume represents a snapshot of the state of the art in writing research methodology at the beginning of the 21st century. Because the research frontier is being advanced with such speed, it would be foolhardy of us to attempt to predict what contemporary methods will be like ten years hence.

Paradigms shift in every discipline. Perhaps the new paradigms will be wholly unlike anything presented in these pages. Undoubtedly, they will be more sophisticated and powerful, but we have every reason that many of them will have evolved from natural extensions of some of those described in this book.

4. OVERVIEW

The tools and techniques described in this book focus only on real-time methods. This was an intentional design decision on our part because, in the last decade, the development of writing theories has occurred primarily as a function of new computer-based methodologies that have enabled researchers to build appropriate new paradigms for understanding writing. Furthermore, this improvement of our understanding of writing has also led researchers to link writing theories with mainstream thinking about cognitive psychology.

We hope this book can be used as a tool book or handbook for investigating writing, either by designing experiments or by studying text production in real-life environments. After reading a chapter, many readers should be able to immediately implement each technique described in the book. This is not to say that some methods (for example, those described by Levy and Ransdell in Chapter 2 or by Kellogg, Olive, and Piolat in Chapter 3) can be used without the user having some computer programming expertise or access to a consultant who has these skills. Nor is it to say that certain methods, particularly Latent Semantic Analysis described by Foltz and Landauer in Chapter 7, cannot be used without significant additional background reading for the reader to establish full competence in the techniques.

Accordingly, this book focuses both on theoretical and methodological questions related to the use of these computer-based techniques and on how to implement them. Each chapter presents the theoretical background that directed the development of the method, the procedure and minimum equipment requirements for conducting a prototypic analysis of writing sessions, some ways to analyse the data obtained with these techniques, and discusses how the basic method can be varied to answer research and/or educational questions.

We have directed the book to a variety of audiences for writing research, but primarily aimed it to those whose objective is to understand the writing process either in laboratory or in traditional applied and field writing contexts. Thus, although the book mainly addresses basic research questions, it may prove to be useful to practitioners (see, for example, Perrin's chapter) and writing instructors (see, for example, Foltz and Landauer's chapter).

The experimental methodologies presented in the following chapters illustrate how recent technological advances have provided new insights about the process of writing and how writing research can be related to current theories in other fields of psychology. The three next chapters (2, 3 and 4) present techniques that allow researchers to collect data about written language production at general level, for example, without investigating one particular processes or type of text. For instance, these techniques and methods provide information about the relationship between writing and the human memory (Chapter 2) or about the dynamic of writing (Chapters 3 and 4).

In Chapter 2, Levy and Ransdell present a memory loading technique they designed to explore the relationship between written language production and working memory as conceptualised by Baddeley and Hitch (1974). They have implemented a dual-task technique that closely mirrors the original methodology used by Baddeley and his collaborators. The particular material of the dual-task Levy and Ransdell present allows researchers to engage specifically only one working memory subsystem at a time (*i.e.*, the central executive, the phonological loop and the visuo-spatial sketchpad). Further, their procedures overcome the criticisms levied at Baddeley *et al.*'s interpretations of his research on human memory. More generally, they enumerate a set of guidelines that researchers may find thought-provoking as they design new memory loading tasks and useful in avoiding pitfalls that occurred in early investigations. To conclude their chapter, Levy and Ransdell describe how their findings provide better insight about the relationship between the different working memory subsystems and the writing processes, and how they extend Kellogg's (1996) model of writing.

In Chapter 3, Olive, Kellogg and Piolat describe the use of reaction times with verbalization – the triple-task technique – to analyse the dynamic of writing, for instance, the time course of the writing processes and their respective attentional cost. In the initial variant of the triple-task technique (Kellogg, 1987a, 1987b) participants are asked to compose a text while they simultaneously perform a reaction time task with a directed retrospection. In Levy and Ransdell's (1994) variant, writers are engaged in a thinking aloud task instead of a directed retrospection. Then, Olive, Kellogg and Piolat present a series of experiments that examine the conditions under which the data collected in dual-task conditions can be interpreted, and, referring to Ericsson and Simon's (1993) research on verbal protocols, they addressed the issue of the reactivity of the thinking aloud task of the technique. Olive, Kellogg and Piolat also review experiments that used the triple task technique. This review examines the effect of knowledge, verbal skill, audience, working memory differences, writing strategies, and medium of production on the time course and cognitive demands of the writing processes. They conclude that writer-specific factors affect mainly cognitive effort (allocation devoted to the writing processes) whereas situation-specific factors have a strong impact on time processing (the temporal organization of the writing processes).

In Chapter 4, Schilperoord analyses the cognitive status of pauses in discourse production. Pauses have long been considered as a fruitful way to explore the underlying temporal structure of language production. In this perspective, Schilperoord considers the empirical status of pauses during writing in light of psycholinguistic research on oral language production. He presents a detailed description of techniques used to sample pause data and how to analyse them. Maintaining that pauses are overt reflections of cognitive processes, Schilperoord argues that pauses reflect mental operations related to formulation and monitoring of language production and particularly that clauses seem to be a relevant unit on which production is based. He discusses how pauses are linked to structural feature of texts and how interpreting pause times, location and scope has to rely on a dynamic model of text production. To conclude his chapter, Schilperoord presents statistical techniques used to analyse pause data. He shows how a mean and frequencies analysis of variance and covariance of pause data allow him to test a cascade model of production in which planning occurs hierarchically at different levels of the text. In sum, Schilperoord provides readers with the criteria that must be met in order to sample data during the writing process, to analyse these data, and to carefully interpret them.

One of the techniques that are proposed by Schilperoord to collect pause data consists in recording the writing activity. The impact of computers has been so increasingly important in the study of writing not only because word processors have become more popular and thus have changed the relation between the writer and the medium of writing, but also because even the simplest word processor allows the recording of all action made by writers. This technique, called keystroke recording, provides data about the content of the text as well as the dynamic of writing by recording temporal parameters of a writing session. The next two chapters (5 and 6) illustrate the use of keystroke recording methods to investigate text revision.

In Chapter 5, Kollberg and Severinson Eklundh show how the understanding of the revision process has been greatly influenced by the development of computerized technology. They present a computer-based tool – S-notation – that provides a better understanding of on-line revisions using keystroke analyses of a writing session. S-notation is a useful procedure that records all typing actions made by writers during a writing session. It facilitates analysis of the distance between revisions and episodes of revisions. Used in combination with S-notation, the Trace-it software represents and provides a mean to explore revisions that occurs during a writing session. For example, it allows moving from revision to revision, replaying the entire writing session and listing all revisions following some criterions specified by the researcher. S-notation and Trace-it are thus instruments that can help to deeply describe individual strategies that writers exhibit.

In this perspective, in Chapter 6, Perrin presents a case study of a professional writer, a journalist. Aimed at analysing writing in the workplace, the computer-aided technique described by Perrin, called Progression Analysis, provides information that combines knowledge of the situation, keystroke analysis, and retrospective interviews to reach an interpretation of writing strategies in their context. Perrin's chapter combines, in a field context, many of the techniques addressed in earlier chapters; particularly S-notation described by Kollberg and Severinson Eklundh in Chapter 5. It also extends to a normative analysis of these strategies, as they appear in a case study, and suggests how news journalists might improve their writing. Perrin principally focuses on the progression of a writing session and thus illustrates how writing occurs in several episodes to adjust to its goal. He argues that episodes of writing in his case study were mainly consequences of coherence problems detected by the writer. Finally, Perrin shows how Progression Analysis helped to discover why problems detected in the text of this journalist were related to the particular writing strategy this writer used. In this sense, Progression Analysis can help to understand how writing unfolds and to help coach professional writers in their workplace.

All techniques and method described in the previous chapters were implemented for the on-line study of text production. However, as Bonin and Fayol argue in Chapter 7, writing also implies lower-level cognitive processes such as those involved in lexical access. Bonin and Fayol present on-line methodologies that have been initially developed for studying spoken language – the picture naming task, the interference paradigm and the priming paradigm – that they adapted to investigate the written production of isolated words. Their goal is to illustrate how these three techniques provide knowledge about the nature of the representation involved in the production of isolated words. By providing examples from spoken and written production experiments, they address issues related to the obligatory phonological mediation in producing isolated words and to the time course of activation of the semantic, orthographical and phonological representations of words. This chapter shows how the study of written language production can benefit from empirical and theoretical data related to the spoken production of language. It thus extends the relations between the study of writing and topics of current concern to mainstream cognitive psychology.

Whereas the previous chapters are principally focused on basic research techniques (except Perrin's Progression Analysis), Foltz and Landauer in Chapter 8 showcase a tool that can be designed both in an applied and basic research context. Foltz and Landauer describe Latent Semantic Analysis (LSA) that serves both as psychological theory of human word learning and as a practical tool for scoring essays, training in summarization, and analysing text coherence and acquisition of knowledge from texts. Numerous automated techniques have been developed for analysing texts, but the main characteristic of LSA is that it generates a representation of the semantic information contained in a text. LSA uses statistical techniques (a form of factor analysis) for extracting relations among words in the text. The similarity between two texts, or two passages of text, or between one text and a prototypical one can be evaluated. Applications of LSA to writing analysis are thus numerous and are just becoming to appear. Landauer and his collaborators have already investigated some of the potentiality of LSA. For instance, they have specifically addressed the issue of essay scoring that may well constitute a crucial topic for the experimental study of written language.

Writing research has often been neglected by cognitive psychologists because of its lack of development of theoretical models. But as we noted earlier in this chapter, this fact is due in great part to the technical and methodological difficulties associated with the study of writing. We hope that this book will represent an important resource for conceptualising and designing new experiments. Particularly, we hope that tools and techniques described should stimulate future research on writing in the next decade and that this will result in finer theoretical models of writing.

WRITING WITH CONCURRENT MEMORY LOADS

C. MICHAEL LEVY* & SARAH RANSDELL**

** University of Florida (USA), ** Florida Atlantic University (USA)*

Abstract. This chapter presents a theoretical context that can guide readers in the development of memory-loading tasks useful for studying written language production. The guidelines for and specific examples of these tasks illustrate how systematic testing can be conducted to evaluate the predictions of a modern theory of writing whose structure and functioning depend upon the involvement of working memory.
Keywords: working memory, concurrent memory load, dual-task paradigm, secondary task, phonological loop, visuo-spatial sketchpad, central executive, theories of writing, *d'*

1. OVERVIEW

For much of the last quarter of the 20th century, during a period when research flourished on the underlying cognitive processes involved in reading, thinking, and problem solving, there was comparatively little scholarly work that focused on the psychological processes of writing. Levy (1997) attributed this imbalance partly to a failure to develop new theories and to extend mainstream theories so that interesting new questions about writing processes might be posed and answered. Another factor that contributed to the imbalance was a paucity of methodologies that researchers could adopt to make systematic studies of writing processes more tractable. Several years ago, the growing international group of European researchers on writing met North American researchers during a Writing Conference in Utrecht (1994). In retrospect, this conference may have been a catalyst for revitalizing global interest in writing processes (Levy & Ransdell, 1996a; Rijlaarsdam, Van den Bergh, & Couzijn 1996a, 1996b). This ensemble provided frameworks for new theoretical conceptions and the results of new methodologies that would have been difficult to imagine before personal computers began to revolutionize how people communicated.

One of our greatest professional challenges was to explore the interface between written language production and contemporary thinking about human memory, especially that component conceptualised as *working memory*. Historically, human memory is an area that has been extraordinarily rich theoretically and empirically. Clearly, writing processes needed access to memory, where rules of orthography and syntax must be stored, together with the individual's mental lexicon and knowledge of the

C. M. Levy & S. Ransdell (2001). Writing with concurrent memory loads. In: G. Rijlaarsdam (Series ed.) & T. Olive & C. M. Levy (Vol. eds.), Studies in Writing: Volume 10: Contemporary Tools and Techniques for Studying Writing, p. 9-29.

world. Exactly how memory, particularly working memory, was involved in text production received relatively little attention of the research community until about 1980, when Gregg and Steinberg's influential book was published.

This chapter explores some ways that we have addressed this issue that have relied largely upon what some have called a dual-task paradigm. The emphasis of this book is on methods used to study writing, but every chapter in this book has at least an implicit link to a model of written language production. Although the links between theory and method are intentionally explicit in this chapter, the explications of the underlying theories are necessarily brief.

The dual-task paradigm is so-named because people are asked to perform a primary task (such as composing a text) while simultaneously engaged in a secondary (or loading) task that is portrayed as having less importance. Nevertheless, people are encouraged to perform at their best on both tasks. The rationale for dual-task experiments stems from a view of human cognitive systems either having limited processing capacities or limited resources that can be invoked at any moment in time. Thus, it is argued if Task A can be performed well alone or simultaneously with Task B, then Task A uses less capacity or fewer resources than Task C that exhibits performance decrements when it is done concurrently with Task B. Accordingly, the magnitude of the degradation in performance of Task A by a second task is used to index the extent of the individual's processing capacities or resources that Task A requires. The relationship between the magnitude of the performance decrement and the utilization of the underling capacity or resources is assumed to be positive and direct.

Dual-task paradigms have been widely used for many years to address basic science issues and applied domains, such as vigilance and attention (Broadbent, 1958; Cherry, 1953; Kahneman, 1973; Moray, 1959). Their use to study cognitive processes in written language production is relatively new (see, for example, Chanquoy & Negro, 1996; Bonin & Fayol in this volume; Levy & Ransdell, 1994, 1995, 1996b; Negro, Levy, & Chanquoy, 2000; Olive, Kellogg, & Piolat in this volume).

It is important to note that the secondary task in a dual-task paradigm can have at least two distinct functions for the research. In some contexts, the secondary task parameters are held constant, and the researcher assumes that the task has no influence on the performance of the primary task. Examples of this use of a secondary task include gathering think-aloud protocols and directed retrospection, both of which are discussed by Olive, Kellogg, and Piolat in this volume. In a different context, the one used in the present chapter, the secondary task is used as both an independent and a dependent variable. That is, characteristics of the task are systematically manipulated in order to determine their effects on the primary writing task; these manipulations are assumed to engage different components of working memory differentially or to different extents. Further, as we shall show later, measuring the performance on the secondary task, it is possible to determine the extent (if any) that the primary task has upon it.

This chapter will explain how several new memory-loading tasks have been deployed in a writing research program. It will also provide a tutorial for further elaborating the methodology that includes coding and human factors considerations. The chapter also provides new empirical data to show how a well-articulated model (Kellogg, 1996) can be evaluated and concludes with ideas for new avenues for scientific inquiry or writing processes.

2. A THEORETICAL FOUNDATION

We began a series of studies of this interface by transposing methodologies devised by Baddeley and his associates (*e.g.*, Baddeley & Hitch, 1974; Salame & Baddeley, 1982; Vallar & Baddeley, 1984) to investigate the interactions among human memory processes. One of these interactions posited a master-slave relationship between a central executive and two subordinate components, a phonological loop and a visuo-spatial sketchpad. The slave systems had been postulated to support the central executive by offloading from it the processing of special categories of information. When Baddeley and Hitch presented a memory task (designed to engage the central executive), performance deteriorated systematically when participants were simultaneously exposed to secondary tasks. A secondary 'task' that involved only the presentation of speech — that the participant could ignore and certainly to which the participant was never was asked to respond — disrupted memory minimally. However, when the task required remembering discrete, unrelated information, performance on the main memory task was seriously impaired. Although Baddeley and others have used these data to support his model of memory, others have challenged this interpretation. However, his critics have never wholly dismissed the idea that memory was involved in different ways or to different extents as secondary tasks were added to a primary task.

Our initial studies of writing closely mirrored the methodology that Baddeley *et al.* designed for their studies of memory. That is, participants were asked to write an essay either in silence, while irrelevant speech was played, or while they attempted to remember a string of digits. A pattern of findings emerged from the analyses of writing protocols and the written products that was consistent with those Baddeley *et al.* had reported earlier in studies of memory.

Having established that there was an orderliness to the data that would have been anticipated by Baddeley, our challenge was to develop more refined methods that would enable us to overcome the criticisms levied at Baddeley's interpretations of his own data. Some of the more serious challenges are not aimed specifically at Baddeley's work but on the question of the meaning of most data collected using a dual-task paradigm (*e.g.*, Navon, 1984; Navon & Gopher, 1979). The focus of this chapter will be on some of the ways that we have addressed these challenges.

A central assumption underlying the use of a secondary task to assess its effects on a primary task is that the two tasks performed simultaneously combine in specifiable ways to use capacity or resources that, in turn, influence observable measures in predictable ways. Researchers often assume that any effect of the addition of a secondary task will be an immediate degradation of the primary task but that performance continues at a constant (but diminished) level. This assumption is rarely tested empirically. As a consequence, the theoretical interpretations are ambiguous when the average performance of a group that experiences both a primary and a secondary task is compared to a control group that performs only the primary task. The situation is not all improved by comparing the average scores on some dependent variable for a group that performs a primary task alone, then later performs the same task together with a secondary task.

Consider the hypothetical data shown in Figure 1. We depict three different hypothetical situations in which a primary and a secondary task are each performed alone over an arbitrary period of time. Then, the participants are asked to perform the primary and secondary tasks simultaneously, and the performance on the dual tasks is measured over an additional (but arbitrary period) of time. Each is measured on its own scale and, for convenience, the performance on the primary task is graphically represented as greater than is the secondary task. We also made the simplifying assumption that all intertask, within- and between-subject variances were unchanged from the beginning of the testing period to the end.

The top panel shows that participants exhibited stability in their performance of both the primary and secondary tasks when each was done alone. When the participants were first required to perform the tasks simultaneously, performance on the primary task immediately declined, but remained stable afterwards. Performance on the secondary task was unchanged. The immediate change in performance on the primary task that is time-locked to the initiation of the requirement to perform both tasks simultaneously argues that this requirement is the cause of the decline. The fact that the decline is stable across time periods measured later, during which the dual task requirement is still in place, lends further support to this cause-effect relationship. Presumably, if the dual-task performance requirement was suddenly abolished, performance on the primary task would immediately revert to the higher level that it exhibited early in the measurement period testing series (*e.g.*, during Epochs 1–4).

The middle panel also shows that participants were able to perform the two tasks alone in a very consistent and stable way. Here, however, when the participants began to do the tasks simultaneously, performance on both tasks immediately declined. For each task, this new level of performance remained at a constant level thereafter.

The bottom panel shows a very different pattern of activity. During the period when each task was being measured alone, performance on each task became better as additional practice with the task occurred. As in the previous example, performance decreased immediately when the two tasks were first undertaken simultaneously. However, unlike either of the previous examples, performance systematically improved. More importantly, because the slopes were different, the improvement occurred at different rates for the two tasks. The underlying complexity increased because the rates of improvement were not identical with those observed when the tasks were accomplished alone.

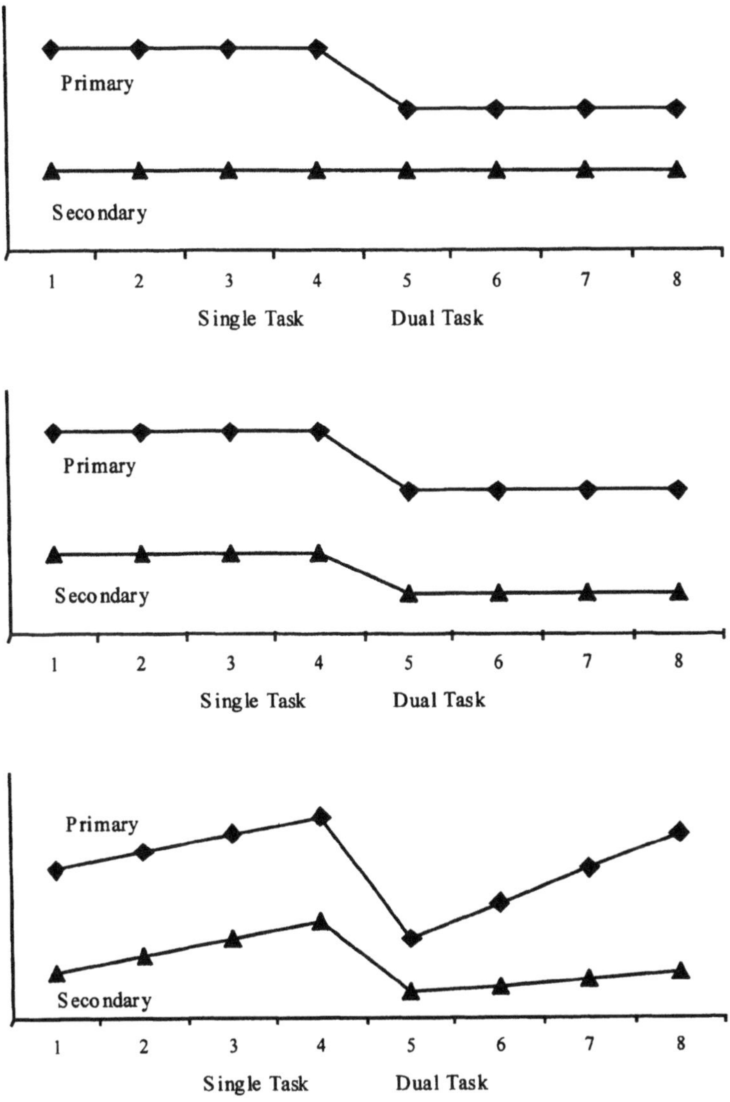

Figure 1. Potential outcomes when primary and secondary tasks are done alone or together. During Epochs 1–4 on the x-axis, the individual performs the primary and the secondary tasks in isolation for a specific, but arbitrary, duration. During Epochs 5–8, the two tasks are first performed simultaneously. The y-axis represents performance measures on each task.

The importance of these three examples derives from the fact that researchers often report only the mean score on a specific dimension for a task done alone, and compare this to performance of the same task when the research participant also is engaged with a secondary task.[1] Rarely is performance on the secondary task measured in either condition. Indeed, with some secondary tasks, such as the irrelevant speech task, no responses are required, and thus there is nothing to measure or report.

Although the hypothetical data exhibited in Figure 1 suggest rather different psychological mechanisms at work, in each graph the average scores for the primary task during the single task phase are identical. More importantly, the average scores for the primary task during the dual task phase are also identical across the three examples. Consequently, a researcher reflecting on the outcomes with access only to those average scores might be led to conclude that the addition of the secondary task mirrored similar cognitive processes in the three situations. Because the examples in Figure 1 were designed to enable us to argue otherwise, we concur generally with previous critics of the dual-task paradigm (*e.g.*, Fisk, Derrick, & Schneider, 1986; Howe & Rabinowitz, 1989; Navon, 1984; Navon & Gopher, 1979) who argue that the data may sometimes be uninterpretable. A focus on an aggregate performance measure, collapsed over time, leads to one of these uninterpretable situations.

One of the serious criticisms of early work in text production research using dual tasks was that the techniques for differentially loading the hypothesized components of memory confounded stimulus properties and response demands with the assumed processing by those components. The irrelevant speech manipulation, for example, was assumed to involve the phonological loop in some low-level processing of the speech. The manipulation required the presentation of a continuous, meaningful narrative, but required no overt response from the participant. In contrast, the concurrent digit load task, designed to stress the central executive, required the participant to memorize a series of discrete digits, maintain them in memory while engaged in the primary task, and later to report them aloud. It should now be clear that it is difficult to compare the writing process or product outcome measures for these two manipulations, owing to the very different stimulus properties and response requirements.

With a clear understanding of the pitfalls in research using dual-task paradigms, it is possible to design experiments that may give a less ambiguous picture of the underlying psychological processes. In the next section, we suggest ways to approach the design of research on writing using dual tasks that avoid some of those pitfalls.

3. SPECIFYING AND MEASURING PERFORMANCE ON SECONDARY TASKS

3.1. Specifying secondary tasks

The considerations discussed in the previous section led to four guidelines for developing secondary tasks to present to writers while they generate text (Levy, White, Lea, & Ransdell, 1998):

---

1 Of course, in order to determine the reliability of the differences (if any), standard errors must also be calculated and assessed.

1) The secondary tasks should not become automatic during the period of time when the data are collected. The rationale here is that automatic processes are presumed to occur without conscious and deliberate effort and would, therefore, presumably require very few resources or working memory capacity. The top panel of Figure 1 may be a classic example of an automatic secondary task that requires minimal resources. Performance on it is identical whether it is performed alone or in conjunction with another task that is deemed more important or critical.
2) The tasks should have similar underlying structures involving the equivalent requirements for input and output. Ideally, the stimuli presented and the responses demanded should be identical for all of the tasks being compared. The sole variable that distinguishes the secondary tasks should be the rules that writers use for deciding when and how to respond appropriately.
3) The need to select and execute a specific response should occur equally often in each of the different secondary tasks. Further, the responses must not occur so frequently as to bring performance on the primary task to a halt. However, they need to be scheduled to occur often enough to yield sufficient data to enable monitoring performance over time.
4) The various secondary tasks should be of comparable difficulty. In the absence of demonstrable equality, the tasks should be able to yield sensitive and continuous measures to enable researchers to make statistical adjustments for differential difficulty.

In an early set of experiments explicitly designed to incorporate many of these guidelines, Lea (1998) presented irrelevant speech to university students while they endeavoured to give immediate free recall to sets of 5–9 consonants. Although this irrelevant speech manipulation requires no overt response, Lea was able to generate interesting data by holding the speech content constant, but varying the characteristics of the speaker. For one situation, Lea himself tape-recorded the message in a conversational manner for later playback. For another, a tape was made using a text-to-speech computer program that produced an intelligible, but emotionally flat rendering of the content. For the control condition, no exogenous sounds were introduced. At issue was whether the hypothesized phonological loop operated in an all-or-none or a continuous, graded fashion. Baddeley and Hitch's (1974) discussions suggested the former. Speech sounds, regardless of meaning, are postulated to have obligatory access to the phonological store, and to engage the phonological loop by virtue of its structural nature. Jones, Miles, and Page (1990) had shown that, in detecting spelling and typographical errors during proofreading, participants performed more poorly when they heard irrelevant, but meaningful, speech compared to participants who heard the same materials played backwards. The performance of the second group was no different in Jones *et al.* (1990) from a third group that heard no tape. Because reversed speech has almost no phonological resemblance to normal human speech, it could be argued that participants detected at some level the absence of useful or meaningful information, eliminating the need for further processing by any system, including a phonological loop.

Lea (1998) argued that, if a phonological loop operated in a graded fashion, then it is possible that speech that minimized nuance, inflections, and pauses that differed in length might produce a reduced load on a working memory. This reasoning suggested that the two tapes identical in content would produce different working memory decrements relative to conditions in which no irrelevant speech was presented, results suggesting that the phonological loop might operate as a pool of resources rather than as a unitary structure.

Our more recent approach has been to use a series of secondary, memory-loading tasks that presented the identical stimuli and required the identical overt response. The tasks differed only in the mental operations that the participants were to perform. Our decisions about which specific mental operations on which to focus were driven in part by an interest in evaluating some claims and implications of a relatively new theory of writing (Kellogg, 1996) whose theoretical origins were directly traceable to Baddeley and Hitch's (1974) theory of working memory.

As briefly noted above, Baddeley postulated the existence of a pair of memory components – a visuo-spatial sketchpad and a phonological loop – whose primary function was to offload some local processing of visual/spatial and speech-like information from a central executive, in much the same way that a graphics card and a sound card lessen the demands on the CPU chip of a modern personal computer.[2] In Kellogg's extension of this basic conceptualisation to writing, additional assumptions became essential. For example, Kellogg argued that the visuo-spatial sketchpad contributed to text production by enabling writers to arrange and rearrange ideas and structures prior to generating text. Thus, the primary contribution of the visuo-spatial sketchpad was to facilitate planning operations. In contrast, Kellogg argued that the phonological loop had little or no influence on planning, but, instead, was instrumental in formulating and translating processes, particular in the translating and monitoring subprocesses. The central executive was involved in all writing processes at some level with the exception of the programming and motor aspects of execution for individuals whose cursive (or typing) skills were well developed. For such individuals, then, Kellogg claimed that these aspects were automatic.

Against this background, we developed a series of tasks that would both meet the formal specifications, described earlier, for an ideal ensemble of secondary tasks and enable an evaluation of some important claims made by Kellogg's theory. The primary task was always text production. In most studies, we have used a standard set of topics, such as 'Describe the best college course that you have ever taken' or 'Describe the house or apartment that you lived in before you began college.' The topics were always chosen to enable undergraduates to generate a substantial amount of text within a relatively short period of time (for example, 10–15 minutes) and without the need to access other materials. In addition, we almost always include an incentive, such as a prize to the person whose work is judged best, in order to maintain motivation for writing at a moderately high level. (Within our student writers, there is agreement that they would prefer to have their work entered into a competition where one of 100 students would win a single $100 cash prize than for each to be guaranteed one dollar for their essay.)

---

2 At the time that Baddeley began publishing this conception of working memory, the notion of independent processors for graphical and acoustic information was some years away. The CPU was responsible for virtually all processing.

In a typical experiment, students write two essays. They always are asked to write the first essay unimpeded by the need to perform a secondary task. In these experiments, the stimuli that would be displayed in the secondary task appear, but the writer is not told how to respond to them. In fact, writers are specifically told to focus on their writing task and to ignore the stimuli presented in the corners of the screen.[3] Writing takes place within a special-purpose computer program that resembles a simple word processor, but which records every keystroke and the time that it occurred.[4] The top panel in Figure 2 displays how the screen might look during the first few minutes of the writing task.

The participant is then typically given 5–10 minutes of practice with what will become the secondary task. During this period, the program prevents the participant from typing anything in the writing window, requiring attention to the characters shown in the corners of the screen. In one series of experiments, the same large character appeared in each corner of the screen. The character in this set of experiments was a Roman alphabetic letter that could vary along these dimensions:

- Case (uppercase or lowercase),
- colour (red, green, or blue),
- font (normal or italic),
- location (normal or positioned lower than the normal by about 50% of the height of an uppercase character),
- phoneme (all characters with the long 'e' in common versus those that did not involve this phoneme).

After 3 s, all four characters shown simultaneously changed in case, colour, font, location, and phoneme. During the baseline measuring period for this task, participants used any finger they wished to press any of the function keys (marked F1–F12) whenever a critical event occurred. The nature of the critical event was linked to the memory components specified in Baddeley's theory so that they could later be tied to the writing processes described by Kellogg. These events had in common the requirement that the participant respond as indicated when one of the following occurred:

- Adjacent characters were the same case, colour, or font or occurred in the same location. The assumption is that this task required the involvement of the visuospatial sketchpad.

---

3 Actually, in many studies that we have conducted, the first task presented to half of the participants was the writing task described. When this task was complete, they began a period of time during which they focused on the secondary task alone. The remaining participants performed the experiment with the temporal order of these tasks reversed. None of our data has shown an order effect or an interaction of order with any other variable. Furthermore, we have found no evidence that the presence of these characters in the periphery of the screen influences any product or process dependent variable compared to a condition where no peripheral characters appear on the screen during the writing-only task. In other words, without an explicit need to attend to those stimuli (such as a need imposed by a researcher) participants can effectively ignore those changing stimuli.

4 During the 1990's our undergraduate students became highly computer literate. All of our participants in these studies could accurately type 25-30 words per minute, which was faster than they could form words using pen and paper.

- Adjacent characters contained the long 'e.' To make this determination, the participant presumably had to retain in working memory some phonological properties of the previous letter long enough to compare it to the currently visible letter. The assumption is that this task required the involvement of the phonological loop.
- Adjacent characters could form a two-letter English word. Because font and case (as well as location, colour and phonemic properties) were irrelevant, participants should have responded when they saw the second letter of 'm*Y*' or '*b*E.' The assumption is that this task primarily involved the interaction of the central executive with a mental lexicon represented in long-term memory. It may also involve conflicts with well-learned reading skills, but, within the context of this model, those conflicts would nevertheless have to be resolved by or within the central executive.

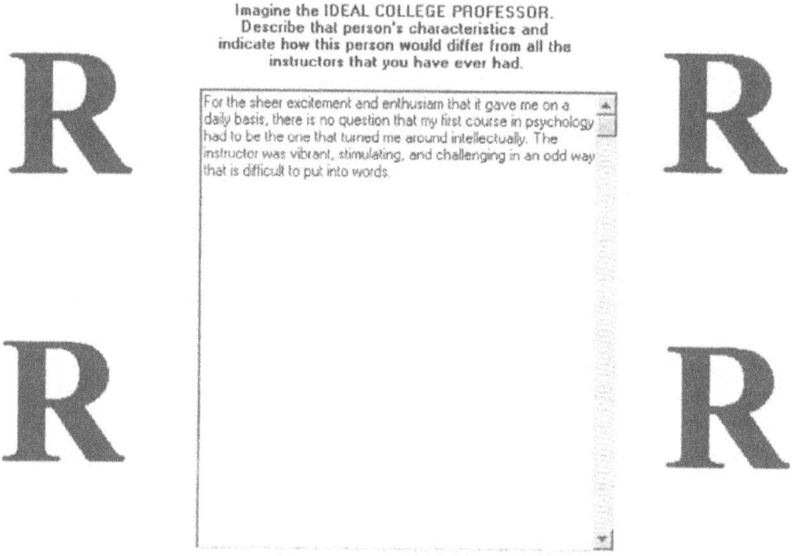

Figure 2. A representative screen showing the writing topic (top), writing text windows (middle) and secondary task stimuli (corners).

The stimuli are sequenced so that the critical event occurs, on the average, about every 15 s, but on a random basis the interval could be longer or shorter by as many as 5 s. The final task for the participant is to write a new essay (with a different topic) at the same time as the secondary task, just practiced, is performed. Writers are reminded to produce the best essay that they can within the 15 minutes allowed, while they maximize their performance on the secondary task. In keeping with our objective to devise generalizable experimental design principles, we sought also to develop a response measure that would be applicable across a wide range of such tasks. This is discussed in the next section.

3.2. Measuring performance on secondary tasks

In the simplest of secondary tasks that requires an observable response, the response can be a vocalization (as in thinking aloud protocols) or key press that reflects (1) writers' assessments of their mental states at moment the response was made (as in Kellogg's triple-task procedure or (2) the writers' detection of a critical event having occurred in the secondary task. Olive, Kellogg and Piolat (in this volume) discuss the treatment of data in the thinking protocol and directed retrospection tasks. We focus here on the detection tasks.

Analyses of this task were based on signal detection theory (Green & Swets, 1966), a methodology long used in engineering, psychophysics, and recognition memory. In the category of secondary tasks described here, each response can be initially categorized as correct or incorrect. More importantly, the responses can be classified as one of four different types, depending upon the state of the secondary stimulus at the time of the response. Consider Table 1, below.

Table 1. The four response categories in a signal detection paradigm.

Response	*Presence of a Critical Stimulus* Yes	No
Yes	Hit	Miss
No	False alarm	Correct rejection

If a participant responded by pressing one of the designated keys before the next letter appeared (allowing for a 3-second response latency), the response was labelled a 'Hit.' When one of the designated keys was pressed at other times, the response was labelled a 'False Alarm.' Within signal detection theory, Misses and Correct Rejections are irrelevant.[5] Hits and False Alarms were aggregated over various time periods, depending upon the experiment, ranging from 25 to 100% of the total time spent on the task. Although there are several ways to determine *d'*, a straightforward one involves the following Excel equation,

5 Misses are irrelevant because the proportion of Hits plus the proportion of Misses must always sum to 1.0. A similar situation exists for the sum of the proportions of False Alarms and Correct Rejections.

=NORMSINV(hit probability) - NORMSINV(false alarm probability)[6]

The resulting value, *d'*, is a pure number that measures individuals' sensitivity in performing the task, uncontaminated by their criterion for responding.

4. CODING CONSIDERATIONS FOR DESIGNING SOFTWARE TO STUDY WRITING USING SECONDARY TASKS

The programs described in this chapter were written in Visual Basic, using a third-party timing control that permitted millisecond resolution. Any modern object-oriented language, such as C++, Delphi, or HyperCard would also be appropriate. The language needs to provide the programmer with label objects for presenting instructions, essay topics, and visual stimuli; multiple timers to control the duration of the presentation of secondary stimuli, feedback, and the length of the session as well as to measure the temporal occurrence of each keystroke. The discussion below is intended to guide readers in developing their own versions of the tasks we describe using whatever programming language they prefer. Researchers whose programming skills are above the novice level may wish to skip the remainder of this section and proceed to Section 5.

4.1. Selection of stimuli

Given a secondary stimulus with known properties (physical location, font, case, character name, acoustic properties, etc.), selection of the next secondary stimulus to display requires distinctive programming checks, depending upon the secondary task in use. Consider the task requiring the participant to respond when two characters appear sequentially in the same colour. The program must ensure that the next stimulus will always have a different colour than the current stimulus *except* when the timing routine indicates that the next stimulus is a critical one. In that case, the colour of the next stimulus must be the same as the current one, but all other properties must change. The programming logic is straightforward whenever the task involves signalling a repetition of two temporally contiguous stimuli that share the same colour, location, font, or case. The programming algorithms are necessarily somewhat different when the task involves identifying successive characters that have a specific acoustic feature (*e.g.*, the long 'e' phoneme) or semantic characteristic (*e.g.*, form an English word).

In the case of the task requiring participants to signal the occurrence of two letters that shared an acoustic feature, we defined two arrays of stimuli. One contained all of

6 The NORMSINV function returns the inverse of the standard normal cumulative distribution, which has a mean of 0 and a standard deviation of 1.0. Although the probability of a Hit or a False Alarm can assume values of 0 or 1, the NORMSINV function returns an indeterminate value if either of these situations occurs. Accordingly, when the Hit rate was 1.0 or 0.0, it is necessary to substitute approximate values (such as 0.9999999 or 0.0000001) to enable the function to return a legal value.

the letters that shared the feature (*e.g.*, 'b', 'c', 'd', ... 'z')[7], and the other contained all the other letters (*e.g.*, those in which the feature was absent).

- The program initially selected one character at random for presentation.
- If the character came from the second array, the next character was randomly selected, subject to the constraint that successive alphabetic stimuli always differed in name.
- If the character came from the first array and the next trial was *not* scheduled to be a critical trial, then the program randomly selected a character from the second set. However, if the timer indicated that the time had come for a critical event, the next character was selected from the first array.
- When the timer controlling the onset of critical events fired, an internal indicator (or 'flag') was set that forced the selection of a character from the first array. This flag remained set until a second stimulus element was shown from the same array. Then the flag was reset.

  In the case of the task whose critical event was the presentation of the second letter of a two-letter English word, the underlying programming logic was constrained by the need to make character changes quickly and 'on the fly.' This effectively ruled out the potential for testing whether the next character generated by the program would successfully pass through an independent spelling checking program. Accordingly, we again formed two arrays. The first consisted simply of all two-letter combinations that formed English words. The second consisted of a 2000-letter randomly generated string that was carefully inspected to ensure that it contained no embedded 2-, 3-, or 4-letter English words. For each participant, the program entered the second array at a randomly selected point between the first and 1000th character, and presented the letters in sequence until a timer signalled the need to interrupt the proceedings for the presentation of a pair of letters that formed an English word.
- The word array was then scanned to determine if the currently displayed character was the first letter of any English word. If it was, the second character was selected from any of the two-letter words that could be formed using the displayed character as the initial letter.
- If the large array contained no two-letter English word beginning with the current letter, the program randomly selected one of the words in the array of two-letter English words, and presented those letters in sequence. The program then scanned the large array of random letters for the next occurrence of the second letter of the English word that had just presented in order to determine what character to display next, thereby ensuring that another two-letter English word was not inadvertently presented.

---

7 In British English, the last letter of alphabet is pronounced 'zed.' However, in American English, it is pronounced 'zee.'

5. HUMAN FACTORS AND EXPERIMENTAL CONSIDERATIONS FOR SPECIFYING SECONDARY TASKS IN WRITING RESEARCH

5.1. Responses to secondary stimuli

Care must be taken to minimize the influence of external factors that might impede the participant's ability to respond quickly and accurately to the demands of the secondary task. For example, in some of our early studies (Levy & Ransdell, 1995), we asked writers to respond as quickly as possible to a tone. Not wishing them to have to move their fingers from the keyboard to press a response button, we placed the button on the floor. Surprisingly, the participants spontaneously volunteered nothing aloud about this rather strange request, and their response latencies were generally quite fast. Some participants, however, confided during their debriefing that they sometimes experienced pain in their toes owing to the need to keep them elevated above the button between responses. As a consequence, our more recent studies have asked participants to make the critical response to the secondary task using any of the function (Fl–F12) keys that appear as a horizontal row of keys immediately above the row of numerals at the top of their keyboard. This enabled them to use any finger on either hand to respond to a critical event.

5.2. Frequency of occurrence of critical event

The issue of 'when' to present a critical event in a secondary task is also a critical consideration for researchers. Presenting them too frequently raises the possibility that the research participant will devote full attention to the secondary task, reducing the opportunities for proficient text generation. Presenting the secondary stimuli too infrequently decreases the reliability of the estimates of hit and false alarm probabilities, the principal performance measures for the secondary tasks. Empirically, we have determined that a good trade-off between these two competing influences is reached for our skilled adult writers when the critical events occur about four times a minute. In practice, we schedule the events to occur on a random basis between 10 and 20 s apart to eliminate the possibility of writers developing an internalised schedule that would enable them to predict when the critical events will occur.

5.3. Size and placement of stimuli

The stimuli used in the secondary task need to be clearly visible to participants, wherever their gaze is directed within the writing window. In our configuration, these stimuli were positioned in each corner of the screen. The width of the characters was determined so that the italic 'M' and 'W' (the widest letters) would almost completely fill the space between the border of the screen and the edge of the writing window. Their height was based on a constraint that the characters be as tall as possible, yet when the upper character was in its lower position it could not overlap visually the position of the lower character in its upper position. The visual angle subtended by the secondary stimuli depended upon the distance that writers held their heads from the screen, the fact that the height of uppercase characters was generally greater than lowercase characters, and that the width depended upon the character being displayed. On average, each character subtended approximately 6° vertically and horizontally.

5.4. Feedback

Because keyboards vary substantially in the tactile and auditory feedback they provide when keys are struck, consideration needs to be given to the possibility that a keyboard assigned to participants may provide less feedback than they are normally accustomed to having. The consequence of this possibility is that writers may not always be confident that they have succeeded in completely depressing the appropriate key to signal that they have detected a critical event in the secondary task. We discovered that this often caused writers to press the selected function key repeatedly, as if to ensure that the program would detect at least one of the keystrokes. The program, of course, detected all of the repetitions. It is straightforward to arrange for a program to count no more than one response per critical target (hit), but keystrokes occurring when no target was visible were, by definition, false alarms. Discriminating between genuine false alarms and false alarms caused by a writer's repeated striking of a function key is therefore problematic. We considered presenting an auditory cue whenever the program detected the striking of a function key. However, we rejected this solution because we often need to test several writers who, while not within the visual field of others, could mistakenly interpret the auditory cue from a nearby computer as coming from their own. Accordingly, we provided feedback visually: Whenever the program detects a user striking a function key, it displayed for 500 ms. a brightly collared border around the window used for entering text.

6. RECENT RESEARCH USING THESE SECONDARY TASKS TO STUDY THE ROLE OF WORKING MEMORY IN WRITING

As noted earlier, one of our guidelines for designing secondary tasks specified a need to be able to establish that the controlled processing that invariably occurs at the onset of the task does not become automatic with repetition during testing. Controlled processes are assumed to be demanding of cognitive resources; automatic processes to need few such resources. In the report one of Lea's (1998) experiments, using stimuli similar to those displayed in Figure 2, writers' detection of a critical event was measured frequently during 20-minute single-task baseline and dual-task (writing + secondary task) sessions. The measured d' changed in only small, unsystematic ways across 5-minute epochs once a task began. When, however, the requirement was imposed to perform two tasks simultaneously, d' values on both tasks immediately declined. That is, Lea's data closely mirrored the results for the secondary task displayed in the middle panel of Figure 1, suggesting that the class of tasks that we described earlier was unlikely to become automatic during testing periods lasting up to 20 minutes. Analyses of the each of the five secondary tasks described above similarly showed no change in d' unless and until the task was performed simultaneously with a writing task. Here, too, the patterns for d' closely resembled the middle panel of Figure 1. Levy and Ransdell (1995), using a simpler tone-detection task, found no evidence to support the development of automaticity when writers composed for 60-minute sessions over a period of 10 weeks. We have now examined several hundred protocols collected over nearly a decade using both simple and complex decision requirements as well as both comparatively short-term and long-term assessments. This examination revealed no detectable signs that these secondary tasks can show a cognitive metamorphosis from one that is highly controlled to one that is automatic within the temporal parameters of our experiments.

Another performance-based consideration in the guidelines detailed earlier was that the tasks designed to differentially load components of working memory would be equivalent in difficulty. For conceptual convenience and to yield greater statistical power, we have collapsed the data from the six conditions into three. Because the tasks involving case, colour, font and location all required a decision based on the visual or spatial properties of the stimuli, the data from these were combined into a single group (Levy, White, Lea, & Ransdell, 1998). The single-task *d'* for this group did not differ from that of the group asked to make a judgment based on the phonemic similarity of adjacent characters or the group whose positive decision was determined by the formation of two-letter English words.[8] Performance on the secondary task immediately declined to a stable level when writers were asked to simultaneously write and perform the secondary task. However, the decline of nearly one standard deviation unit was comparable for the three groups. Because each mean was based on more than 100 observations, the absence of differences approaching statistical significance lends support to the thesis that the equal-difficulty guideline for the secondary task (alone or in conjunction with the primary task) was satisfactorily met. The remaining guidelines for similar input/output requirements and frequency of occurrence of critical events, but for different decision rules, were satisfied methodologically.

Kellogg's (1996) theory provided a basis for making predictions about the effects of manipulating a secondary task on planning, translating, programming, executing, reading and editing processes as different loads were placed on a visuo-spatial sketchpad, a phonological loop or a central executive. Many of experimental outcomes were consistent with Kellogg's model. However, several outcomes that have been recently replicated using other variations of these tasks either were novel because the model contains nothing to anticipate them or were not entirely consistent with the model.

6.1. Representative findings consistent with Kellogg's model

When any of the six secondary tasks described earlier in this chapter was added to the research participants' text production task, decrements were observed for every writing process measure: fluency, execution speed, overall planning and reviewing time, and initial planning time. Because most of these measures were collected as the writing unfolded in time, it was possible to track the participants' performance as a function of time. Invariably, the pattern that emerged when performance on the secondary

8 This suggests that the (intuitively more cognitively complex and difficult two-letter word) task was no more difficult to perform alone than any of the simpler taks when they were performed alone.

task alone was compared to when it was conducted in combination with writing yielded outcomes that closely resembled the second panel from the top in Figure 1. Thus, each of the secondary tasks impaired writing performance measures, consistent with an interpretation that depends upon each of them making demands on a limited capacity working memory system. Kellogg's (1996) theory makes this basic assumption, but provides opportunities for evaluating much more focused hypotheses. It was also generally the case, as shown in the middle panel of Figure 1, that performance on the secondary task was impeded when it was performed simultaneously with the primary writing task. Thus, in general, while writers worked hard to focus on text production, their cognitive loads were so strained by the demands of the dual tasks that performance on both tasks suffered.

Methodologically, one of the most straightforward assumptions to evaluate is Kellogg's claim that the visuo-spatial sketchpad is involved only in the planning process. Planning has been shown to occur throughout the writing process (*e.g.*, Hayes & Flower, 1980, 1983; Kellogg, 1987a, 1994; Levy & Ransdell, 1995). Its occurrence is readily identifiable using thinking aloud protocols (Hayes & Flower, 1983; Levy & Ransdell, 1995) or via directed retrospection (Kellogg, 1987a, 1987b; Levy, Marek, & Lea, 1996) or the triple-task described by Olive, Kellogg, and Piolat (this volume). In the paradigms described in the present chapter, planning is best indexed by pauses between words, sentences, and paragraphs, but the presence of pauses is no guarantee that essay-specific planning is occurring or, for that matter, that any planning is occurring. When writers re-read their texts, for example, they will generally stop moving their pens or making keystrokes. In contrast, the initial pause that occurs between the presentation of the writing topic and the first sign of text production is a purer measure of planning because, by definition, no other writing process (*e.g.*, translating, programming, executing, reading or editing) will have been initiated.[9] Our secondary tasks designed to differentially load the visuo-spatial sketchpad increased initial planning time nearly 50% compared to the writing-only condition, which is an amount reliably longer than observed when any of the other secondary tasks (*i.e.*, those designed to engage the phonological loop or the central executive) were deployed.

Ignoring the initial planning time, but considering all other times during which the writers paused yields a measure that includes both further planning and re-reading. Re-reading is associated with a need to reassess the writing plan as well as to edit what has been composed to that point.[10] Given the relatively brief period of time allowed for writing these essays, the failure of writers to make substantive editorial changes was not surprising. Many otherwise good spellers ignored obvious typographical errors. Nevertheless, compared to the secondary tasks designed to engage the central executive and the phonological loop, when participants wrote while performing a visuo-spatial secondary task, they paused for longer durations even after

9 In our studies, writers are initially given general instructions about their task. The presentation of the display showing the topic of the essay is a signal that they may begin writing.

10 As writers composed, each of their keystrokes was captured and marked with its time of occurrence. This enabled us to compare what was typed during the writing session with the final version of the essay shown on the screen at the conclusion of the session to determine when and where editorial changes had occurred.

text production had begun, and maintained this pattern throughout the remainder of the writing period.

Finally, the quality of the essays, determined by trained judges blind as to the testing conditions, showed pervasive effects when a secondary task was introduced. However, in accord with our studies using irrelevant speech and digit-loading tasks (Ransdell & Levy, 1996, 1998), the data again showed the greatest decrement to be associated with the secondary task designed to most heavily involve the central executive.

6.2. Findings unanticipated by Kellogg's model

With strong ties to Baddeley and Hitch's (1974) theory, Kellogg's model of writing depends to certain degree upon the internal integrity of the model of working memory underlying it. One of the assumptions that can be drawn from Baddeley and Hitch is that the visuo-spatial sketchpad and the phonological loop slave systems are unitary structural components that operate at any moment in a binary, all-or-none rather than a graded fashion. As mentioned earlier in this chapter, Lea (1998) compared a number of measures collected within-subjects when participants were tested either in the absence of irrelevant speech or in the presence of irrelevant speech produced by a human or by a software text-to-speech generator, or to a silent control. In every measure when irrelevant speech was associated with lower levels of performance, the speech generated by the software had reliably less deleterious effects than the same content delivered by a recorded human voice. Moreover, in those conditions, the computer-generated irrelevant speech produced results that were no different from the silent control condition. These results suggest a weakness in the unitary, all-or-none assumption about the nature of the phonological loop in the Baddeley and Hitch conception of working memory. However, Kellogg wisely chose not to develop his model so that its conceptual viability would stand or fall on the empirical soundness of every component of the Baddeley and Hitch theory. The finding that the phonological loop can be engaged in varying degrees by external stimuli may, in fact, provide additional flexibility to models of writing that can treat a concept such as phonological loop as a varying pool of memory resources.

6.3. Findings not consistent with Kellogg's model

In one series of studies (Levy, White, Lea, & Ransdell, 1998), writers who were exposed to the six secondary tasks described earlier were also given tests of serial recall with and without the need to perform the concurrent secondary task. Serial recall was evaluated immediately following the presentation of 15-item word lists taken from Rœdiger and McDermott (1995). Although the performance on the secondary tasks performed simultaneously with the study of the words suffered immediately and equivalently across the ensemble of concurrent tasks, recall of the words depended upon the nature of the secondary task. The best recall occurred in the presence of the secondary task designed to involve primarily the central executive. Recall was less satisfactory when participants were responding to tasks designed to involve the visuo-spatial sketchpad or the phonological loop. This pattern of findings is not consistent with an interpretation of the Baddeley and Hitch (1974) model that envisions a system capable of quickly and automatically routing visual or spatial and phonological information to specialized memory subsystems for independent processing. Instead, the findings suggest that when visuo-spatial or phonological processing is required, the central executive either does not immediately and automatically pass control to the appropriate slave system or it maintains an interaction with the slave systems on an ongoing basis. It should be noted that these findings contrast with those reported earlier by Baddeley and his associates who engaged the phonological loop with irrelevant speech and the central executive with a digit-memory task. As we have suggested earlier in this chapter, these secondary tasks differ in many critical ways, making claims about the mechanisms by which each operates in a single experiment open to alternative explanations. To the extent that Kellogg's (1996) depends upon the solidity of Baddeley and Hitch's assumptions about the distinctive roles of the visuo-spatial sketchpad, the phonological loop, and the central sketchpad, these data may have negative implications for Kellogg's model.

Some writing data from the same series of experiments reported by Levy, White, Lea, and Ransdell (1998) may also have troublesome implications for Kellogg's model. One example centres upon the primary role of the visuo-spatial sketchpad, assumed to be planning. We believe that a reasonable inference from the model would be that the only secondary tasks to influence initial planning time would be those that involved the visuo-spatial or central-executive decisions. In fact, inconsistent with the expectations from the model, the secondary task designed to engage primarily the phonological loop also produced significant increases in initial planning times.

As another example, recall that the execution process of writing is assumed to be automatic for skilled typists. In this situation, few cognitive resources are required, suggesting that the working memory central executive and its slave systems might not be implicated. It might therefore be reasonable to anticipate from Kellogg that none of the secondary tasks used here would have any influence on the speed of the writer's execution[11]. Our data show, however, that each of the secondary tasks reliably slowed the writer's execution speed from 15 to 30% compared to a writing-only baseline condition. Once again, the effects were immediate and sustained through the remainder of the writing session.

Patterns similar to the memory task have emerged in some clever conceptual replications of the dual-task writing experiments of Levy, Ragosta, White, Lea, and Ransdell (1998) that were designed by Joseph Ragosta in our laboratory. He substituted icons of ordinary playing cards for the changing letters. In one variation, participants were to respond (pressing any F1–F12 key) whenever consecutive cards were the same colour, a task that was assumed to principally engage the visuo-spatial sketchpad. Other participants responded when a 'Joker' appeared; this task, in which the critical card was neither red nor black, was designed to primarily engage the cen-

11 In order to obtain as pure a measure as possible of writing execution speed, we reduced the words per minute calculated across the writing session by the time spent pausing between words, sentences, and paragraphs. The value remaining reflected the time to type the word on the keyboard after he writer had decided what the word should be.

tral executive. As in the earlier experiments, writing process measures deteriorated more when the participants were engaged during text production with the phonological task than with the central executive task.

It should be noted, however, that in all of these studies using the guidelines for designing secondary tasks described earlier in this chapter, the pattern of writing quality observed in our research using the irrelevant speech and digit load tasks was replicated. That is, although writing quality deteriorated whenever a secondary task was introduced, the judged quality of the essay was declined most from baseline conditions when the secondary task primarily engaged the central executive. This dissociation between the outcomes for writing processes and the written product may be due to writers in laboratory experiments making a strategic decision to maintain quality at all costs (Ransdell & Levy, 1996, 1998).

7. SOME FUTURE DIRECTIONS FOR WRITING RESEARCH

Every scientific methodology that we know about has links that either explicitly or implicitly link it to at least one theoretical view of a scientific domain. The dual-task methodologies described in this chapter are no exception. They were expressly designed to evaluate the validity of assumptions made in a model of writing that was, in turn, an extension of a model of human memory. Having said this, we argue that the guidelines that we discussed for creating secondary tasks can be transposed to aid in the creation of entirely different tasks that might enable future researchers to evaluate very different theories of working memory or of text production.

Olive, Kellogg, and Piolat (in this volume) discuss how other multi-component tasks, such as thinking aloud protocols, and their triple task, can be used to productively to help understand writing processes. We have reported elsewhere (Levy, Ragosta, White, Lee, & Ransdell (1998) about the use of yet another variation of these tasks that focus on the contribution of working memory to writing. Specifically, we devised a set of procedures[12] that loaded working memory by re-mapping the keyboard well-known to skilled typists. In a typical experiment, they were told that two of the most-frequently used letters in English (the 'i' and 'e,' whose keys are located at opposite ends of the US keyboard, but on the same row) were 'broken.' As a result, whenever they needed to type an 'e,' they had to press the key marked with the tilde ('~') symbol and whenever they needed to type an 'i,' they had to press the key marked with the pipe ('|') symbol. The alternate symbols were on the same ends of the keyboard as their 'broken' counterparts, but two rows up. Neither of the alternate symbols was likely to be used in the generation of an English-language essay. The scientific rationale for this 'broken keyboard' technique was to de-automatize the highly overlearned motor sequences mastered years ago by skilled typists. In effect, an element of conscious, deliberate control could be introduced into an overlearned and highly automated task. This enabled us to evaluate an assumption explicit in Kellogg's theory that the motor aspects of producing written text by skilled writers required no working memory resources.

---

12 These procedures were based in part on a suggestion by Robert Madigan (1997, personal communication).

There are, of course, many other ways that the contribution of memory can be varied and studied as writers produce text. For many years, we have asked writers to generate essays on topics selected because each participant brought to the laboratory life experiences that enabled them to write continuously for 20 to 30 minutes on the subject matter without needing access to external materials. The drawback to this procedure is that writers bring different experiences with them to the laboratory, making the content of their essays necessarily different. This, in turn, contributes variance to the decisions that judges must make about the quality of the final products. We have recently begun exploring a variation that minimizes this problem. It involves the presentation of interesting, but novel, material to the participants to study for 15 to 20 minutes in anticipation of their writing about the content to a peer. An audiotape or video could alternatively be used to deliver the information, enabling the researcher to control the amount of time that the participant was exposed to each element of information. If the auditory or visual information was presented via computer software, the participant could be allowed to re-play any portions. The researcher might later use the information collected from such repetitions to better understand the participant's representation in LTM of the content used to generate the essay.

It is difficult to imagine a theory of writing processes that did not need to make a fundamental assumption about the involvement of human memory. As our understanding of memory systems develop further, we should anticipate that we can use tools such as those outlined in this chapter to better understand the contribution of memory to writing. These tools can give researchers a powerful way to directly manipulate the functioning of memory so that its role can be systematically enhanced or diminished in accessing ideas, lexicons, syntax, orthography, and phonology. In this way, our understanding of the often ephemeral, unconstrained process of writing may be strengthened.

8. ACKNOWLEDGEMENTS

This chapter could never have been written without the insights, inspirations, and sweat contributed by Joseph Lea, Joseph Ragosta, and Katherine White. Ron Kellogg, Thierry Olive, Mark Torrance and an anonymous Dutch reviewer were generous in offering constructive feedback that helped us to craft the final version of this work. Any remaining flaws are our responsibility.

THE TRIPLE TASK TECHNIQUE FOR STUDYING THE PROCESS OF WRITING

THIERRY OLIVE*, RONALD T. KELLOGG**
& ANNIE PIOLAT***

** CNRS & University of Paris VIII (France), ** Saint-Louis University (USA),
& *** University of Provence (France)*

Abstract. In this chapter, we first present two variants of a technique of secondary reaction time task and verbalization task that allow researchers (1) to estimate the general temporal organization of the writing process, (2) to analyse the recursiveness of writing and (3) to measure the amount of resources allocated to the writing processes (Kellogg, 1987b; Levy & Ransdell, 1994, 1995). Next, we present a series of experiments that evaluated the validity of the method. We then synthesize studies that used the triple task method to address questions concerning the way by which situation-specific or writer-specific factors affect functional characteristics of writing. We describe results from experiments that investigated the role of writers' knowledge, type of text planning, writing medium and cognitive capacity on resources allocation to the writing processes and on their temporal organization. Finally, we delineate how the triple task technique can be varied to answer future research questions.
Keywords: secondary task, verbalization, think-aloud protocols, working memory, cognitive resources, writing processes, dynamic of writing,

1. INTRODUCTION

A central issue in cognitive research on text production concerns the dynamics of writing. Planning ideas, translating the planned content into sentences, and reviewing ideas and text are three basic production processes. The dynamics of writing refers both to the temporal organization of these processes during a writing session and to their cognitive demands (Piolat & Olive, 2000). To state it simply, researchers study 'when' a process is activated and its 'cost.' It has long been established that planning, translating, and reviewing do not occur in linear order (Hayes and Flower, 1980). They are instead recursive, with one process calling upon another, as when translating an idea into a sentence prompts the writer to engage in further planning. Writing processes interweave and the pattern of their activation reflects the writer's strategy for coping with the task demands. Consequently, how writers perform should depend on factors that affect when writing processes are activated during a composition (Rijlaarsdam & van den Bergh, 1996b).

T. Olive, R. T. Kellogg & A. Piolat (2001). The triple task technique for studying the process of writing. In: G. Rijlaarsdam (Series ed.) & T. Olive & C. M. Levy (Vol. eds.), Studies in Writing: Volume 10: Contemporary Tools and Techniques for Studying Writing, p. 31-59.

With respect to the cost of a process, it has long been recognized that writers must juggle simultaneous demands (Flower & Hayes, 1980) that often overload working memory resources (Grabowski, 1996; Kellogg, 1996, 1998, 1999; Lea & Levy, 1999; Levy, 1997; McCutchen, 1994, 1996; Ransdell & Levy, 1996; Torrance & Jeffery, 1999). Indeed, writing processes are resource-limited. Consequently, exploring the allocation of cognitive resources to the writing processes highlights how writers deal with working memory limitations as a function of the demands of the task.

The present chapter describes the use of a triple task technique designed to answer questions about the time course and cost of the writing processes. Writing a text is the primary task and detecting auditory probes as rapidly as possible is the secondary task. The tertiary task assesses the contents of the writer's working memory at the time when an auditory probe occurred through the collection of verbal protocols. One variant uses directed retrospection (Kellogg, 1987a, 1987b) and another uses thinking aloud protocols (Levy & Ransdell, 1995) to achieve this. Each variant has is own advantages and focus. However, the two are based on the same design: secondary RTs to the probes are associated with the writer's activity. The variables collected allow the researcher (1) to estimate the general temporal organization of the writing process, (2) to analyse the recursiveness of writing and (3) to measure the amount of resources allocated to the writing processes.

First, we detail the design, material, procedure and dependant variables of each one of the two variants. Then, we present a series of experiments that evaluated the extent to which the method is reactive and valid. It is argued that both variants of the triple task method are useful research tools. Although the validity of the verbal protocol method is more valid than directed retrospection, it is also potentially more disruptive of working memory resources needed for writing. Conversely, the directed retrospection is less reactive, but also it sacrifices detailed information about the nature of the writing processes. Before concluding, we synthesize several studies that used the triple task method and provided new data about invariant functional characteristics of writers. Specifically, we suggest that planning and reviewing tend to demand more cognitive effort than translating, but more time is typically devoted to translating during composition. Further, individual differences in domain-specific knowledge, verbal ability, audience representation, and working memory capacity affect the time and effort allocations. Similarly, time and effort allocations are further affected by situational factors, such as the medium of production. We end by trying to delineate how the method can be modified to answer future research questions.

2. THE TRIPLE TASK TECHNIQUE

The general design of the method involves measuring the allocation of working memory resources using reaction time (RT) to an auditory probes and coupling these measurements to specific writing processes engaged in during composition. The procedure calls for participants to focus attention on composing a text composition and to respond as rapidly as possible to auditory probes distributed in a variable interval schedule. This secondary task technique is based on the assumption that the primary and secondary tasks compete for a limited pool of attentional or working memory resources (Kahneman, 1973; Kerr, 1973; Power, 1986). Therefore, performance in the secondary task decreases, as the demands of primary task increase. The greater the performance degradation in RT to the auditory probes compared with single task, baseline RT to the same stimuli, the greater the cognitive effort required by the writing processes. Such a dual task technique is commonly used in cognitive psychology, so the unique advantage of the triple task technique lies in the addition of the third requirement. To couple the RT data with specific writing processes, the writers are asked to think aloud or to categorize the contents of working memory as they write.

The original variant of the triple task technique was proposed by Kellogg (1987a, 1987b). With this method, after each probe detection, participants perform a directed and immediate retrospection about their thoughts at the moment the probe occurred. This kind of verbal protocol is an example of what Ericsson and Simon (1993) called concurrent probing, in which information still available in working memory is reported. For this purpose, participants are requested to choose among response categories referring to particular writing processes. In the second variant of the technique (Levy, 1997; Levy & Ransdell, 1995), while composing with a word processor, writers are engaged in a thinking aloud task, verbalizing information in the current focus of attention. The probe RTs are then associated to writing processes that are identified by analysing both the verbal report of the writer and the data of a keystroke record program.

2.1. Directed retrospection protocols

2.1.1. General design

The primary task requires the composition of a text and the secondary RT task requires the detection of auditory probes (*e.g.*, tones or beeps). When participants hear auditory probes during the composition of a text (the primary task), they are asked to say 'stop' as quickly as possible whenever they detect such a probe (RT secondary task). A voice-operated relay interfaced with a computer recorded the time from the presentation of the probe to the detection response in milliseconds. The spoken response has the advantage of freeing both hands for either writing in longhand or typing on a word processor. Another alternative is for the writer to click a mouse button with the non-dominant hand that is free during handwriting.

After probe detection, the writers are asked to identify the mental process in which they were engaged when they perceived the probe. Because they are given response categories to choose among, their immediate retrospection is directed, unlike the undirected form used in thinking aloud protocols. Specifically, they choose among four response categories (for example, planning, translating, reviewing or other) by pressing a labelled button on a response box or labelled keys on a computer keyboard. The writers are first trained to identify their thoughts as examples of the four categories.

Although a finer grained distinction among processes could be used, a small number of possible choices helps to insure reliable categorizations. It may be difficult for writers to distinguish between generating ideas and organizing ideas, for example, but both thoughts could be labelled accurately as planning. At the same time, the validity of the method suffers to a degree by combining two distinct sub-processes into the broader category of planning. Another strength of the method is that the participant decides which category best fits their thoughts at the moment. With verbal protocols, the researcher must make this decision from examining the writer's statements and other behaviour.

In theory, the immediate, directed retrospection task makes it possible to find out which mental process was interrupted by the auditory probe. That is, the writer could have been planning, translating, reviewing or thinking of something unrelated to the three basic writing processes when the auditory probe occurred. Thus, the extra time it takes to detect the auditory signal and to say 'stop' can be taken as a measure of the degree of effort or capacity associated with the writing process interrupted by the signal. An RT interference measure is computed for each participant subtracting from the mean or median RT associated with each process, the mean or median baseline RT obtained when participants responded only to the auditory probe task. Furthermore, by analysing the mean frequency with which the writing processes are reported, the directed reports provide an estimate of the processing time devoted to planning, translating, and reviewing.

2.1.2. Procedure

The experimental procedure involves the following steps: the directed retrospection training, the collection of baseline RTs, and the experimental task in which writers perform a composition concurrently with RT probes followed by retrospection. For 30 minutes of composition, the total length of the experiment is between 60 and 90 minutes.

During the first step of the experiment, the participant is trained in the method of directed retrospection. The experimenter begins with instructions that define the writing processes under investigation (for example, planning, translating, and reviewing). The number and nature of writing processes can be varied as a function of the research goals. Nevertheless, a category unrelated to the writing process must be systematically used (for instance, 'other'). This unrelated category is for all thoughts that do not fit the defined writing processes (*e.g.*, daydreaming). The instructions then continue with examples of thinking-aloud protocols to illustrate further each writing process. Next, participants are required to categorize several examples of thinking-aloud protocols. Each time an error occurs, the experimenter provides feedback to correct the participant's understanding of the meaning of the different categories.

During the second step of the experiment, the reaction time task is introduced. Participants are informed that during the composition they would occasionally hear an auditory signal ('beep'). They are asked to react as quickly as possible to these beeps by saying 'stop' or by clicking the mouse with their non-dominant hand while handwriting with the dominant one. After delivering these instructions, a series of single-task RTs are collected. Generally, when 30 RTs are collected, the first five trials are treated as warm-up signals and the mean baseline RT is calculated from the 25 other RTs. The probes are distributed in a random interval with a mean interval of once every 10 s and a range of 5 s to 15 s. During the composition, probes are distributed with a mean interval of once every 30 s and a range of 15 s to 45 s[1].

1 Note that Kellogg's procedure samples the writing processes only about every 30 s, whereas Levy and Ransdell's procedure allows a much finer temporal resolution (every 1 s).

In the last step, directly after the collection of the baseline RTs, the experimenter reads the writing assignment and gives the topic of composition to the participant.

2.1.3. ScriptKell: A software for implementing the triple task

In his first studies Kellogg (1987a, 1987b, 1988, 1993) used a PASCAL program for implementing the triple task technique, but it was not designed in a flexible way that allowed one to vary parameters of the experiment. ScriptKell is a computer-assisted experimental tool that has been designed to easily modify Kellogg's technique (Piolat, Olive, Roussey, Thunin, & Ziegler, 1999). This software can be used to investigate writing and other complex cognitive activities. It runs on Apple Computers with Macintosh environment (system 7.0 or higher). It is programmed in Hypertalk in a HyperCard 2.3 environment. Since version 1.0, ScriptKell has been compiled and thus can be used without HyperCard.

ScriptKell has been designed so as each critical parameter of the triple task technique can be freely adapted to the experimental goals. Thus, it is possible to specify the essential parameters of the procedure and the global configuration of the secondary tasks. ScriptKell should, therefore, facilitate the realization of experimental designs to address new questions concerning the functional characteristics of writing and other complex cognitive activities.

When ScriptKell is started, the program displays a configuration window that allows the experimenter to specify the multiple parameters of the experimental procedure by selecting or not the different secondary tasks. For example, it is possible to choose only the baseline RT task, the writing task, the directed retrospection task or all three. Furthermore, the entire configuration of these secondary tasks can be defined (*e.g.*, duration of the baseline RT phase, interval between the probes, number and nature of response categories during the directed retrospection task, response keys, auditory signals, writing duration, etc.) for any given experiment. By default the program gives the values of the parameters that had been used in the previous session. The selected parameters can be saved in file that is located in ScriptKell's folder. With this function, particular parameters can be loaded at any time.

In the baseline RT task, participants are presented only with a number of probes (auditory signals) that they have to detect as rapidly as possible. But instead of reacting by saying 'stop' into a microphone in Kellogg's procedure, with ScriptKell participants react to the probes by clicking on the computer mouse with their non-dominant hand. The baseline RT task allows measuring the mean baseline RT of each participant against which the RTs in the triple task procedure can be compared. The probes are pseudorandomly distributed in an interval that can be specified by entering its inferior and superior boundaries (in seconds). The experimenter also needs to specify the total number of probes and the number of final probes that are used to calculate the baseline RT. Speeded responses are given by clicking on the computer mouse. In the secondary RT task, participants perform a primary task and a secondary RT task to auditory probes. Again, inferior and superior boundaries are entered to specify the distribution interval. The duration of the composition is either unlimited or limited. In the last case, the experimenter can define its duration (in seconds) depending on the goals of the experiment.

In the secondary RT task, participants often fail to detect a probe. To handle such omissions, ScriptKell offers two options: the experimenter either chooses a delay after which the program emits a new probe or a reminder one. In the directed retrospection task, participants are asked to choose one or several categories that best reflect what they were doing when they were interrupted by the probe. The experimenter can specify the number of response categories (maximum 12). In addition, responses categories are labelled and responses keys are assigned to each category. It is important to note that ScriptKell allows participants to choose one or several categories after each probe. As participants may occasionally forget to perform the directed retrospection task, the program offers several options to launch or not a new probe.

ScriptKell automatically records and analyses the different variables of Kellogg's procedure (number of reactions, frequency of category choices, mean RTs, mean difference scores). The data of each participant are saved in a text file that is located in ScriptKell's folder. In the first section of the spreadsheet, summary information about the participant and the experiment is given, such as the participant name and identification and the date and time at which the experiment started. In the second section, the parameters and the results of the baseline RT task are given (*i.e.*, the interval between probes, the number of probes used for the computation of the mean baseline RT and the mean baseline RT). The third section deals with the overall results. The program gives the relevant parameters, the total number of responses, the mean RT associated with each category (with their standard deviation) and the mean difference score. All responses are then listed in chronological order along with their corresponding measures: the time since the beginning of the composition, the time since the last probe, the corresponding RT, the difference score, the subprocess identified with the directed retrospection and the designation time (time between the response to the probe and the identification of the retrospection category). In a fourth section, the data are broken as a function of the categories that were selected in the retrospection. Finally, in order to investigate changes in performance over time, the total writing time is broken into three and four equally parts, and all analyses are provided separately for each part (see Figure 1).

2.2. Thinking aloud protocols

2.2.1. General design

The method implemented by Levy and Ransdell (1994, 1995) is similar to Kellogg's variant. The focus of these authors is also to study the time course of the writing processes and the cognitive effort of writers but in order to identify the writing processes interrupted by the probe, they simultaneously analyse thinking-aloud protocols and keystroke recording protocols of the composition.

Date : Mer 02 juin 2000 11:30:37
Participant name : Standard-$n°15-Patrick-E+

——————— BASELINE RT TASK ———————

Interval between beeps : from 5 to 15 sec.
Computation of the mean baseline RTs with the 5 last beeps
Detail of the RTs (sec) : 0.6/0.633/.../0.433/0.417/0.317
Mean baseline RT (sec) : 0.483 sec.

——————— WRITING TASK ———————

Interval between beeps From 15 to 45 sec.
Total number of recorded reactions : 26

Chronology		Delay	RT	RTp.	Retrospection	DT
0	: Start					
23	23	0.767	0.284	Planning	2.033	
46	21	0.905	0.422	Translating	1.167	
...						
775	24	0.983	0.500	Reviewing	1.517	
809	32	1.067	0.584	Reviewing	0.95	
816	: END					
Means		0.977	0.494		1.178	
Sd			0.142		0.231	

——————— ANALYSIS BY THIRD ———————

Planning

	1st :	2nd:	3rd:	TOTAL:	
Nb designations:	5	1	1	7	
Mean RT	0.933	1.0	1.067	0.962	
Mean RTp	0.450	0.517	0.584	0.479	(sd =0.172)
Mean DT	1.22	0.633	1.983	1.245	(sd=0.582)

Translating
...

Reviewing
...

——————— ANALYSIS BY QUARTER ———————
...

Figure 1. A sample of an individual protocol provided by Scriptkell.

Thinking-aloud protocols are an important source of data for psychologists. For example, such method helped researchers to identify a number of basic subprocesses involved in writing, such as planning, translating and reviewing (Hayes & Flower, 1980). Thus, by providing direct information about the way writers manage the writing processes during a composition and by giving a state-by-state description of the activity, thinking-aloud protocols are also helpful to build empirical models of the cognitive system (Hayes & Flower, 1983). But by combining data providing both from thinking-aloud protocols and keystroke recording protocols of the composition it is possible to precisely identify the writing processes as they unfold in real time. Indeed, researchers can discriminate between difficult categories by comparing the two kinds of protocols. For example, revision and reviewing processes can be identified with the verbal protocols but cannot be easily discriminated. The presence of writing activity in the keystroke recording protocol is evidence of revision activity. Furthermore, computer-based recordings of a composition allow a second by second description of the writer's activity.

Thus, in Levy and Ransdell's variant of the triple task technique, while participants compose a text, they are at the same time engaged in a thinking-aloud task and a secondary RT task. Besides collecting the verbal and resource allocation protocols, an unobtrusive written protocol is obtained from keystroke recordings.

2.2.2 *Procedure*

Although Levy and Ransdell (1995) asked participants to compose during 10 sessions, the procedure is identical whatever the number of writing sessions. Each session begin by a two-minute phase in which writers perform a secondary RT task in single-task condition in order to calculate the mean baseline RT. During this phase as during the composition, the probes are distributed once every 30 s in mean (in an interval between 15 s and 45 s). Then participants perform the composition phase. Before beginning, the experimenter read the instructions concerning the composition and the thinking-aloud task. They are asked to continuously provide concurrent verbal protocols as they wrote and are encouraged to say aloud every thought that comes to their mind without trying to justify what they write or say. Participants are also asked to continue responding to the tone whenever they heard it. During the composition, each time a 10-seconds silence occurs, the experimenter asks the writer to continue to think aloud. The writers were assigned a new topic for their compositions each week.

2.2.3. *Apparatus*

Writers perform the triple task on a personal computer in a Windows environment. The data are collected and analysed with separate softwares (for a detailed technical descriptions of the apparatus, see Levy & Ransdell, 1994, 1995). The typical screen layout provides an area occupying three fourths of the screen that the writer uses to compose his text. The writers use Notepad, a word-processing software including only the basic text editing functions (cut, copy and paste).

Each writing session is recorded with a videotape connected to the computer. An interface (Simulscan) converted the VGA signal provides by the computer for the monitor into an NTSC (or PAL) signal that is field directly to the videotape. The verbal protocols are recorded by directly plugging a microphone to the videotape recorder. By this way, the unfolding of the writing session can be seen back and forward or paused.

The secondary RT task is implemented using Beeper, a software developed for this purpose. Beeper runs in the Windows environment as a background task while a writer is using any other Windows application. It sounds aperiodically a tone in a variable interval of 30 s. Pressing a key or a secondary mouse (since the writer's hands are usually engaged with the keyboard a footswitch is placed on the floor) provides the detection signal of the tone.

Once the data are collected, trained judges analyse the written and verbal protocols by coding the nature, unfolding and the duration of the writing processes under investigations (for instance, planning, generating text, reviewing and revising). Levy and Ransdell (1995) employed a computer-aided analysis of the protocols, which is a helpful mean to deal with this large amount of data. EventLog (Henderson, 1989) was used to code the verbal and written protocols. This software allows one to easily code in predefined categories the protocols as they unfold second by second. However, as several raters are needed to code the protocols, a critical point concerns the interrater agreement on the nature of the writing processes that is coded. To circumvent this problem, Levy and Ransdell have developed Agree, a software specifically designed to calculate an index of the interrater agreement. The software compares the coding of protocols by pairs of raters and gives an index expressed as a percentage (for a description of this index, see Levy & Ransdell, 1994).

2.3. Dependent variables

The two variants of the triple task technique provide data aiming at describing the dynamic of writing under two general angles: the temporal organization of the writing processes and cognitive effort allocated to the writing processes. Thus, two types of raw data can be analysed.

The analysis of the temporal organization of the writing processes is provided by the verbalization data (directed retrospection or thinking-aloud protocols) and is aimed at describing 'processing time' allocated to the writing processes (Kellogg, 1987a, 1988). At a general level, the temporal organization of the writing processes can be described simply by calculating the percentage of processing time allocated to each writing processes. For instance, for each subject, the number of times a particular process has been reported through directed retrospection or identified with the verbal and written protocols is divided by the number of time all the writing processes have occurred. However, these data only take into account the number of time the different writing processes occurred. Levy and Ransdell (1995) also calculated the mean duration of the writing processes by looking at one second intervals in their protocols.

Still, it is more interesting to analyse processing time as a function of the unfolding of writing and the total composition time can be divided into several phases. Then, the allocation of processing time to the writing processes can be analysed according to these writing phases (note that each one of the previous variables can thus be analysed as a function of the writing phase). This distinction provides two kind of analysis. A first analysis concerns the pattern of time processing in one single phase of all the writing processes. In other words, it is related to the following question: 'In one phase of the composition, which process is prominent and how processing time is allocated to the other processes?' and is aimed at providing intra-phases comparisons of the different writing processes. This analysis is carried out by dividing, for each process, the number of times they occur during a specific phase by the total number all the writing process have been identified in this phase. Then, the percentages of each writing process in one specific phase are compared.

A second analysis concerns the pattern of time processing of one writing process through all the writing phases. In other words, it is related to the following question: 'Through a composition, how evolves the allocation of time processing for one single writing process?' and is aimed at providing between-phases comparison. Thus, this analysis is carried out by dividing the number of times one single writing process occurs during all the writing phases by the total number this writing process has been identified in all the phases. Then, the percentages of time processing for this specific process at each phase are compared. Thus, it is possible to determine which process dominates at a particular moment of a writing session and how a particular process is engaged through the writing process.

At another level of inquiry, the temporal organization of the writing processes can be studied by analysing the recursion of writing processes. From the analysis of verbal protocols, Hayes and Flower (1980) have shown that the activation of each writing processes (*i.e.*, planning, translating, and reviewing) was repeatedly interrupted by the others. In order to highlights this recursion, Levy and Ransdell (1995) constructed what they called a matrix of transitional probabilities. A matrix of transitional probabilities describes the shifts between a writing process and the others (for example when a writer shifts from planning to translating or from reviewing to planning). These matrices are build by dividing the number of times a writer shifts from a process to another by the total number all the writing processes occur during a predetermined period of writing and are independent of the absolute frequencies of occurrence of writing processes. These matrices contain all possible shifts among all possible combinations of the writing processes. For instance, Levy and Ransdell (1995) selected ten minutes time frames and, hence, were able to compare the changes in the matrices during a single session of composition, between different writing sessions and between different writers. Thus, matrices of transitional probabilities offer a new means to investigate the recursiveness of writing.

Finally, with the triple task technique the allocation of working memory resources or cognitive effort can be analysed. Indeed, the secondary RT technique is based on the principle that participants have to simultaneously perform two tasks that compete for limited working memory resources. The duration of a secondary RT is assumed to reflect the amount of working memory resources allocated to the primary task, here writing. Therefore, by calculating the mean RT associated to a writing process by the mean of the directed retrospection or with the verbal and written protocols, the longer the RT, the greater resources are allocated to this process. Finally, although it has not been yet studied, it is possible to analyse the pattern of changes in cognitive effort of the writing processes through the composition session by comparing the RTs in different writing phases.

In summary, the triple task technique allows one to approach the question of the temporal organization of the writing processes through directed retrospection or verbal protocols. Thus, it is possible to analyse the allocation of processing time during a composition session and the recursive features of writing, as well as momentary cognitive effort.

3. REACTIVITY AND VALIDITY OF THE METHOD

A critical issue with the triple task technique is whether it disrupts or misrepresents the writing processes of interest. Indeed, writing has often been considered as an overloading cognitive task. It is possible, therefore, that with this technique writers cannot allocate a sufficient amount of cognitive resources to the composition task. Also, interpreting the outcome of experiments with dual task requirements can be problematic if certain assumptions are not met. Finally, the validity of verbalizing or categorizing thoughts is potentially troublesome.

Ericsson and Simon (1978) contented that verbal protocols were valid measures of cognition if the contents of working memory could be reported without recoding the information (Level 1) or if already heeded information simply required recoding into a verbal format (Level 2). In their view, the greatest problems with obtaining reliable information occurred when the experimenter asked participants about information that is normally not processed or paid attention to. In this case (Level 3), participants needed to infer or generate information in order to comply with the experimenter's instructions. Another important source of validity problems lies in delaying probes until after the task is completed. This, of course, runs the risk of participants forgetting what they did and invites them to reconstruct the important processes and make inferences to fill in gaps in their recall.

The triple task method uses immediate testing as writers compose with both verbal protocols and directed retrospection. Hence both variants avoid the forgetting problem. Planning, translating, and reviewing processes involve a wide variety of representations that differ with respect to their explicitness and ease of verbal coding (Flower & Hayes, 1984). Either verbal protocols or directed retrospection might be unsuitable in writing tasks if most of the information available in working memory requires recoding, inferencing, or generating in order to yield reports. It will be argued here that this is not a serious problem in writing, although for verbal protocols and directed retrospection each have their own advantages and disadvantages. It will also be argued, in the next section, that the use of secondary task RT in the triple task method is acceptable and yields interpretable results.

3.1. Potential problems with secondary reaction time tasks

3.1.1. Interpreting secondary reaction times

Secondary RTs tasks have been designed to account for the allocation of cognitive resources on cognitive tasks (Kahneman, 1973; Kerr, 1973). However, the interpretation of performances in dual-task conditions has often been critiqued (see for example, Navon, 1984). For example, Howe and Rabinowitz (1989) have claimed that performance in dual-task conditions is uninterpretable. They argued that the performances observed in such situations couldn't be attributed univocally to the cognitive demands of the primary task. They claim that the dual-task methodology complicate the analysis of cognitive demands since the adding of a secondary task multiply the interactions between the different processing. For their part, Fisk, Derrick, and Schneider (1986–87) argue that dual-task performances are interpretable only if three methodological criteria are filled.

According to the views of Fisk *et al.* (1986–87), the first criterion that dual-task designs must meet regards performance stability. Following these authors, performance in the primary task (here writing) has to be not affected by the secondary task (here the RT task). Piolat, Roussey, Olive, and Farioli (1996) addressed this question by comparing text produced when writers performed only a composition (single task situation) with a conditions in which writers performed the triple task technique. Piolat *et al.* (1996) evaluated the effect of the secondary task on the number of final words, on the fluency, on the syntactic complexity (number of words by sentence) and on the number of revisions. They observed no significant difference on the number of words, on the fluency, on the number of revision or on the syntactic complexity. Furthermore, Piolat *et al.* (1996) compared the mean cognitive effort in dual task situation (composition with secondary RTs) and triple task situation (composition, secondary RTs and directed retrospection). Theme of the text and experimental conditions (*e.g.*, number of auditory probes, interval between probes, instructions) were similar to those of Kellogg (1988). Results showed that there were no significant difference between the dual-task condition and the triple-task condition in terms of cognitive effort. In an additional relevant study, Penningroth and Rosenberg (1995) compared a group of individuals who performed the secondary RT task as they wrote a story with a writing only control group. Subjective ratings of attentional overload and ratings of the coherence of the stories written did not differ. Surprisingly, the holistic quality ratings obtained were reliably higher for the RT group compared with the control group.

The second criterion proposed by Fisk *et al.* (1986–87) concerns the stability of cognitive demands of the secondary task throughout the procedure. Indeed, in the case of an incidental learning on the secondary task response, the observed decrease of the RTs might be attributed to this learning and not to a lower cognitive effort involved by the primary task. Olive (1997) addressed this question with the triple task technique by comparing the first RTs to the last RTs and did not observe any difference between these RTs. He concluded that cognitive resources allocated to the secondary RT task were constant and that variations of duration of the RTs could be attributed univocally to modifications of the cognitive demands of writing and not to changes in the secondary task's demands.

The third criterion identified by Fisk *et al.* (1986–87) concerns the pools of resources of the primary and secondary tasks. For these authors, performance on dual-task can be interpreted only if the two tasks share the same pool of resources. Although this question has raised controversial discussions on the structure on the cognitive system (see, Lea & Levy, 1999), our purpose is not to decide among the different hypotheses that have been proposed. Nevertheless, it is possible to show that the two tasks share a common pool of resources if modifications of the RTs are observed as a function of the difficulty of the composition task. Olive (1997) reviewed the experiments using the triple task technique and showed that RTs varied when the difficulty of the composition task was manipulated.

In sum, adding the RT task and the directed retrospection does not modify the text produced by the writers. Writers perform the RT task only or the directed retrospection immediately after does not influence the cognitive effort associated to the writing processes. Furthermore, the demands of secondary RT task remain stable through the composition and the two tasks draw their resources from a common pool. Thus, as the triple task technique meets the three criteria of Fisk *et al.* (1986–87), we argue that performance on both the composition task and the secondary RT task can be interpreted without ambiguity concerning their respective cognitive demands.

3.1.2. Importance of instructions

Another question that can be raised against the interpretation of secondary RTs concerns the focus of the participants on either the primary task or the secondary task. This question was addressed after Piolat, Roussey, Olive, and Farioli (1996) observed that writers who received an elaborated training to the directed retrospection task were slower in the RT task (624 ms) than writers who were trained according to Kellogg's original procedure (393 ms). Their result suggested that the nature of the training instructions to the directed retrospection task could have resulted in focusing the writers to this task and consequently could have resulted in increasing their cognitive effort. This interpretation was supported by the analysis of the time participants took for choosing among the response categories (writing, planning, reviewing, or other). Writers who received the more elaborated training were significantly longer in choosing the labels in the directed retrospection than writers who were less extensively trained (1.85 *vs.* 1.2 s).

Farioli and Piolat (1999) addressed this issue by comparing the effect of instructions that focused participants on one of the three tasks of the triple task technique (the composition task, the RT task, the directed retrospection task). They analysed how these instructions should affect both the allocation of time and effort to the writing processes. They observed that writers who focused on the secondary probe task showed shorter RT than writers who focused on the writing task, but did not observe any difference between conditions when writers were focused on the composition and on the directed retrospection. Furthermore, the allocations of time to planning, translating, and reviewing did not vary with the instructions, nor did the time it time it took to identify the writing process interrupted by the probe.

The previous findings show that intentionally focusing on one of the three tasks can force changes in the cognitive effort devoted to the other tasks (Fisk, Derrick, & Schneider, 1986–1987). In such cases, the participant may only have a small margin in allocating his or her resources to each of the three tasks and does so based on a subjective evaluation of the experimenter's demands (see also the concept of 'cognitive balance' in Glynn, Britton, Muth, & Dogan, 1982).

3.1.3. Probe timing

A further constraint of the triple task technique is the choice of the time interval with which the probe interrupts the writing process. In two studies, Olive (1997) and

Piolat, Roussey, Olive & Farioli (1996) addressed the question of whether the choice of a particular time interval affects the text produced by the writers, the cognitive effort of the writing processes and the allocation of time processing to theses processes. In Piolat *et al.*'s (1996) experiment, three groups were given the triple task technique but under different time intervals. In the high-rate group, writers experienced short intervals between probes (auditory probe every 15 s varying between 10 and 20 s), in the average rate group, writers experienced medium intervals (auditory probe every 30 s varying between 15 and 45 s), and in the low-rate group, writers experienced long intervals (auditory probe every 45 s varying between 30 and 60 s). The results showed that the temporal organization of the writing processes was not significantly affected by variations of the interruption interval. Furthermore, the text produced in the three experimental groups did not differ. In contrast, secondary RTs were significantly affected by these variations. The RTs were longer in both the low-rate and high-rate groups than in the average rate group (low-rate = 525 ms, high-rate = 502 ms, average rate = 393 ms). Thus, it seems that varying the interval between the auditory probe affects the distribution of cognitive resources across the different tasks.

Without interpreting these results any further (see Piolat *et al.*, 1996) it seems that the choice of the interruption interval is an important feature of the design of the triple task procedure. For example, it is clear that the choice of this interval may affect writers' performance as a function of their expertise; the less experienced the writer, the higher the probability that critical interruption intervals produce what is often referred to as the cognitive overload during writing.

3.2. Potential problems with verbal protocols

Although verbal protocols have raised several discussions, this method has been widely used in cognitive psychology (Ericsson & Simon, 1993; Russo, Johnson, & Stephens, 1989; Wilson, 1994), and particularly for the study of writing (Smagorinsky, 1994). From the seminal works of Hayes and Flower (1980; see also Swarts, Flower & Hayes, 1984; Hayes & Flower 1983), verbal protocols have also been used to study for example, second language writing (Cumming, 1994) and spelling strategies (Varnhagen, 1995). Furthermore, this method allows one to relate the temporal organization of the writing processes with text quality (Breetvelt, van den Bergh, & Rijlaarsdam, 1994). Thinking-aloud protocols have also enabled one to identify the different writing processes and the type of knowledge associated with their activation in novice writers (Burtis, Bereiter, Scardamalia, & Tetroe, 1983) and, associated with a simultaneous analysis of pauses, in expert writers (Kaufer, Hayes, & Flower, 1986). As the two variants of the triple task technique resort to verbal protocols either by asking participants to categorise their activity with a directed retrospection (Kellogg, 1987b) or with a concurrent thinking-aloud (Levy et Ransdell, 1995), it is thus necessary to evaluate the advantages and inconveniences of these methods.

3.2.1. Concurrent versus delayed protocols

Ericsson and Simon distinguished different types of verbal protocols according to the moment when participants produced it and whether the information was still in the active focus of attention. They contended that think aloud protocols ask a participant to verbalize information that is currently in the focus of his or her attention. Similarly, concurrent probes, to use Ericsson and Simon's (1993) terminology, call for an immediate retrospection about information still within working memory. In contrast to these variations of concurrent protocols, delayed probes assess information only after the task has been completed; Ericsson and Simon referred to these after-task questions as retrospective protocols. As an example, writers might be asked to categorize their thought processes after they have finished their text (Schumacher, Clare, Cronin, & Moses, 1984). Consequently, these protocols could be distorted through forgetting and reconstruction of the activity. These phenomena will largely depend on the delay between writing and the protocol task (Ericsson & Simon, 1993; Gufoni, 1996).

The terminology used here distinguishes between thinking or talking aloud and directed retrospection that take place immediately after the occurrence of a probe. In both cases, the information reported is either still in the focus of attention or, at least, still in working memory. But we question whether it is reasonable to claim that all verbalized information is still in the focus of attention whereas immediate or concurrent probes for a categorization response are not attended but available in working memory. We see no strong basis for determining whether the verbal protocol or the categorization response is based on currently heeded information or information recently heeded and still in working memory. Consequently, we contrast two kinds of concurrent probes – verbal protocols and directed retrospection taken together – with delayed retrospective probes. Do concurrent versus delayed probes have different effects on the nature of the information that is collected?

Levy and Ransdell's variant of the triple task technique uses thinking-aloud protocols. To test their validity, Levy and Ransdell (1995) and Levy, Marek and Lea (1996) compared the content of concurrent verbal protocols with those of delayed retrospective categorizations. Levy and Ransdell (1995) observed that writers were not able to recall well the processes they activated during the composition, even when they exhibited a high-level rate of confidence. They observed, in the best case, that sixty percent of retrospective categorizations matched the processes identified in the concurrent protocols and only 10% in the worst case. Unlike delayed retrospection, concurrent retrospection occurs within one or two seconds after detection of the auditory probe. It should be less subjection to the hazards of forgetting and reconstruction that likely bias experiments using delayed probes.

3.2.2. Directed or undirected protocols

Another major difference between the two variants of the triple task technique concerns the way writers identify the writing processes. Indeed, while Levy and Ransdell's instructions ask writers to report their thoughts freely, Kellogg's instructions require that writers identify their thoughts in terms of pre-determined categories of processes. This design raised at least three questions. The first one is related to the information provided by the retrospection task: do writers' categorizations provide valid insights into their own activity? The second question directly deals with the training of the directed retrospection: are writers sufficiently trained to identify the writing processes they activate? Finally, the third question raised by the method is that in the majority of the experiments already conducted, writers only categorize one process, although several may be activated in parallel.

If the products of planning, translating, and reviewing are not readily accessible to conscious report, then concurrent directed probes may not provide a valid picture (Ericsson & Simon, 1993). The validity issue was initially tested by Kellogg (1987a, note 6, 1987b) who observed a substantial agreement between writers categorizing their own verbal protocols as examples of planning, translating, and reviewing and a trained judge categorizing the same report. After thinking aloud while composing, the writers received training on using the three categories and then listened to a recording of their verbalizations. Despite that nearly 20 minutes passed from the end of the writing task to the stage of categorizing the verbalizations, a mean of 82% of the participants' categorisations matched the experimenter's categorisations of the same verbalizations. Presumably, this figure provided a low estimate of agreement given that forgetting probably occurred over the 20-minute retention interval. Thus, the results provided a validation of the directed retrospection task.

A second study of the validity of directed retrospection assessed whether the categorizations are subject to distortion because of forgetting or because participants respond randomly (Levy, Marek, & Lea, 1995). The writers were given a large number of categories (15, including 'other'), as in a study by Schumacher *et al.*, and instructed to retrospect concurrently with composing when auditory probes occurred. Then, at the end of a 20-minute writing session they reviewed a videotape of the entire writing session. At the points when probes occurred, they were asked to recategorize their thoughts at that point in the composing process. Levy *et al.* found that some writers matched their earlier categorizations about 75% of the time. However, others showed little consistency, not much better than random responding. This suggests that any delay in categorization risks seriously distorting the validity of the data. Such forgetting effects may be less severe, though, when only three categories are used.

Levy *et al.* also tested whether metaknowledge about the writing process influences the pattern of responses given to directed retrospection. For example, the general notion that writers first plan, then write, then revise could cause exactly this pattern to occur regardless of the true contents of working memory. If that is so, then even categorizing the behaviour of someone else writing ought to show the same pattern. So, Levy *et al.* had participants decide whether the research assistant was engaged in planning, translating, reviewing, or other activities whenever an auditory probe occurred as the assistant appeared to be writing. The results showed a flat pattern of responses over time: planning, translating, and reviewing were reported equally often as the writing session progressed. Thus, metacognitive knowledge appeared to have little effect when tested in this manner.

Levy and Ransdell (1995) suggested that with directed retrospection writers overestimate the amount of time they spend reviewing, because of metacognitive beliefs that reviewing is common. During composition their verbal and written protocols revealed little if any reviewing. In contrast, self-reports given on a survey about their typical composing process revealed that nearly a third of their time and effort was spent on reviewing. This outcome could be interpreted to mean that self-reports of any kind, including directed retrospections, are subject to distortions inherent in the writers' metacognitive beliefs about writing processes.

However, Levy and Ransdell underscored that the self-reports they analysed were convergent with the pattern of temporal organization of the writing processes that Kellogg observed (1987a, 1987b, 1998). Planning ideas and their relationships is relatively more pressing early in writing and reviewing later in the task. Translating commonly occurs during all phases of a writing session. These temporal patterns are unique for each process and have been observed now in studies using directed retrospection (Kellogg, 1988; Levy & Ransdell, 1995; Piolat *et al.*, 1996), undirected verbal protocols (Levy & Ransdell, 1995; Penningroth & Rosenberg, 1995; Rau & Sebrechts, 1996), and videotaped observations of writing behaviour (Levy & Ransdell, 1995; Breetvelt, van den Bergh, & Rijlaarsdam, 1994). The absolute magnitudes of the time estimates given to writing processes are not identical across studies, possibly because of differences in the measurement technique, writing topics, and other procedural matters. Nonetheless, all these studies have found that planning decreases over a writing session and reviewing increases, while translating occurs frequently throughout composition. That different retrospective and observational methods converge weakens the case that the patterns reflect beliefs rather actual working memory allocations.

Although metacognitive beliefs could certainly influence self-reports, one would expect them to do so when no little or no information is available in working memory. This could readily happen when answering a survey question about typical writing processes. It may be very difficult to retrieve information about how working memory resources were actually allocated in a particular past writing task. But with an immediate report collected as one writes, this kind of distortion ought to be less likely. Also, metacognitive beliefs did not seem to affect categorizations of someone else's writing behaviour, when the individual has no access to the writer's working memory (Levy *et al.*, 1995). Although further tests of whether metacognition distorts directed retrospection are needed, the evidence does not suggest that this is a serious weakness of the directed retrospection variant of the triple task technique.

The focus here has been on potential problems in identifying writing processes correctly using directed retrospection. It must be noted, however, that the technique solves the segmentation problem encountered with undirected, think aloud protocols. At times, there can be multiple ways to divide a think aloud protocol into segments that define a process. It is up to experimenter to determine the best way to proceed. With directed retrospection, the writer segments his or her thoughts to fit a single process category. Thus, the writer rather than the experimenter takes care of the segmentation problem.

3.2.3. Training of directed retrospection

Piolat, Roussey, Olive, and Farioli, (1996) observed that writers frequently showed some difficulties in labelling their mental activity in the directed retrospection. They investigated the role of training for successful performance in this task. Two groups of 20 participants were tested. The first group received Kellogg's original training. The second group received two training sessions. The first session was a discussion group of three hours in which participants were confronted with their usual way of writing and learned to label their writing processes according to Kellogg's categories. In the second session, one week later, they were submitted to Kellogg's original training. Although some differences were found in the RTs and in time of categorization, the two groups did not differ in the use of the different writing subprocesses. This result suggests that Kellogg's original training is sufficient and that with such training writers are able to correctly categorize their activity.

Finally, should more than one categorization response be given, to reflect parallel processing? The directed retrospection task, as it was originally implemented, asked participants to categorize their activity with only one label (or process). From a theoretical perspective, with this technique researchers implicitly assume that writing processes are sequentially activated. Kellogg (1987a, 1988) indicated in the description of his experimental procedure that writers should choose, among all mental processes, the one that appears the most dominant at the time the auditory signal occurs. Kellogg (1994, 1996) admitted that some processes might be fairly complex and difficult to classify into only three categories. This complexity may stem from writers' capacity to engage in several subprocesses in parallel. Evidence of such a parallel activation was found by Levy *et al.* (1996: 548) who showed that 8% of concomitant protocols concerned at least two processes.

Pélissier and Piolat (1998) assessed if asking writers to account for their mental activity with only one process biased the results obtained with the triple task technique by setting up two experimental conditions. In the One-Choice condition, writers were requested to choose the most important process during the retrospection task. In the Two-Choices condition, writers were requested to categorize their mental activity with one or, if they thought it was necessary, two processes. A strong consistency in terms of time processing and cognitive effort was observed between the two experimental conditions 'One-Choice' and 'Two-Choices.' Furthermore, these authors observed that the most frequent pair of processes associated by the participants was Translating and Executing, followed by Evaluating and Revising. By contrast, Planning and Reviewing were found to be relatively autonomous. The high cost of these processes in working memory, particularly as concerns reviewing could explain this serial activation. From these findings, Pélissier and Piolat (1998) concluded that the standard paradigm of the triple task provide highly reliable data.

3.2.4. On the reactivity of verbal protocols

The issue of the reactivity of verbal protocols deals with the effect of these tasks on the writing activity itself. Do they transform the writing process? Kellogg (1987b) compared 30 writers engaged in directed retrospection with 30 control writers who composed as a single task. Despite the adequate statistical power, no reliable differences were observed in either writing fluency or quality. Kellogg (1987b) concluded that concurrent directed retrospection is not reactive.

As for thinking aloud, Ransdell (1990, 1995) observed that participants engaged in a concurrent thinking-aloud task were slowing their composition. They produced fewer words and sentences per minute than participants composing in silence did. However, the final number of words and the syntactic complexity were not affected.

Levy and Ransdell (1995) noted, with writers who compose different texts during several sessions, that the slowing of their participants was temporary. Eventually they were able to rapidly produce text at their normal level of fluency while they concurrently thought aloud.

It could be, then, that thinking aloud only increases the duration of pauses and even that effect might be eliminated with further practice. However, Stratman and Hamp-Lyons (1994) analysed the consequences of thinking-aloud protocols on writers' ability to detect and to revise errors included in a text. They observed that, relative to silent writing, thinking aloud slightly decreased the rate of fixing problems in sentence cohesion while augmenting the detection of ambiguous pronominal reference.

Further, Janssen, van Waes and van den Bergh (1996) carefully examined the effects of thinking aloud on the length and frequency of pauses at different levels of text structure and in different kinds of writing tasks. They observed an increase in the duration of pauses both on a complex task of writing a business report and on a simple explanatory assignment. However, they further observed that in the complex task correlations between pauses within sentences, between sentences, and between paragraphs were much higher when thinking aloud than when writing silently. The length of pauses to plan, translate, or review within sentences was highly predictive of pauses between sentences and between paragraphs only when writers were thinking aloud. Although this difference was not observed in the simple task, the result strongly suggests that thinking aloud can alter the nature of the writing process. It does more than just lengthen pause durations.

If thinking aloud is hardest to do in complex tasks, then its use may be limited. Rymer (1988) had difficulty in getting professionals to think aloud while engaged in real, as opposed to artificial or laboratory, writing tasks. Of nine scientists studied by Rymer, only five were willing to try thinking aloud while composing a scientific paper on their work. Two of those dropped out immediately while a third quit after several attempts at talking aloud while trying to do serious work. A fourth persisted but his protocol included only the words he had drafted, long pauses, and occasional explanations of his silence. Thus, only one scientist remained in the study who could provide a good verbal protocol while writing on the job. In theory, directed retrospection should fare better given that writers are not required to continuously articulate their thoughts. However, it is unknown whether the interruptions of once every 30 s, on average, are also problematic when writers engage in real-world tasks with serious personal consequences. Further studies with both variants of the triple task are needed with professional writers accomplishing actual writing assignments.

On theoretical grounds, Ericsson and Simon (1993) differentiated three types of verbal protocols. At Level 1, they identified simple verbalizations that are direct translations of the inner-speech. At Level 2, they described verbalizations that include categorizing thoughts. At Level 3, they identified verbal protocols that try to explain thinking activity and require inferences and the generation of content. In Levy and Ransdell's (1995) thinking aloud procedure, participants presumably perform Level 1 verbal protocols. Similarly, in Kellogg's procedure writers are directed to retrospect about information currently in the focus of attention or available in working memory.

It is necessary in this procedure to recode the information as one of three process categories, a Level 2 kind of verbal protocol.

Ericsson and Simon's (1993) analysis of the effects of these types of verbal protocols led them to conclude that protocols from level 1 and 2 do not affect the primary task, except in its rate of execution. Providing a protocol slows processing but does not in theory change its character. They concluded that only protocols from level 3 modify the activity because they require more cognitive resources than the previous two. If one accepts their view, then both the verbal protocol and directed retrospection variants of the triple task should be non-reactive.

Two points may cloud this theoretical picture, however. First, participants probably also filter information with the directed retrospection procedure and report thoughts unrelated to writing as the 'other category.' It seems likely that a similar filtering process occurs with think aloud protocols. It is difficult to believe that writers articulate every thought that passes through their minds no matter how unrelated it may be to the task at hand. Scanning for particular kinds of information is an example of a Level 3 verbal report, which may be at times taint the writer's characterization of the contents of working memory. Second, if one accepts the portrayal of writing provided by Flower and Hayes (1984) it is also likely that at least some representations used in writing require recoding into a verbal format (Level 2) or even inferences and generation (Level 3). A preverbal, image generated during planning, for example, either must be ignored or recoded in order to talked about. It is a fine line as to whether this involves a simple recoding of information or active generation of content that goes beyond the original fleeting image. One possible advantage of the directed retrospection method is that participants need merely recognize that such an image occurred as part of planning. The recoding problem in this case is inherently simpler.

These two points emphasize the difficulty of deciding on theoretical grounds whether a complex cognitive activity can be captured through verbal protocols without altering the activity of interest. Russo, Johnson, and Stephens (1989) argued against making such claims on theoretical grounds and called for empirical checks in each task. For their part, Russo *et al.* showed that the accuracy of performance in certain tasks (*e.g.*, simple addition and a choice between two gambles). For writing, it appears that, when the task is complex enough, thinking aloud may begin to alter the nature of the processes in addition to increasing the frequency and duration of pauses. Directed retrospection has not yet been shown to do this, but further work is required before reaching a definitive conclusion.

3.3. Conclusions on methodology

It appears that the triple task technique allows one to measure important features of writing processes without fundamentally altering those processes, at least in laboratory situations. Neither the functional characteristics of writers nor the quality of the text produced in triple task situations are influenced. People are able to respond to auditory probes and to either think aloud or categorize writing processes while concurrently focusing on the primary writing task. Categorizing thoughts during writing into a small number of categories appears to be a reasonably valid approach, whereas a large number of categories can confuses writers. Obviously, the fewer categories used, the less informative the experiment will be in detailing the subprocesses of writing. This does not mean that a large set of categories must be used to gain more information. Rather, it means that the directed retrospection has been designed to track accurately the time course of a small number of categories (about 3–5). The think aloud procedure is also a reasonably valid approach for many if not all of the representations held in working memory during text production. With respect to reactivity, it seems likely that the requirement to articulate every thought that enters awareness is more reactive than categorizing thoughts every 30 s or so. But more evidence is needed on this point. The primary form that reactivity takes in writing while thinking aloud is a slowing of the process. However, some evidence suggests that when the writing task is sufficiently complex, thinking aloud may begin to disrupt processing and the same outcome could apply to directed retrospection.

The secondary RT method, as it is commonly used, meet the criteria defined by Fisk *et al.* (1986–87). Therefore, the secondary RTs can be interpreted without any ambiguity on their interpretation. Undirected retrospection or thinking aloud may be most susceptible to disrupting writing, but verbal protocols clearly open an interesting window for researchers. Only verbal protocols provide the kind of rich detail that characterizes high-level cognition. Finally, it seems that verbal protocols alone are not sufficient. Thus, it is essential to analyse both verbal and written protocols in order to obtain convergent data. Because verbal and written protocols are on-line recording of composition, they provide more reliable and valid information than could be obtained only from the final text or from the writer's retrospections obtained after the task is completed. Kellogg's procedure offers the same advantage of collecting retrospections that are fresh in working memory as the writer composes rather than after the fact, when only long-term memory representations can be retrieved.

Comparatively, the directed retrospection procedure does not provide a convergent picture of writing behaviour, as does the think aloud procedure with the simultaneous analysis of verbal and written protocols. On the other hand, verbal and written protocol analyses are markedly more labour intensive than are the analysis of the writer's directed retrospections. Studies using verbal protocol analysis in reasoning, problem solving, and writing have traditionally been limited to small sample sizes as a consequence. It is possible to test hypotheses demanding large factorial designs using Kellogg's variant. Furthermore, writers are not obliged to use a word processor with Kellogg's procedure offering the option of studying handwriting versus typing on a word processor (see Piolat & Olive, 2000). And, it is important to note that word processors can affect writing strategies, and particularly planning and revision processes (see section 4.2; Kellogg & Mueller, 1993; Olive, Piolat, & Polge, 1997; Piolat & Blaye, 1991).

The central point is that verbal protocols and, specifically, the triple task provides a powerful method for portraying the processes used by writers as the task unfolds. It provides a much richer set of data than can be provided by a behavioural protocol of keystrokes and pauses alone. Either technique for collecting verbal protocols captures many, but probably not all, of the kinds of representations held in working memory as writers plan, translate, and review text. It is important to recognize that verbal protocols of any kind provide only a useful approximation of the thoughts that enter the writer's mind during text production. But compared with using only behavioural observations of motor output, the approximation can be quite useful indeed.

4. EXPERIMENTAL FINDINGS

In general, with directed retrospection researchers have been principally interested in studying the effects of endogenous writers' characteristics (*e.g.* their level of knowledge) or of writing conditions (*e.g.*, specific pre-writing tasks or writing medium). By contrast, the thinking aloud method has brought forward the diversity and stability of individual writing strategies. Nevertheless, researchers that used the two variants of the triple task technique have also been interested in the relationship between the cognitive functioning of writers and the quality of their text. Because our purpose here is to briefly describe findings obtained with the triple task technique, their theoretical contexts and relations to text quality are not presented. In this section, we begin with the general functional characteristics of writers observed with the triple task technique. We then turn to ways in which situation-specific or writer-specific factors affect these characteristics.

4.1. General functional characteristics

The triple task technique provides estimates of the cognitive effort and processing time devoted to planning, translating, and reviewing. Consequently we can ask whether one process dominates the others at particular points in time and whether these relationships change as writing progresses. Finally, it is of interest to examine the shifts among processes in terms of a matrix of transitional probabilities.

4.1.1. Cognitive effort

Several studies have investigated cognitive effort during writing by analysing secondary RTs. Thus, Kellogg (1987a, 1988) has shown that the cognitive effort associated with planning and revision was greater than for translating. This result was also observed by Olive, Piolat, and Polge (1996). Kellogg and Mueller (1993) replicated this same pattern for individuals composing on a word processor, but observed little difference among processes when writing in longhand. Piolat, Roussey, and Rous (1996) also did not observe any difference between the writing processes in terms of allocation of effort. In contrast, Levy and Ransdell (1995) observed that planning and translating required more effort than reviewing and revision processes required. Using Kellogg's procedure, Piolat *et al.* (1996) and Olive, Piolat, and Roussey (1997a, 1997b) did not observe differences between revision and translating but observed a greater effort associated with planning.

The results reported in these studies do not converge in any simple fashion, suggesting that the allocation of resources to writing processes probably varies with the specific demands of the task and the knowledge and interest of the writer. A systematic study of these factors is needed to sort out the variables that affect the pattern of allocation. In broad terms, though, it appears that planning and reviewing can often be more resource-demanding than translating ideas into sentences. Even if translating is not fully automatic, its lighter demands on working memory can be partially explained by noting that translating subprocesses are also involved in the production of spoken language (Fayol, 1992, 1997; McCutchen, 1996). On the contrary, by their nature, planning and revision processes have to be highly controlled (Fayol, 1992, 1997; Kellogg, 1996; McCutchen, 1996).

The allocation of cognitive effort to the different writing processes can also be studied as the writing session unfolds. A limiting factor here is obtaining enough RTs per process to allow meaningful comparisons. Given the changes already documented for the way processing time is allocated to writing processes, it is likely that effort also varies. For example, the text already produced can induce a decrease in effort allocated to planning because writers better anticipate the content it remains to integrate in the text produced so far (for a similar analysis of pauses, see Foulin, 1995). Furthermore, changes in the effort allocated to a writing process can have an effect on the effort allocated to the other writing processes. Indeed, a decrease in resources allocated to a process provides more available resources that, consequently, can be allocated to other writing processes.

For example, planning a writing narrative text should be less effortful than planning a persuasive text (Kellogg, 2001). Narrative schemas are acquired at an early age and are heavily practiced throughout childhood in listening to and telling stories (Mancuso, 1986). In contrast, schemas for argumentation and persuasion are weakly developed in all but the highest ability college students (Britton, Burgess, Martin, McLeod, & Rosen, 1975). Kellogg (2001) observed that the RT interference score associated with planning was reliably indeed lower when writing a narrative compared with a persuasive text. The working memory resources unneeded by narrative composition were not devoted exclusively to planning, however. Instead, the cognitive effort devoted to translating and reviewing also was lessened in narrative relative to persuasive composition.

4.1.2. Processing time

Based on the directed retrospection task or on the analysis of both verbal and written protocols, the experiments cited above have also investigated the question of the allocation of processing time. For instance, Kellogg (1987a, 1987b, 1988) has shown that translating was activated during about half of the time of a composition, that planning was activated during 30% of a composition and that revision was activated during 25%. Olive, Piolat and Polge (1996) and Piolat *et al.* (1996) reported similar results. However, with a finer-grained analysis and by dissociating reviewing from revision, Levy and Ransdell (1995) observed that writers devoted 40% of the processing time to planning, 45% to translating, 8% to reviewing and 6% to revision. For their part Penningroth and Rosenberg (1995) and Piolat, Roussey and Rous (1996) reported a similar allocation of processing time for translating but a lower one to planning (10%) and an important to revision (about 40%). Because different independent variables were manipulated in these experiments (that affected principally writing strategies), the outcomes were not identical. Nevertheless, a general pattern of the time spent planning, translating, and reviewing is discernible.

Translating processes seem to be the more activated throughout a writing session. Writers generally devote 40% to 50% of their time to translating. This finding is stable and does not seem to be affected by situation-specific or writer-specific factors. On the other hand, planning and revision processes appear to be heavily affected by these factors (see section 4.2).

In order to analyse changes during a composition, the allocation of processing time has also been studied as a function of the writing phase. For example, Kellogg (1987a, 1987b, 1988) divided the total composition time in thirds and analysed the pattern of allocation of time into each writing phase and the changes of each writing processes across the different writing phases. In general, whatever the writing phase, writers allocate more processing time to translating. On the other hand, as the composition unfolds the time devoted to planning decreased and that devoted to revision increased (for similar results, see Penningroth and Roth, 1995; and Piolat, Roussey, & Rous, 1996).

Finally, analysing their data about the allocation of time processing with a temporal resolution of 5 s, Levy and Ransdell (1995) reported similar but more detailed results. About two thirds of the way through a 40-minute composition, their participants shifted from a principal activation of planning to a strong activation of translating, with 85% of the verbal reports indicating sentence generation. However, reports of translating then begin to gradually decrease, while the time devoted to revision begins to increase, from a low of 3% revision at the beginning of the session and to a high of 10% at the end of the session. The allocation of processing time to reviewing follow the same pattern as that of revision, except that it begins its increase starting about one fourth of the way through the composition.

Levy and Ransdell (1995) also analysed the mean duration of a period of activation of the writing processes (a period being defined by the beginning and the end of the activation of a process). They have shown that the mean period of translating was about 7.5 s and that the mean periods of planning, reviewing and revision was about 2.5 s. They also examined the mean number of periods independently of their duration. Writers generally produced about 46 periods of planning and about 37 periods of translating but only 15 periods of reviewing and 21 of revision.

4.1.3. Matrices of transitional probabilities

As indicated above, the triple task technique has provided strong insights about general functional characteristics of the process of writing for different writers, and particularly about the allocation of time and effort to the writing processes. One remaining question concerns the stability of these allocations of working memory to writing processes over time, for multiple writing assignments of the same basic type. Levy and Ransdell (1995, 1996b) examined this question by asking the participants in their experiment to compose short essays on a different topic during each of 10 writing sessions. The writers were given 40 minutes to write each essay. These authors observed that an individual's writing profile of time allocations across sessions was surprisingly regular, and particularly for planning and translating. The multiple R2 was greater than .80 when the first nine writing sessions were used to predict the allocation of time processing during the last writing session. For each writer, Levy and

Ransdell (1995) compared the matrices of transitional probabilities (the shifts between a process and another) across sessions of composition and across 10-minute periods within a writing session. Their analysis revealed that the profile of transitional probabilities shown by a given writer, what Levy and Ransdell called a 'writing signature' was stable within an individual writing session and across the sessions. It is unclear at present whether a given 'writing signature' changes when the type of discourse is varied, say, from essays to narratives.

The previous findings show that the triple task technique has provided new data about invariant functional characteristics (Kellogg, 1988; Levy & Ransdell, 1995, 1996b). Some general features of the process of writing have been described. In the next section we present how situation-specific or writer-specific factors affect these patterns of allocation of time and effort.

4.2. Writers' inter-individual differences effects

4.2.1. Domain-specific versus verbal knowledge

So far, not enough studies have been conducted with the triple task technique to reach firm conclusions about differences between individuals in domain knowledge or linguistic skills. For example, the effect of topic knowledge on the allocation of time and cognitive effort was first investigated by Kellogg (1987a). In his experiments, participants were divided into two groups of low- and high-knowledge based on how they scored on a test of topic knowledge. Results showed that high knowledge writers engaged less cognitive effort in the writing than low-knowledge writers did. On the other hand, the allocation of processing time to the writing processes was not affected by the writers' level of knowledge.

More recently, Kellogg (1998) reported evidence that domain-knowledge indeed can reduce RT interference scores, but seemingly not verbal knowledge. Participants wrote narratives about a half-inning of baseball and were divided in high and low knowledge conditions using Voss, Vesonder, and Spillich's (1980) procedure. The subjectively rated quality of the narratives was independently affected by verbal ability as well as domain-specific knowledge. However, the RT interference scores were affected only by domain-specific knowledge, with no interaction between these factors.

On the other hand, Olive, Piolat and Roussey (1997a, 1997b) also investigated the effect of topic knowledge and of linguistic skill with the triple task technique. They found that the level of topic knowledge of the writers interacted with their linguistic skill. When they composed a text about a familiar topic, low-skilled writers did not allocate more cognitive effort to the composition than high-skilled writers did. But when composing on an unfamiliar topic, low-skilled writers engaged more cognitive effort than did high skilled writers.

An interesting interaction was also observed on the pattern of temporal organization of the writing processes. Low-skilled writers planned more their text and spent less time translating when composing about a familiar topic than composing about an unfamiliar one. Inversely, high-skilled writers planned less and spent more time translating when composing about a familiar topic. As suggested by Olive *et al.* (1997b) these patterns of processing time reflect the activation of knowledge-telling versus knowledge-transforming strategies. It appears that the level of topic knowledge of writers may not only mediate such strategies, but also by their verbal skill.

4.2.2. Writer's representation of the audience

In oral language as in written production, attention directed to the verbal production depends on the different parameters of the communicative context. Among these parameters, Piolat, Roussey and Rous (1996) manipulated the social status of the audience. The participants of their experiment were asked to write a letter either to a friend or to the university president about an increase of university fees. Their results revealed that the social status of the addressee of the letter affected both processing time and cognitive effort. More precisely, writers revised their text more when the social status of the addressee was high, the university president. This task driven difference in working memory allocations was already apparent in the first two sentences of their writing. Thus, the cognitive effort of the writers is also dependent on writers' representation of the context of production.

4.2.3. Working memory capacity differences

So far we have considered ways in which momentary allocations of working memory resources vary depending on the specific writing process and knowledge differences among writers. Another key question is whether individual differences in working memory affect these allocations. Piolat and Fruttero (1996) investigated this issue dividing the writers into two groups of low- and high-WM, according to their score on a 'writing span' test. This was based on the speaking span test of Daneman and Green, 1986 and on the writing span test of McCutchen, Covil, Hoyne and Midles (1994). The 'writing span' test consisted of detecting a misspelled word in sentences and to memorize it; similar steps were followed for the other sentences (2, 3, 4, 5, or 6). Finally, participants were requested to recall the words and to insert them in a story. Participants were then asked to produce a text with the triple task technique.

The main result showed that low-WM writers showed higher RT interference scores during writing than high-WM writers did. Moreover, writers' working memory capacity affected the allocation of processing time to the different writing processes. In low-WM writers, more processing-time was allocated to planning in the two first thirds of the composition whereas high-WM writers immediately translated their text. This set of data suggests that WM capacity induces the use of different writing strategies.

4.3. Situation-specific effects

4.3.1. Pre-writing strategies

Beyond writers' inter-individual differences, the triple task technique also allows one to evaluate how writers adapt to different constraints in the writing task. For example, Kellogg (1987b, 1988, 1994) examined the effect of pre-writing strategies. In his first experiment, where participants performed the retrospection task without collecting RT to the probes, participants had to compose either with an outline or with no outline. Furthermore, in each group, half of the participants produce a rough or a polished draft. As Kellogg expected, the factors he manipulated affected the allocation of time processing to the writing processes. In a second experiment, Kellogg compared three groups of writers (no-outline *vs.* written outline *vs.* mental outline) that performed the triple task technique. He also observed effect of the pre-writing task on the pattern of allocation of processing time but no effect on writers' cognitive effort. Planning and reviewing processes principally accounted for the writers' strategic adaptations of processing time to the pre-writing task manipulation. From these findings, Kellogg (1988) concluded that writing strategies controlled processing time and not effort.

4.3.2. Writing in second language

Barbier (1998; Barbier, Piolat, & Roussey, 1998) analysed the allocation of processing time and cognitive effort for students that composed a text either in their native or in a second language. In this study, by contrast to Kellogg's original procedure of the triple task technique, participants were asked to label their mental activity by choosing one of six response categories. The categories were: (1) 'I was paying attention to spelling', (2) '...word choice', (3) '...grammar', (4) '...ideas', (5) '...text organisation', or (6) '...other things'. The results reported by Barbier (1998) indicated that the label 'I was paying attention to word choice' was more frequently chosen in the foreign language than in the native language. In contrast, the option 'I was paying attention to ideas' was more frequently chosen in the native language than in the foreign language. Barbier's findings shown that language expertise and familiarity has a direct effect on the extent to which the writing processes were used.

4.3.3. Medium of production

The question of whether the writing tool can restructure the writing process is important in the context of the triple task technique because Levy and Ransdell's request writers to compose their text with a word processor. This question, however, is also important in the current context of computers development. Kellogg and Mueller (1993) have shown that writers using a word processor devoted more effort to planning and reviewing than when writing longhand. Writers also devoted more processing time to reviewing in the early phases of composition when using the word processor. This was particularly true for those highly experienced with word processor. For example, Olive, Piolat, and Polge (1997) compared the effect of word processor on journalists who used word processor daily in their writing to experienced students. They reported that students showed no differences in terms of cognitive effort as a function of the writing tool. The same results were observed for the journalist, except for revision processes. Journalists devoted more effort in the longhand condition than when they used a word processor.

In contrast, Olive *et al.* observed significant effects of the writing tool on the allocation of processing time. For the journalists, when writing by hand, a different writing process dominated in the three composing phases (cf. Kellogg & Mueller, 1993). When writing with a word processor, the journalists used in a recursive way the three writing processes in each composing phase. In contrast, in the students, the medium did not affect in a notable way the time allocations to writing processes; however, they did review more with a word processor relative to longhand.

Kellogg and Mueller's (1993) and Olive *et al.*'s (1997) and other findings in the literature suggest that writing as it occurs in longhand is restructured when using a word processor. However, other studies are necessary to better understand the impact of word processor on the functional characteristics of writing.

In sum, the experiments that have been reported in the previous section have investigated the effects of inter-individual differences by examining writers' working memory capacities, writing tasks involving different kind of knowledge (topic, linguistic or discursive knowledge) and different writing situations (composition strategies, medium). In a synthetic way, it is important to note that these potential sources of variation differently affect the allocation of cognitive effort and/or the general pattern of temporal organization of the writing processes. From the results of these experiments, one can identify three general groups of factors that seem to affect the writing process in different ways:

1) Writer-specific factors (domain-specific knowledge, working memory capacity) mainly influence cognitive effort but do not seem to affect the allocation of time processing to the writing process. In particular, a high availability of knowledge of the writers about the topic of composition induces a lower cognitive effort.
2) Situation-specific factors (pre-writing strategies, outline) mainly affect the allocation of time processing. The temporal organization of planning and translating processes are principally affected by the way writers organize their composition.
3) Finally, linguistic (or verbal) knowledge and the medium of production appear to have an effect on both processing time and cognitive effort.

5. CONCLUSION

The main goal of this chapter was to present the triple task technique and to assess its contribution to basic research on writing. A review of the literature suggests that the triple task technique yields valid insights into writing processes and affects neither the unfolding of these processes nor the quality of the text produced. Thus, experiments that manipulated writers-specific and situation specific factors provided strong insights about the dynamic of writing. And, even if the method provide information mainly about resources-demanding writing processes and does not allow to study automatic processes involved in the text production, several important issues about the process of writing can still be explored. For example, a major issue that should be deeply studied concerns the development of inter-individual writing strategies and how writers adapt these strategies to different constraints of composition. Do these strategies result from the efficiency of the writing processes or are they determined by writers' working memory capacities?

Finally, to support the development of more fine-grained theoretical descriptions of the processes involved in writing (*e.g.*, Brown, McDonald, Brown, & Carr, 1988; Hayes, 1996; Kellogg, 1996), researchers should not be restricted to use only the same three or four response categories as in Kellogg's original retrospection. For example, in order to study the subprocesses of revision, Roussey (1999) used six labels for the directed retrospection (reading to comprehend text, reading for problem detection, detecting a problem, diagnosing a problem, searching for a correction, revising) that characterized the revision process according to Hayes, Flower, Schriver, Stratman, and Carey (1987)). Roussey's findings showed that more cognitive effort was allocated to improving the semantic coherence of the text than for improving the surface of the text. In addition, more processing time and effort was allocated to the processes related to text comprehension (reading for comprehension, reading for problem detection, detecting and diagnosing a problem) than to those related to production (searching and making the correction). As showed by this research, one of the main advantages of the triple task technique lies in the possibility to modify the number and the content of response categories of the directed retrospection task depending on the cognitive activity under investigation and the particular research objective. Such an easy to use technique should greatly improve our understanding of the dynamic of the cognitive processes involved in writing.

6. ACKNOWLEDGEMENTS

The authors wish to express thanks to Michael Levy and Sarah Ransdell for many helpful comments on earlier drafts. Any remaining flaws are our responsibility.

A copy of ScriptKell can be obtained without charge from the first or the third author: thierry.olive@univ-paris8.fr; Annie.Piolat@up.univ-mrs.fr.

ON THE COGNITIVE STATUS OF PAUSES IN DISCOURSE PRODUCTION

JOOST SCHILPEROORD

Discourse Studies Group, University of Tilburg (Netherlands)

Abstract. This chapter discusses some aspects concerning the cognitive status of pauses in research on discourse production. It starts with a concise review of some of the 'canonical' studies on language production in which the pause analytical methodology is adopted. Section 2 discusses methods of collecting pause data and constructing pause databases. Section 3 addresses one key issue: The empirical status of pauses. First, it is shown that the relation between pauses and cognitive processes in discourse production can be maintained by looking at what happens in the immediate neighbourhood of pauses. Based on an analysis of actual transcripts, four kinds of pauses are distinguished: Pauses signalling retrieving, pauses signalling monitoring and pauses signalling repairing processes. Secondly, this section discusses how pause time variances can be interpreted in terms of underognitive processes, and the section concludes with a discussion of how pauses are related to text structural characteristics. The fourth section discusses various statistical methods for analysing pause data, showing the kind of research questions that can be addressed by each method.
Keywords: Pauses/pausing, pause analysis, scope of pauses, locations of pauses, pause time, hesitation, text production, discourse analysis, discourse structure, planning, retrieving, formulating, monitoring, repairing, units of production, paragraphs, sentences, clauses, constituents, mean length, frequencies, variance, covariance.

1. INTRODUCTION

Traditionally in psychology, the time lapse between a stimulus and a response is taken to be *response time*, that is, the time needed to produce a response to a given stimulus. If it can be argued that producing a response Y for a certain stimulus X requires a particular amount of cognitive energy, then the more time it takes to produce Y, the more cognitive energy was required to do so. In this respect, the study of *pauses in language production* fits within the stimulus-response paradigm. Take a look at the transcript in (1) taken from a corpus of *dictated* letters of practising lawyers.[1]

1 The examples presented in this chapter are all taken from this corpus. A description of the corpus and sampling methods can be found in Schilperoord (1996). Throughout this paper, I will use transcript examples all taken from this corpus. When possible, I have skipped the original Dutch text.

J. Schilperoord (2001). On the cognitive status of pauses in discourse production. In: G. Rijlaarsdam (Series ed.) & T. Olive & C. M. Levy (Vol. eds.), Studies in Writing: Volume 10: Contemporary Tools and Techniques for Studying Writing, p. 61-87.

(1) Mijns inziens is het van belang om (....) de arbeidsovereenkomst in te kleden
In my view it is important to (...) arrange the about contract

Having expressed the conjunction 'om' (*to*) the language producer interrupts the flow of language, pauses and then continues the production process by expressing 'de arbeidsovereenkomst in te kleden.' Assuming such interruptions come about involuntarily, it can be inferred that right after having expressed 'om,' the language producer detects the need to produce a continuation while he apparently does not have a continuation available at the time. Detecting the need to continue can hence be considered *a stimulus* and thus, producing the desired continuation is *the response* to that stimulus, while the length of the intervening pause between detection and continuation is *response time, i.e.* the time required to produce the response. The crucial assumption is that a pause reflects some kind of cognitive process the language producer engages in, in order to find a suitable continuation. However, these not only are statements that have to be argued rather than merely postulated. They also raise various questions, such as: Why is a pause inserted precisely at that time? How can we validate the assumption that pauses reflect cognitive processes? What other determinants of pauses are there? What precisely *is* the nature of the response? Is it only the determiner 'de,' or does it concern the entire phrase 'de arbeidsovereenkomst in te kleden'? How can we be sure that the length of a pause indeed represents the time needed to produce the continuation? And so on.

This chapter seeks to find some plausible answers to these questions, and some solid grounds warranting the assumptions as mentioned. Finding appropriate answers to these questions and proper motivations for using pauses as data in cognitive research on language production is important, because these matters are all located at the heart of the pause-analytic methodology. We should therefore handle them with care.

My plan of attack for this chapter is as follows. The first section presents a concise overview of some of the canonical pause analytical studies in psycholinguistic research on language production. The section is meant to provide the reader an impression as to the kind of research issues that have been addressed within this paradigm. Section 2 is a rather instructional section on how pause databases can be sampled, and what is needed in order to construct a database. Section 3 raises various methodological issues. Briefly stated, it addresses the issues mentioned before. Section 4 is devoted to a description of various statistical techniques to analyse pause databases. Section 5 concludes this chapter.

A final introductory remark on pause types. Pauses come in many flavours. Especially in conversational contexts, various types of pauses can be distinguished. Generally speaking, pauses belong to a broad class of different types of hesitation phenomena, including, for example, restarts, self-corrections and both filled and unfilled pauses. What unites these phenomena is that they all imply a deviation from a continuous, and entirely linear process of speech production. If speakers or writers would never pause, or would never make errors that need correction, then we as researchers would be deprived from a rich source of evidence as to the underlying cognitive framework in language production. Fortunately, as everybody knows from their own experience, pauses and other hesitation phenomena make up an unalienable part of any process of spontaneous language production, be it oral or written, thereby providing us a 'window' to what happens in the minds of people when they speak or write. Moreover, various authors assume pauses, especially those occurring within interactional contexts, not only to reflect thinking processes on the part of the speaker, but ascribe to these hesitation phenomena all sorts of interactional, rhetorical or socio-psychological functions (cf. de Beaugrande, 1984; Clark, 1995). Clark, for instance, assumes that speakers insert pauses deliberately in order to make their language more comprehensible for interlocutors. So in his view, pauses have interactional origins, rather than cognitive. Admittedly, pauses present us with a multi-determined phenomenon. The present chapter, however, will be confined to pauses occurring within *monological contexts*, and, more specifically, to pauses in written text production processes. In addition, the chapter is confined to one particular kind of pause: the 'silent' pause. Therefore, we simply define pauses from a perceptual point of view, that is, we regard them as 'silences in the speech of a person' (O'Connell & Kowal, 1983) or 'moments of scribal inactivity' (Matsuhashi, 1981). As indicated, Section 3 discusses the conditions that are to be met in order to interpret such silences or moments of scribal inactivity as signals of cognitive processes in text production.

2. PAUSE ANALYTICAL RESEARCH

> 'Hesitations in spontaneous speech occur at points where decisions and choices are being made. On this basis, the patterning of hesitations should provide clues as to the size and nature of the encoding units which are operative.'

David Boomer, who wrote these words in his 1965 paper on units in language production, was one of the first psycholinguists who adopted pause analysis and applied this method to a corpus of spontaneous speech in order to learn about the cognitive processes and structures underlying the production of speech. The quotation adequately indicates the importance of pause analysis for the study of language production, be it oral or written, spontaneous or planned. Pauses are assumed to reflect moments in the course of producing a stretch of speech or text where the producer engages in thinking about what to say next, how to say it, or to evaluate what has been said. By carefully examining the locations and durations of pauses, insights can be gained into the nature of these processes and their temporal organization. This section provides a synopsis of research on pauses in language production so as to provide the reader an impression of how such research is conducted, and what research issues are at stake. We do so by discussing a few 'canonical' papers on pauses: Boomer (1965), Henderson, Skarbek and Goldman-Eisler (1966) and Butterworth (1975).

Boomer's paper *Hesitations and Grammatical Encoding* (Boomer, 1965) nicely illustrates the focus of interest in the early days of psycholinguistics: the production of (isolated) *sentences*. In addition, the study reflects the theoretical issue that has long dominated and still is dominating the field: the search for the characteristic 'unit' of production. Pauses testify to that issue as follows. If indeed a particular unit of encoding speech underlies production, then such a unit should have its linguistic counterpart: words, phrases or even longer sequences of language. Moreover, one might hypothesize that pauses, taken to be reflections of underlying processes of preparing subsequent speech, will be predominantly located at the *boundaries* of linguistic correspondences of the operative encoding unit. So, the research strategy is then to hypothesize, on independent grounds, a certain encoding unit, and to see whether the above mentioned expectation about pause locations is borne out by the data: a transcribed corpus of spontaneously produced speech. The null hypothesis predicts pauses to be distributed randomly across linguistic units (whatever they are). In Boomer's study, the so-called *phonemic clause* is put forth as the basic unit by which speakers encode and produce language. A phonemic clause is a phonologically marked macro segment, containing one and only one primary stress, and ending in a terminal juncture. However, according to the examples Boomer discusses, phonemic clauses roughly correspond to main clause structures. Boomer's corpus consisted of about 1600 of these structures. An example is given in (2).

(2) $_1$and $_2$the $_3$weather $_4$was $_5$hot

Each pause and hesitation was tabulated by its location, as either 'between' phonemic clauses (position 1), or at one of the subsequent within-clause positions (positions 2 to 5). One surprising finding was that, contrary to his hypothesis, Boomer found largest proportions of pauses at the second position. In other words, there is a strong tendency for speakers to pause right after the first word within the phonemic clause. After that word, chances for pauses to occur at the subsequent locations (3 to 5 in (2)) drop considerably.[2] Although this finding is not entirely consistent his initial hypothesis, Boomer interpreted his data as supportive to the clause-as-unit hypothesis. He proposed a two-stage encoding process according to which the speaker first decides upon the 'larger' units, such as 'grammatical decisions' (Boomer, 1965: 156), and then selects 'smaller' units, *i.e.* lexical choices. The reason for pauses to occur predominantly after the first word is accounted for in terms of speech management and the restricted amount of attentional resources. Boomer states:

> The initial word in a phonemic clause sets certain constraints for the structure of what is to follow. The selection of a first word has in greater or lesser degree committed the speaker to a particular construction or at least a set of alternative constructions, and has also foreclosed the possibility of other constructions. (ibid, pp. 156)

So, by uttering the first word, the speaker commits himself to a certain (structural) continuation. This may have some memory advantages: lexical search can now occur 'guided' by the already activated clause structure. Ever since, Boomer's findings have been confirmed by many other pausological studies on sentence production (*e.g.*, Ford & Holmes 1978, Ford 1982, Schilperoord 1996, 1997).

At about the same time Boomer's paper was published, Henderson, Skarbek and Goldman-Eisler published a paper in *Language and Speech* (Henderson, *et al.*, 1966) in which they reported a pause distributional phenomenon that is since known as *temporal patterns in spontaneous speech*. Using a corpus of spontaneously produced monologues, they observed that pauses occurring in such longer stretches of speech

---

2 This finding was replicated in Schilperoord (1997, 2000). See also Section 4.

tend to cluster, resulting in an alternating pattern of phases characterized by much hesitating and pausing (the so-called *hesitant* phases) and phases characterized by (relatively) fluent speech (the *fluent* phases). The theoretical issue at stake here is whether the lock-step nature by which discourse seems to come about has any cognitive significance. According to the authors, it does. On the basis of the distributional properties they claimed to have observed, Henderson *et al.* put forth a plan-execute mechanism. Pauses are responsive to this mechanism in that hesitant phases signal cognitive planning processes, whereas subsequent fluent phases signal the execution of plans. Henderson *et al.* call this the underlying 'cognitive framework' in language production. So the observed time patterns suggest a psychological relationship between hesitant and fluent phases. If so indeed, this would imply that speakers plan discourse fragments that extent over several clauses, a feature that cannot be accounted for by models of sentence production per se. At any rate, such models fail to account for the distributional properties of pausing Henderson *et al.* observed.

Henderson *et al.*'s conclusions as to this 'underlying cognitive framework' have, however, been heavily disputed. Jaffe, Breskin and Gerstman (1972), for example, doubted whether the cyclic nature of pause distribution bears any relevance to the cognitive processes operative in language production. They noted that the clustering of pauses was observed only by the eye, and not tested statistically. Moreover, they showed the cyclic patterns to be present in randomly generated time series data as well. In his reply, Henderson (1974) proposed treating the cyclic patterns (or *cognitive rhythms*, as they were termed by the time) as a research hypothesis, with Jaffe *et al*'s objections representing the null hypothesis. He called for further, independent evidence favouring the hypothesis. This further evidence was provided in a later study by Brian Butterworth (1975), one that was based on a much closer look at some of the *structural* features of the produced monologues. Butterworth had subjects talk on ordinary matters such as academic life. Using the Henderson *et al.* plotting procedure, he observed the same alternating patterns of hesitating and speaking in his monologues. However, to this he added evidence based on the 'semantic structure' of the monologues. He asked independent judges to segment the produced monologues according to so-called 'idea units.' Judges were not given any definition of 'idea units' and were asked to decide for themselves what they considered to be idea units. If at least half of the judges picket out a certain location to be a boundary between two idea units, such a location was considered to represent a semantic structural juncture in the discourse. These junctures were subsequently correlated with the cyclic temporal patterns. After all, if the hesitant phases indeed signal planning on the part of the speaker, these phases can be expected to coincide with the semantic structural junctures. In other words, idea units can then be treated as planning units as well. This correlation indeed turned out to be significant (Butterworth, 1975: 81).

However suggestive these findings may be, Butterworth himself points out the main flaw of his research method: its dependency upon informal intuitions about the semantic units structuring the discourses. He therefore calls for adopting a 'semantic formalism' in order to segment and structure the discourses. Schilperoord and Sanders (1997, 1999) took this call to task, and ascribed structural descriptions to a sample of *written* texts based on a procedural technique for analysing the hierarchical structure of discourse. They indeed found pause distributional patterns to correlate systematically with the structural features of the discourses. Hesitation occurs mainly at 'heavy' breaks in texts, whereas fluency was mainly found at the more peripheral junctures between text fragments. This suggests further evidence that pause patterns are indeed responsive to planning-execution processes in discourse production.

This section has highlighted some of the methods and research issues in pause analytical studies on language production. It has shown, first, what issues are considered relevant (the 'unit' issue, distributional properties of pauses and their cognitive significance), and, second, some of the relevant research variables: pause frequencies, pause times and pause distributional properties. In the next section, the issue of collecting pauses and constructing a pause database will be addressed.

2.1. Collecting pause data

Methods to collect data in order to study language production processes can be categorized according to two criteria (Van der Pool, 1995). The first one typifies the *moment* at which such data are collected with respect to the actual process studied: data can be gathered on line or off line. The second criteria concerns the way the data relate to the actual process: they can either be *extrinsic* with respect to the process, or *intrinsic*, simply because they are an indispensable part of the process. Sampling thinking-aloud protocols presents an example of online, extrinsic data. Protocols are willingly and consciously provided for by subjects while they are performing on some production task. In this respect, they may intrude upon the process under study (Janssen, Schilperoord, van den Bergh, van Waes, & van Wassenaer, 1994). Text analysis is an off-line, intrinsic method, whereas collecting data from interviews is an off-line, extrinsic method. According to these criteria, sampling pauses hence is an *online and intrinsic* method of sampling process data. Pauses are typically sampled *during* the process of language production, and subjects need never be asked to provide pauses.

We start this section by briefly discussing the kind of language material that is best suited for pause sampling methods (2.1.1). We then turn attention to two sampling methods, one that makes use of old-fashioned recording equipment, and one that makes use of modern computer applications (2.2 and 2.3). After this, we proceed by discussing some of the principles of database constructing. As will turn out to be the case: the way a pause database is constructed heavily depends on what one wishes to learn about the process under study. This section (2.4) therefore only exemplifies ways of constructing databases.

2.1.1. Materials

The choice of material obviously depends on what specific research questions one wants to address, whether one's interest concerns written or oral language production, whether one is interested in monological or interactional speech, and so on. Generally speaking, *simple* and *spontaneous* production processes are best suited for pause sampling, that is, speech production that goes easily and smoothly. This does not foreclose the possibility to study *written* text production processes by means of the pause analytical method, as I have shown in Schilperoord (1996). One may use *professional dictation* of highly routinized production tasks in order to collect data relevant to written text production. A useful system of dimensions to categorize language production tasks can be obtained by categorizing production tasks in terms of the presence or absence of pre-planning, problem-solving, and so on. If, for example, the writing process one wants to study is characterized by intensive problem-solving and massive editing or revising on the part of the writer, with actual language production being but one aspect of these processes, it will soon prove impossible to relate pause data to ongoing processes (see also Section 2.4). In that case, one should seriously consider adapting other research methods, such as think-aloud protocols.

2.2 Auditory recording of pauses

The simplest way to sample a pause database is by making visual or auditory records of spontaneous or planned speech. The difficult part of it concerns detecting and measuring pauses. Both auditory and visual recordings can be made of conversations, monologues, rehearsed formal speech, or, as in my own research, professional dictation. All one needs is recording equipment and the permission of the speakers to record their speech. Visual records have the additional advantage of allowing one to collect pause data from 'silent' production modes, such as typing or handwriting[3]. Trouble starts as soon as the tapes have been collected. In general one should use computer programs in order to both *detect* and *measure* pauses. The GIPOS-program, designed by IPO, for example is a very useful tool for detecting and measuring pauses. The program represents recorded speech as oscillograms. Waveforms, consisting of amplitudes (speaking) and bars (pausing), are projected onto a time track and by manipulating various cursors to points of transitions between amplitudes and bars, pauses can both be detected and measured. Detection proceeds by using both the oscillograms and the original tapes. Accordingly, pauses can be located relative to their surrounding words. Measuring proceeds by establishing the duration of a pause. The necessity of this rather time consuming method is that ear-detection of pauses often leads to wrong decisions with regard to their actual locations (people often 'hear' a pause between two successive phrases, even if it is actually located after the first word within the second phrase), whereas manual measurements of pause times turn out to be hopelessly insecure and unreliable.
Typed transcripts of the materials recorded can thus be used to collect, detect and measure pauses, but there are computer systems allowing one to construct the database automatically.

2.3 Keystroke recording methods

Since the 1980s, computers have become an increasingly important tool for the study of writing processes. Various so-called *keystroke recording programs* have been developed. Such log programs produce a chronological, real time record of keystrokes and they automatically measure the duration of intervening pauses. This sampling

---

3 Although the problems of detecting and measuring pauses even grow in complexity with this sampling method (see Van Waes, 1991).

method is, of course, strongly tied to a particular production mode (you cannot keylog oral production), but it has the obvious advantage that records of processes are being produced in an unobtrusive and automatic way. It provides databases that can be directly subjected to statistical programs in order to analyse the data. The most sophisticated keystroke logging program up to date that I know of is called *S-notation* (Severinson Eklundh & Kollberg, 1994; Kollberg & Severinson Eklundh, this volume). The program provides a full fledged, real time representation of the way the writer has propelled the text through space and time by registering all keystrokes, pauses, online revisions and the like. The database can be readily analysed in SPSS. The program has been primarily designed to study the process of on-line revisions made by writers, and its application in actual research testifies to this, but obviously, it can be used to collect pause data as well.

Despite these benefits, keylogged pause databases have some serious flaws. It is the very nature of the way production data are sampled (that is, by having subjects type texts on a personal computer) that may seriously distort the data. Consider a pause that has been key logged. Even under optimal conditions, this pause may reflect widely different processes. For example, the writer may have paused in order to *read* previously produced text, or she/he may have been *thinking* about what to say next. Noticeably, in any known model of writing processes, reading already produced text on the one hand, and thinking about how to continue on the other, are considered *different* processes, serving *different* purposes in the course of writing. Revision and planning are not the same, but the recorded pause does not allow one to tell one process from the other. Things may get even worse though. After all, the program does not rule out the possibility that the recorded pause has nothing to do whatsoever with text production. A pause may be the result of a writer having difficulties in handling the software or the keyboard, or of one who has just been scrolling through the text. In brief: a keylogged pause may not always be a pause, and if it is, it may not always be a production pause.

2.4 Constructing a database

As said before, traditional pause analysis seeks to find out whether systematic relationships exist between a pause location, relative to some variable of interest, and its duration and/or frequency. Descriptive pause analytical research aims at finding out whether pauses falling within some time interval (< .5 s, .5 s < x < 1 s, > 1 s and so on) cluster around certain locations. Quasi-experimental pause analytical research aims at testing hypotheses as to what kinds of locations generate the longest, or the most pausing. In any case, some procedure must be developed in order to label a set of pause data as to how they are located relative to the discourse produced. To this end, both linguistic and discourse analytical techniques have been adopted. For example, because Boomer (1965) was interested in whether or not phonemic clauses represented the characteristic unit of encoding, he located his pause data relative to that particular unit. A pause occurred either *between* two instances of this unit or *within* such unit. This procedure may of course be augmented by various other structurally defined units of interest. For example, in Schilperoord (1996), and Chanquoy, Foulin and Fayol (1995) pauses are located relative to positions such as 'between words,' 'between grammatical phrases,' 'between grammatical clauses,' and 'between full blown sentences'. Butterworth's study on cognitive rhythms employed a method for the analysis of the semantic structure of discourse in order to label pauses relative to such discourse structural units. Schilperoord and Sanders (1997, 1998) employed a procedural account of the analysis of text structure to tag pauses for various discourse structural locations.[4]

To better visualize what a database might look like, consider the rows of figures in (3).

(3)	3	15	124	0	1	0	3440	3	1	
	3	15	125	2110	0	1	0	1	2	

(3) represents two lines of labels, taken from my own database consisting of about 23.000 of such lines. What information do they carry? The ten figures in each line represent eleven variables that were all considered interesting or required to address some cognitive questions regarding written text production. The first variable is the variable 'subject number.' As can be seen, the data concern text production processes performed by the third subject in this study. The second variable is 'text number.' As can be seen, (2) contains data taken from the 15th text produced by Subject 3. The third variable is 'transition number.' By that, I simply refer to number of transitions between words for Subject 3 in text 15. The data in (3) concern the transition from the 123rd to the 124th word and that from the 124th to the 125th word. The fourth variable is 'pause duration.' If no pause occurs at the transition between the two words, this variable receives the value '0.' If a pause actually occurred, it is represented by its duration (measured in milliseconds). The fifth and sixth variable refer to the kind of activity employed before and after the transition. A '1' means that the text producer is 'speaking' (dictating that is); whereas '0' means that he pauses. The seventh variable represents characteristics of the preceding event, in this case: the length of the speaking event that went on during these transitions. The eighth variable refers to the position of the pause with respect to structural units such as 'words,' 'phrases,' 'clauses,' 'sentences,' or 'paragraphs' (which were the five types of location used in this study), and, finally, the ninth and tenth variable represents the category of words surrounding the transitions: function words, such as determiners or auxiliaries, or lexical words, such as nouns or verbs.

A database like this one allows for various types of analyses.[5] Because the constituting unit is the 'transition between words,' I was able, by using variables 3, 4 and 8, to estimate the frequencies of pauses relative to particular location types. This could be achieved by dividing actual pause occurrences for location type X by the sum total transitions of this type. In addition, by using the same set of variables, mean pause durations and pause time variations for various locations types could be estimated, either including or excluding '0-pauses' (cf. Schilperoord, 1996, 92ff).

4 Here we shall not be bothered with the various problems encountered when one actually tags pause locations. This issue will be taken up in the next sections.

5 As this is not the place to report the actual results of these analyses, I stick to mentioning the possibilities. The reader is referred to Schilperoord (1996) for empirical data.

Furthermore, since pause time frequencies and durations are 'nested' within subjects and/or within texts, various subject-specific estimates could be derived from the database, allowing for a distinction between 'within' and 'between' subjects variances, and between 'within' versus 'between' text variances for various measures. As we sampled various production processes per writer, we were also able to test within-subject stabilities of the obtained measures, or within-subject/within-text stability of measures.

In addition, by using variables 9 and 10, the database allowed for estimates of pause frequencies relative to lexical categories. For instance, it was found out that text producers pause more often after a determiner than before this category. Because (3) contains a real time representation of text production processes that were sampled, the development of pause time across production processes could also be plotted. Finally, the examples given here all concern 'row-internal' data. However, by simply looking at data across rows, it was possible to track down various 'pause to pause' relationships (for more details, see Schilperoord, 1996, especially Chapter 3).

I hope this example has made it clear that what you might get from a database depends on what you put into it. However, some assumptions with regard to pause locations, pause times and their cognitive significance have been left implicit up until now. The next section therefore addresses these methodological issues in more detail.

3. THE EMPIRICAL STATUS OF PAUSES

The former section described techniques of sampling and labelling pauses as if it were entirely clear what a pause is, and what cognitive status can be attributed to pauses. This is, however, not the case. Underlying the pause analytical enterprise are various assumptions regarding their empirical status, assumptions that have to be made explicit in order to show what pauses can and cannot tell us about cognitive processes language production. This section aims at doing so. The issue will be addressed both from a *processing* point of view and from a *(text) structural* point of view. We begin by discussing how pauses relate to production processes such as retrieving information from memory, or revising already produced text (Section 3.1). Then we discuss ways of interpreting pause times in terms of cognitive processes (3.2) and finally we discuss how pauses relate to (structural features of) the surrounding text (Section 3.3). This section ends with a discussion of how processing aspects and structural aspects can be combined in order to develop theories of cognitive processes in text production further (in Section 3.4).

3.1 Pauses and production processes

Collecting pause data forces us to define what a pause is. As we already noted, most authors working in the field of pause analysis do so from a *perceptual* point of view. Pauses, then, are 'moments of scribal inactivity' (Matsuhashi, 1981), or 'silences in the speech of person' (O'Connell & Kowal, 1983). Such definitions, however, do not tell us much about how pauses are related to ongoing cognitive processes in (text) production. Let us try to be a bit more precise about this matter and suppose that we have a 'basic' theory of language production processes. This theory posits four types of cognitive processes operative in text production: *planning* text and *retrieving* information from memory; *formulating* information that is retrieved; *monitoring* the text produced so far; and *repairing* already produced text.[6]

Studying these processes means asking questions such as: What is the relative frequency of these processes as they occur in the course of producing text? How are they organized in real production time? Or, are there any typical patterns of processes? As we cannot observe mental processes directly, we are in need of some behavioural correlate of a certain process. If a text producer performs behaviour X, h/she is accommodating process Y. Ideally, each of these behavioural correlates will be unique for the process it signals. This state of affairs can be depicted as follows:

Mental level	1	2	1	3	4
Behavioural level	1*	2*	1*	3*	4*

Here, a *mental* level is distinguished from a *behavioural* level. What happens at the mental level can only be approximated by making observations at the behavioural level. So, we observe that for some time, a text producer performs behaviour 2*, and we infer that during that time he must have been engaged in process 2. Moreover, if we observe that behaviour 2* is replaced by behaviour 1*, we can infer that the text producer switched from process 2 to process 1.

The crucial issue then is: what is the nature of such behavioural types? To address the issue, consider transcript (4) (S = speaking/writing, P = pausing).

(4)		Behaviour	Time
	1. S	*the letter is somewhat unclear*	2.1
	2. P	Pause	1.7
	3. S	*because the other party does speak about a*	3.4
	4. P	Pause	0.9
	5. S	*demand*	1.1

What is happening here? We witness a text producer formulating the beginning of a sentence (lines 1, 3 and 5): *The letter is somewhat unclear because the other party does speak about a demand.* The process is interrupted two times by a pause (lines 2 and 4): one taking 1.7 s and another one taking .9 s. So there are two kinds of behaviours: speaking[7] and pausing.

Let us assume that we can indeed distinguish between speaking and pausing, that is, that these are fundamentally *different* kind of behaviours. Inferring mental processes from such behavioural observations may then proceed by looking how a particular stretch of text production *deviates* from an 'ideal' production process according to

---

6 Almost any cognitive theory of production I know of starts from this distinction. See for example: Levelt (1989) and Flower and Hayes (1981).

7 See Footnote 1.

which the text comes about strictly linearly, and without any sort of interruption. Any such deviation can then be interpreted in terms of some kinds of mental process. Note that in (4) only one type of deviation can be observed: The text producer interrupts the process and pauses. Obviously, what happens during these pauses will have something to do with what immediately follows them.[8] For example, during a pause a writer *activates* as yet inactive information from memory and subsequently expresses that information verbally. Our 'basic' theory refers to this process as *retrieving*. Therefore, we may infer that a pause that is part of the pattern 'speaking– pausing–speaking' reflects a retrieval process at the mental level. We may thus postulate the first type of correlation between what happens at the behavioural level and what is apparently happening at the mental level (to be called 'Type-I pauses,' see 5).

(5)	Type I- pauses	
	behavioural level	*mental level*
	speak–pause–speak	retrieve

Now, let us see what happened after line 5 in transcript (4). This is depicted in transcript (5, L = listening)

(6)			
	5. S	*demand*	1.1
	6. P	Pause	1.2
	7. S	*that this party has on*	3.2
	8. P	Pause	3.0
	9. L	[*that this party has on*]	3.2
	10. P	Pause	1.5
	11. S	*the firm NAME*	4.5

Transcript (6) differs from (4) in one respect. After having paused in line 8, the text producer rewinds the tape and *listens* to an already produced part of his text (see line 9, listening, indicated by brackets). After this, he pauses again (line 10), and then continues production (line 11).

Note that, just like the events in transcript (4), production here is still *linear* in that each new increment is attached to the final word produced so far. Unlike transcript (4) however, this transcript shows *two* types of deviations from uninterrupted production. The writer not only pauses several times, he also listens to a part of the already produced text before he carries on production. The mental correlate of this pattern of behaviours might well be that of *monitoring*, which is posited by our 'basic' theory as well. During the pause in line 8, the text producer may have suspected that something has gone wrong, or at least that something in the already produced text is not in ac-

---

8 For the sake of simplicity, we neglect -for now- the possibility that what happens during this pause will have something to do with what is happening before *it. However, in the final part of this section, this possibility will be considered.*

cordance with his original intention. In order to check whether this is indeed the case, he listens to his own text, decides that it is right after all, and continues production.[9]

Another reason for listening may be that the text producer is uncertain as to how precisely the next increment (12) is to be attached to the last one (8), and in order to refresh his memory of the text already produced, he checks the original text. Both reasons, however, essentially point at the same process: production is monitored, leading the text producer to acknowledge the need to refresh his memory of the text produced so far (Schilperoord & Janssen, 1993). So, we may postulate the second type of correlation between the mental level and the behavioural level (Type-II pauses, see 7).

(7)	Type II-pauses	
	behavioural level	*mental level*
	speak–pause–listen–(pause)[10]–speak	monitoring

Transcript (8) shows what happened after line 11.

(8)	11.S	*the firm NAME*	4.5
	12 P	pause	7.3
	13 S	*but fails to note whether*	3.2
	14 P	pause	1.3
	15 S	*this and that means*	2.5
	16 P	pause	5.1
	17 L	*(but fails to note)*	3.0
	18 P	pause	1.6
	19 S	*whether this means*	1.9

The flow of events in transcript (8) differs from the one in (6) in what happens after a part of the already produced text is listened to in line 17. As can be seen, as a point of continuation, the text producer selects the verb *to note* and after a brief pause (18), he continues by producing line 19. The crucial observation to be made here is that the selected point for continuation is located *before* the original point of interruption in line 13. The net result is that a part of the already produced text is – literally – taken from the record and replaced by a new piece of text. In effect we witness the text producer producing what our 'basic' theory calls a *repair*: the erroneous *this and that* is replaced by *this*. Transcript (7) thus shows three deviations from 'ideal' linear and continuous production: pausing, listening and can best be referred to as *discontinuous* production. This pattern apparently reflects monitoring (the pause in line 16) and repairing (the pause in line 18) an error. Therefore, the third type of correlation between the mental level and the behavioural level can be stated as follows (see 9).

---

9 Once again, things may be more complicated than is suggested here. We return to this in the final part of section 3.1.

10 Parentheses indicate this pause to be optional. The general pattern does not change if this pause is absent. Sometimes text production is continued immediately after listening.

(9)	Type-III pauses	
	behavioural level	*mental level*
	speak–pause–listen–(pause)–disc. speak	monitoring + repairing

Together, (5), (7) and (9) result in the following system of processes and correlated behaviours (see 10).

(10)	*behavioural level*	*mental level*
	speak	formulating
	speak–pause–speak	retrieve
	speak–pause–listen–(pause)–speak	monitoring
	speak–pause–listen–(pause)–disc. speak	monitoring + repairing

So far, so good. We seem to have arrived at a clear-cut system of observational behaviours bearing a one-to-one relationship with the processes our 'basic' theory distinguishes. Unfortunately however, matters concerning this one-to-one assumption are somewhat more complicated than suggested in (10). There are at least three of such complications: (1) It may be that a certain process X has more than one behavioural correlate or (2) that a certain behaviour reflects more than one type of event at the mental level, or (3) that a certain behaviour is a response to a stimulus that is not part of our original 'basic' theory of text production. All these complications impair the validity of pause analytical research and it is therefore necessary that they are discussed here in some detail.

Let us once again take a look at (part of) transcript (8), repeated here as (11).

(11)	11 S	*the firm NAME*	4.5
	12 P	Pause	7.3
	13 S	*but fails to note whether*	3.2

The pause in line 12 is part of the pattern corresponding with the process of retrieving information – it is a Type-I pause. The contents of line 13 are retrieved or the text producer is engaged in lexical search. Either way, we take it for granted that this pause reflects retrieving. The assumption is based on the events flanking this pause, and since nothing special happens here – the text producer interrupts the flow of language, thinks, and continues – the pattern is an instance of (5). But can we be sure of that?

Note that nothing prevents this pause from reflecting not only retrieving, but monitoring processes *as well.* In fact, the safest assumption seems to be that monitoring processes take place constantly, and therefore any pause will have some sort of a 'backward' orientation. If a repair is actually produced, or part of the text is actually listened to, this will only make the monitoring process *apparent*, but we cannot rule out monitoring processes to have taken place simply because no repair is produced. So although inferring the mental correlates of a pause from the events surrounding it is probably the best way to do the job, it nevertheless leaves room for uncertainty of which one should be well aware.

The second complication concerns the possibility that a certain cognitive process X has more than one correlate at the behavioural level. For example, it may be the case that retrieving new information already starts while formulating the current increment. In fact, there is some experimental evidence indeed suggesting this to be the case. Ford and Holmes (1978) conducted a click experiment in which they had subjects talk spontaneously about topics such as 'academic life.' While speaking, at irregular intervals the subjects heard clicks, and were asked to respond to these clicks as quickly as they could by pressing a button. Probe reaction latencies are considered to be a measure of cognitive processing load. A major result of this experiment was that latencies tend to increase towards the end of clauses. This indicates that, while verbalizing a certain clause, subjects already start planning the next one. So there seems to exist some 'spill over' in retrieval processes. Retrieval does not take place exclusively during pausing – it might just as well take place while subjects are actually producing text. This is another reason why the assumption underlying pattern (5) should be relaxed somewhat.[11]

The third complication contributing invalidity to pause analysis is that a certain behaviour X performed by a text producer may be a response to a stimulus that is not incorporated in the 'basic' theory of text production. In principle, any interpretation attributed to a pause should be based on the 'basic' theory. However, consider a situation where a text is dictated, not on a machine, but to a steno typist. Obviously, a lot of pausing will go on, but in this situation (at least some) pausing may be a response to a communicative factor: providing the steno typist opportunities to type the dictated message. This is a factor that clearly falls outside the scope of the basic theory of text production.

Speaking in general, one should always bear in mind that pauses in language production are a multi-determined phenomenon. De Beaugrande (1984) sums up over twenty (!) reasons for speakers to hesitate. These seem to cluster into four major determinants. Apart form cognitive causes, pauses may have physical causes, socio-psychological causes or communicative causes. Whether or not one or more of these causes are actually present within the test situation largely depends on characteristics of subjects, tasks, communicative setting and so on.

Physical causes can never be ruled out, simply since they are an unalienable part of speaking, typing or writing. They originate from breathing activity (in case of speaking), muscular activity (writing, typing) or keyboard activity (typing).[12] What such pauses have in common, however, is that normally they are very brief. To extract them from the database, it is therefore useful to define a 'cut off' value (Dechert & Raupach, 1980). Although chosen somewhat arbitrarily, in case oral pauses are sampled, this value usually equals .25 or .3 s (Schilperoord, 1996), whereas in case writing pauses are sampled it equals about 1 s (Van Waes, 1991).

---

11 *We return to this issue later on when we discuss the relationship between the length of a pause and the 'length' of the processes reflected by pauses.*

12 *Some of these were already discussed in Section 2.4.*

Socio-psychological factors causing a speaker/writer to pause concern, for instance, speaking anxiety, or 'writer's block.' Asking subjects who never have done so to dictate a text is therefore not a wise thing to do. Generally speaking, socio-psychological factors can be ruled out if subjects are allowed to produce texts within 'normal' circumstances, and by having them perform production tasks with which they are well acquainted. Real-life tasks are therefore to be preferred (Schilperoord, 1996, chapter 1).

Finally, communicative reasons for pausing are limited to conversational settings, with more than one speaker present. Speakers pause not only to prepare subsequent speech, but also to provide their interlocutors the opportunity to comprehend the message, or to accomplish a rhetorical goal. In any monological context, communicative pauses can be ruled out.

The considerations thus far result in two 'rules of thumb' that guide pause data sampling. First, use methods to sample data that allow only for a highly restricted set of production behaviours. And second, allow subjects to perform on tasks they are well acquainted with, to be carried out within 'normal' circumstances. In brief, real-life tasks and production circumstances should be employed as much as possible.

3.2 On interpreting pause times

In the introductory section it was argued that pause time can be treated as response time. This is explicitly stated by Butterworth's *pause paradigm* (1980: 156): 'The more the delays' ... [*pause time*] ... 'the more cognitive operations are required by the output.' In its strictest sense, the paradigm entails that pause time equals processing time (cf. Kowal & O'Connell, 1987: 113). A pause of, say 6.4 s, therefore reflects a cognitive process taking 6.4 s. And since processing length is usually considered a measure of processing load, differences in pause times may be interpreted in terms of differences in processing load: the longer the pause, the heavier the load.

Even from this quite simple way of putting it, it will be clear that, in its strictest sense, the Butterworth paradigm can be challenged. Basically, the paradigm encompasses two assumptions, *viz.* that pauses are entirely 'filled up' with processing and that cognitive processing takes place exclusively during pauses. We already discussed the second assumption when it was noted that, for example, retrieving operations may 'spill over' to other kinds of production behaviours, so in this section we confine ourselves to the first assumption.

Can it be maintained that pause time equals processing time? The simple answer is 'no.' As things stands, this position is based on the inaccurate assumption that pause time and processing time are both represented on a rational scale. Pause times are indeed: a pause of 2 s is twice as long as one of 1 s. Furthermore we can estimate interpretable mean pause times, and finally, pauses may last 0 s.

Processing 'times' however, are not represented as such, thereby ruling out most statistical possibilities mentioned. One simply cannot maintain that the processing load reflected by a pause of 2 s is twice as 'heavy' as the processing load reflected by a pause of 1 s. Likewise, it is impossible to maintain that any two pauses taking 2 s reflect equal processing loads. So, although it is possible to project pause times (and durations of other types of behaviour) onto a real time track, processes cannot. Therefore, the relation between pause time and processing time is best being viewed as one having positive monotonicity. This implies that longer pauses reflect cognitive processes that are *relatively* more effortful compared to processes reflected by shorter pauses. Interpretations of differences in pause times should therefore be in accordance with the monotonicity assumption. So, the often reported result that, in producing written texts, people tend to pause longer before paragraphs than before sentences (Chanquoy, *et al.*, 1995; Schilperoord, 1996; Van Waes, 1991), allows us only to conclude that, apparently, planning paragraphs is more effortful than planning sentences.[13]

3.3 Pauses and structural features of texts

This section deals with the methodological question of how pauses are related to the structural features of a text (both linguistic and text structures). To put the issue in perspective, let us once again have a look at a transcript from dictation processes (12).

(12)	1.	that	(6.2)
	2.	neither the actual procedure nor	(5.6)
	3.	the financial picture that (...)	

We are dealing here with two Type-I pauses. After having vocalized the complemetizer '*that*' in line 1, the text producer pauses 6.2 s and then continues by adding '*neither the actual procedure nor*' to the text. Something similar happens after line 2. Section 3.1 made explicit what processing assumptions can be made here. However, justifying such an assumption requires us to address three additional issues: Why is this pause located precisely where it is? Why does it last 6.2 s? What is its scope? We shall deal with these issues in turn.

3.3.1. Pause locations

As we saw earlier (Section 2), an important part of constructing a pause database consists of labelling the precise *location* of pauses relative to the text that is being produced. Pauses may function in terms of various structural characteristics (words, phrases, sentences, paragraphs and so on). Pause analytical research often concerns the question whether, on average, pauses are longer or occur more frequently relative to unit x than unit y. 'Functioning in terms of unit x' then means that a pause occurs right *before* an instance of unit x (a sentence, a clause, and so forth). Regardless of what precise criteria are used to locate pauses[14] relative to the text, conducting this kind of research requires us to make the assumption that the location of any pause coincides with the moment where the text producer has acknowledged its cognitive necessity. The entire enterprise would be senseless if there would exist the possibility

---

13 For further discussion and references on this matter, see Schilperoord (1996, especially chapters 1, 2 and 7).

14 This depends fully on the kind of question one would like to study, or the theory one puts to test.

of *postponing* pauses because such a possibility would imply that the text producer deliberately inserts pauses in the text, just where he likes them to occur. In other words, a prerequisite for any cognitive question to be addressed by means of pause analysis is that pauses are truly *involuntary* responses to a stimulus. We therefore postulate a variant of Levelt's *Main Interruption rule for repairs* (Levelt, 1983) stating that the flow of language is interrupted immediately upon detecting some trouble. The rule is given in (13).

(13) *Rule I*
If a pause is located at location X, its cognitive necessity was detected immediately prior to X.

How does Rule I apply to actual data? Generally speaking, it says that within a string such as [X <pause> Y Z], element Y (say, a word) was not already 'there,' so to say, when X was vocalized/written down, but that vocalization of Y was postponed by, deliberately, inserting the pause after X. So, rule I states this pause to function in terms of [Y], or [Y Z] (I will return to the issue of scope later on). The rule also says that within the string [X Y <pause> Z], the text producer was not already aware of some trouble by the time element X was vocalized. In other words, any delay between stimulus and response is ruled out. Needless to say that if any proof can be produced suggesting Rule I is off the mark, then pause analytical research would be in serious trouble.[15]

3.3.2. Pause times

Section 3.2 discussed some merits of interpreting pause times in terms of cognitive processes and processing load. It was argued that interpreting pause time differences is a matter of monotonicity. It is nevertheless necessary to make the stringent assumption that, with regard to the observed pause time, pause time is involuntary as well. This is made explicit by Rule II (14).

(14) *Rule II*
The length of a pause is the precise time the text producer needs to produce a continuation, to produce a repair, or to monitor the text produced so far.

Rule II can only be maintained if performance on whatever production tasks one employs happens as quickly as possible, so as to ensure that pauses indeed exclusively reflect cognitive processes (apart from reservations discussed in Section 3.2), and not mental activity that is unrelated, or only remotely related to ongoing production.

15 For further discussion on this issue, see Schilperoord (1996: 293-299).

3.3.3. The scope of pauses

This brings us to what seems to me the most complex methodological issue regarding pause analysis: the *scope* of pauses. As can be easily gleaned from the various transcripts presented so far, the length of the increments by which texts are produced varies considerably, both within texts, between texts, within subjects, and between them. The issue of scope can be put into perspective by considering the string of events in (15).

(15) {<pause X> $[..]_1$ $[..]_2$ $[..]_3$ $[..]_4$ <pause Y>}

For the purpose of the discussion to follow, it suffices to assume that (15) depicts a situation in which some Type-I pause (pause X) is followed an increment of four units of some type (say words), after which another Type-I pause occurs (pause Y).[16]

The question now is: What is retrieved during pause X? Alternatively, we can ask: What assumption with regard to its scope can be substantiated? Are we to assume that all units 1–4 retrieved and subsequently vocalized, or only unit 1? Note that Rule I rules out the possibility during pause X that unit 2, or units 2–4 are retrieved, but not unit 1, for that would imply a postponement of unit 1. But what about units 2, 3 and/or 4? Consider the next transcript (16).

(16) 1. justify the / (2.3)
2. far-reaching conclusions (...)

It may be the case that during the pause following line 1, the entire increment 2 (*far-reaching conclusions*) is retrieved. It may, however, just as well be the case that the noun 'conclusion' was already active at the onset of the pause, and that the pause was only 'used' in order to search for the right adjective.[17] In that case, the pause has only functioned in terms of the immediately following element 'far-reaching'; unit 1 in terms of (15). Because this unit belongs to the category of words, we are forced to assume that pauses only function in terms of words, this category being their maximal scope. That is, words come about with or without the need for pausing, but the possibility that pauses may function in terms of units larger than the word is precluded. The only thing we can conclude then, is that pauses reflect lexical search and that some words happen to be the first element of a constituent whereas others are the first elements of clauses and yet others first elements of, say, sentences.[18]

Clearly, this state of affairs is not satisfying. To see why, bear in mind that many pausological studies have sought to find out whether distributional and temporal properties of pauses can be accounted for in terms of *larger* linguistic categories such as constituents or clauses. Such research questions are relevant to the extent that it can be made plausible that some pauses function in terms of words while other function in

16 We will confine the discussion on scope to type-I pauses.

17 See for further discussion: Schilperoord and Verhagen (in press).

18 It would imply that words are the only category relevant for a production theory, which is reminiscent to 'early' psycholinguistic theories of production (cf. Lounsbury, 1954).

terms of, say, clausal structures. After all, if this cannot be maintained, then indeed there would be little use in distinguishing these categories and adopting them as explanatory variables. In other words, the 'only unit 1-assumption' should be abandoned. But how? Example (15) makes clear that we cannot decide to do so, just on the face of it. My proposal will be to turn this matter into an empirical affair. In the remainder of this section, I will outline a procedure for locating pauses relative to various linguistic units. The proposal is not meant to be the final word on scopal issues, but may prove useful in generating hypotheses about the scope of pauses that can be tested statistically.

The proposal is based on the idea that *hierarchical* relations hold between the various units. These hierarchical relations are a decisive factor in generating hypotheses about the scope of pauses. The precise nature of the relations one imposes upon the 'raw' linguistic material is not what matters, at least not here. What matters is that the categories one adopts and the relations between them must have some psychological significance. If they do, they can be employed in order to properly locate pauses and assess their scope. Consider the string presented in (17).

(17) <pause> *In the* <pause> *procedure for* <pause> *the* <pause>

(17) marks the onset of a string of words that, together, constitute a complex PP-structure '*In the procedure for answering clients' mail*'. In Figure 1, the hierarchical phrase structure of (17) is presented.

The type of location and scope of the three pauses occurring within this constituent can now be assessed by defining the location of each pause relative to the maximal projection of the word immediately following that pause. This is shown in (18).

(18)	*pause*	*increment*	*projection*	*scope*
	1	in the	P ⇛ PP	constituent
	2	procedure for	N	word
	3	the	det ⇛ NP	embedded constituent

Underlying (18) lies the following set phrase structure rules of which it can be argued that it represents some 'mental' reality (see 19).

(19)
a. $P^2 \Rrightarrow \text{prep}, N^2$
b. $N^2 \Rrightarrow \text{det}, N^1$
c. $N^1 \Rrightarrow \ldots N \ldots$

Consider pause 1 in (18). As it directly occurs before the preposition 'in,' and because this element projects a PP-constituent (19a), the location of pause 1 is to be defined relative to the level of constituents. Accordingly its scope is hypothesized to span the minimal PP-constituent, so it ranges from 'in' until 'procedure.' Pause 2 occurs right before the noun 'procedure.' Because, based on rule 18b, the determiner 'the' already has projected the NP-constituent, its scope is hypothesized to span until the next 'between-words' pause, or the next phrase boundary (19c). Finally, pause 3 occurs before the determiner 'the,' which projects an NP-constituent (19b). This pause is therefore located relative to the level of constituents, and since the NP is part of the PP, we can hypothesize its scope to span an embedded constituent. Obviously, if one considers the entire PP-constituent the relevant unit, then only pause 1 is located relative to the level of constituents whereas all other pauses are located relative to the level of 'words.' This, however, is a matter of choice. The relevant observation to be made here is that we can locate a pause and hypothesize about its scope by taking into account the hierarchical level of the unit it precedes.

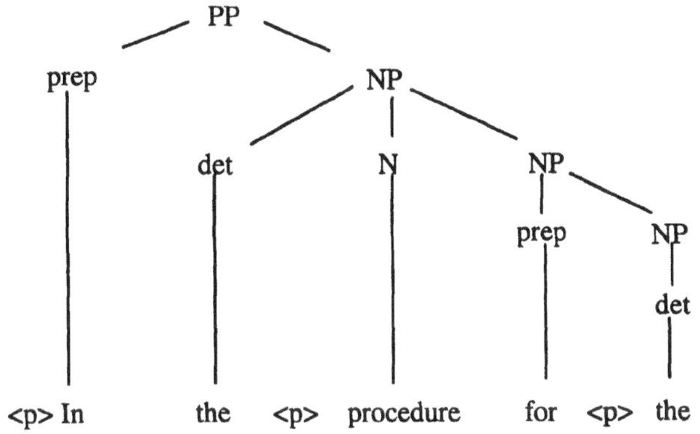

Figure 1. Phrase structure of string (16)

To put matters in more general terms, the procedure for locating pauses and assessing their scope requires us to select a set of text structural features of which it can be plausibly argued that they constitute psychologically 'real' units. Suppose the following set is selected:

Paragraphs,
sentences,
clauses,
constituents.

This set implies that a pause can occupy five kinds of locations: It can be located between paragraphs, between sentences, between clauses, between constituents or within constituents. Note these categories are top-down inclusive: a pause located between paragraphs is also located between sentences, between clauses, and ultimately between words. These hierarchically ordered units or levels also constitute the scope of the pause. Hence, the scope of a pause between paragraphs is hypothesized to span the level of paragraphs, including all pauses occurring within that paragraph. So, pauses themselves are organized hierarchically: They form a *cascade*.

The logic of this assumption can be put in perspective by considering a situation in which we would *not* restrict the scope of a pause to its location level. If we refrain from doing that, we would end up with the unsatisfying situation in which the scope of a pause between sentences (to give an example) would extend up to the level of paragraphs. This state of affairs would clearly contradict Rule I. So the rule determining the scope of a pause can be phrased as follows (see 20).

(20) *Rule III*
The scope of a pause located relative to the text structural featureX_n ranges onto:
1. The next pause located relative to X_n
2. The boundary between X_n a next instance of X_n
3. The boundary between X_n and a higher level unit X_{n+1}

Note 1–3 in (20) represent hypotheses, to be tested empirically, for example by comparing the average durations of pauses at the various locations, or their frequencies. In addition, if indeed empirical evidence for such hypotheses can be produced, this may lead us to adopt a *stack-like* model of pauses. Ultimately, any pause located at, say, the level of paragraphs must reflect at least some activity that has to do with vocalizing the first word of that paragraph, which happens to be also the first element of the first constituent, the first clause and the first sentence (cf. Schilperoord, 1995, 1996). The prediction to be tested, then, is that pause durations vary systematically with their scope and locations: Longest pauses occur between paragraphs, then between sentences, then clauses and so on. This prediction has been repeatedly confirmed by pause time analyses (cf. Chanquoy *et al.*, 1995; Schilperoord 1995, 1996; Van Waes, 1991. See also Section 4 of this chapter).

This rather lengthy section addressed three important methodological issues regarding pause-analytical research. We began by discussing how pauses, combined with other kinds of production behaviours, are related to various cognitive processes underlying text production. We then addressed the issue of pause length, and we concluded this section by discussing how pauses relate to (text) structural features, and what this implies with regard to pause locations and the scope of pauses. The next section sheds light on some statistical methods that can be employed to analyse a pause database.

4. METHODS OF PAUSE ANALYSIS

This section exemplifies three ways of analysing a pause data set. We briefly discuss the most widely used methods of computing *mean durations and frequencies* (4.1). These methods relate pauses to text features. Section 4.2 provides a concise review of analyses of pause time *variances*. This method can be applied in order to study how pauses are related to each other, and the distribution of pause times fluctuates as a function of (real) production time. Finally, Section 4.3 discusses developmental models for the analysis of pause times.

4.1 Mean lengths and frequencies

Traditionally, research on pauses has been mainly concerned with analyses of *pause time distribution* relative to some linguistic category of interest, and to the analysis of *pause frequencies* for particular pre-selected location types. This method has been adopted particularly in the quest for the 'basic' unit of encoding in speech production. If, for example, some unit A consists of two or more instances of unit B, such that $[B_1, B_2, ..., B_n]A$, and A is considered or hypothesized 'more' basic than B, then more pause activity is to be expected between two instances of A than between two instances of B. In addition, pause times will increase at, or towards, the boundaries of any two instances of A. Examples of applying this method are, among many others, Boomer (1965) and Ford and Holmes (1978), who on this basis argue for the phonemic or grammatical clause as corresponding to basic encoding units.

Pause time variances have also been adopted as indications for various levels of speech preparation and planning. Longer pauses are considered to reflect conceptual planning (*i.e.*, content finding and structuring), whereas shorter pauses are believed to reflect planning at linguistic levels (word retrieval, syntactic alignment and so forth). Other dichotomies that refer to the same distinction to be encountered in the literature are macro planning versus micro planning (Butterworth, 1980), distal versus molar planning (O'Connell & Kowal, 1987), and central versus peripheral planning (Goldman-Eisler, 1972). It has on many occasions been shown that pause time distribution is responsive to this distinction and that pause time variances can be explained to a certain extent by it.

However, one should be careful not to draw too sharp a line between these two kinds of speech preparation. After all, any pause, believed to accommodate 'central' voluntary conceptual planning, will, in the end, result in the production of, at least, one word (this was already implied by the 'stack-model' of pauses discussed in the former section). So therefore such a pause can be said to accommodate both kinds of speech preparation, which is, both central and peripheral planning, the former 'spilling over' to the latter. In Schilperoord (1995, 1996) I tested a *cascade* model of text production. The model assumes online planning of text to take place at several levels simultaneously. These levels are constructed top down inclusive in that each unit of planning at some level X_n implies planning at the enclosed levels X_{n-1}, X_{n-2}, ..., X_{n-m}. For example, planning a new paragraph ultimately implies planning the first sentence of that paragraph, the first clause within that sentence, the first phrase within that clause and, finally, the first word within that phrase. Each pause was scored for the highest possible level within the cascade hierarchy. If, at a certain location type, defined as 'between two instances of X,' X being paragraphs, sentences, clauses, phrases and words, no pause occurred, a 'zero-pause' was assigned to it.

Applying this cascade model, I was able to account for over 50% of the observed pause time variances. In addition it could be shown that pause time distribution honoured the hierarchically nested levels: the longest pauses (on average) could be found at paragraph junctures, then between sentences, then clauses, the phrases and, finally, between words. Pause time frequencies showed the same tendency, the estimated proportionate frequencies being 1.00, .95, .68, .60, .53 for paragraphs, sentences, clauses, phrases, and words, respectively.

4.2 Analysis of variance and covariance

The analysis of pause time variances, if it received any attention from scholars at all, has been primarily used to estimate the amount of pause time variance that could be explained by some set of parameters derived from a model, a theory or unit of interest. However, as will be shown in this section, analysing pause time variances can be used in its own right, and reveal much about underlying cognitive processes that would have otherwise have stayed under cover. To show this, I will concisely describe a study that I report about in more detail in Schilperoord (2001).

This study explored not only how pauses behave relative to some textual unit (paragraphs, sentences, or otherwise), but also how they behave *relative to each other*. The goal was to test one crucial assumption implied by the cascade model hinted at in the former section: In the course of text production, writers plan paragraphs 'gist-like,' and then proceed by working out this plan in terms of forming plans for the constituting sentences, which, in turn are decomposed in terms of constituting clauses, and so on. If so indeed, one should expect the kind of processes that go on during a paragraph pause to have much in common with the kind of processing signalled by pauses between sentences, but in addition to have less in common with processes going on during pauses at lower levels. This is not a trivial assumption, because in terms of their *linear order* of appearance a pause between paragraphs will more often have been followed by one at a level *lower* than that of sentences. The cascade model tested, thus assumes that pauses located at *adjacent* hierarchical levels of processing should have more 'in common,' no matter the fact that linearly speaking they are located more remotely than pauses at non-adjacent levels. This hypothesis was labelled the *adjacency-thesis*.

To see how it was tested, consider some pause, occurring between two paragraphs. This pause will, to a lesser or greater extent *deviate* from the general mean estimated for between-paragraph pauses. Such variances in durations can be attributed to local fluctuations in the need for preplanning and varying cognitive demands put on the production system. The same will hold for between-sentence pauses. The theoretical issue can hence be turned into an empirical question by exploring how paragraph-pause variances and sentence-pause variances *covary* or *correlate*. There are three logical possibilities as to how pauses at different locations may covary/correlate: They may correlate positively, negatively, or there may be no significant correlation at all.

Put in terms of processing, the first possibility entails that if, relative to the average length for some superordinate level L_x, pause times at X *increase*, so will pause times at the subordinate level $L_{x-1,2,\ldots n}$. If a text producer uses more time than average to plan a paragraph, he will also use more time to plan the sentences within that paragraph, the clauses within that sentence, and so on. The second possibility represents the reversed situation: If, relative to the average length, pause times increase at level L_x, pause times will decrease at a subordinate level $L_{x-1,2,\ldots n}$. If a paragraph is sufficiently planned, there will be less need to plan the constituting sentences and so on. The third logical possibility entails that there is no significant correlation between pause time variances at the levels L_x and $L_{x-1,2,\ldots n}$. In that case, deviations from the means for different levels are randomly distributed. Planning load at the paragraph level may vary, but these fluctuations will have no predictable import on planning load at lower levels.

The adjacency thesis predicts correlations between levels of processing to be either positive or negative, and, in addition, it predicts correlations to be most significant between adjacent levels of processing. So, 'having much in common' means that variances at the level of paragraphs will covary significantly with variances at the sentence level, no matter whether these correlations are positive or negative. At lower levels – clauses and constituents – these effects will gradually subside.

Table 1. Correlations between levels of processing.

	Estimates			
	Sentence	Clause	Constituent	Word
Paragraph	*.801*	.701	.418	.145
Sentence		*.942*	.808	.467
Clause			*.825*	.497
Word				*1.00*

To test this hypothesis, a correlation matrix was estimated. The results are presented in Table 1. Table 1 shows that, as predicted by the adjacency thesis, correlation estimates are indeed highest for adjacent levels of processing (the italics in Table 1). Local variances at the level of paragraphs do have an impact on processing at the sentence level, but such effects are far less discernable at the clause level, whereas at lower levels they are almost absent. Schilperoord (1996) shows that these results indeed support a cascade model of on line text planning. However, for the present purposes – to illuminate how analysis of variances might be informative as to cognitive processes in text production – it suffices just to present these data and see what can be gleaned from them.

4.3 Developmental models

The former section looked at relations between pauses at different levels of processing, and how such relationships can be explored. This section describes a method of pause time analysis that can be adopted in order to explore relationships between pauses for *a given level* of processing. This method draws on *developmental models of time series data.* To introduce the method, I first have to be more specific as to what research questions can be addressed with it.

As said previously, an issue that has gained much attention in research on language production is whether there exists some basic unit of encoding and whether this unit corresponds to a particular syntactic category. Many studies have provided evidence suggesting that grammatical clauses indeed correspond to such a basic unit of encoding (Boomer, 1965; Ford & Holmes, 1978; Ford, 1982; Holmes, 1988; Schilperoord, 1997). Such evidence is, however, mainly based on analyses of pause durations and frequencies. If some unit A is hypothesized 'more' basic than B, then more pause activity can be expected between two instances of A than between two instances of B. In other words, researchers have mainly looked at what happens *at the boundaries* of some hypothesized unit of encoding.

However, if a certain unit A indeed is a basic unit of speech encoding, then specific patterns of pause activity can be predicted to occur *within* that unit. This prediction can be based on Bolinger's notion of *linear modification*, which he describes as follows:

> Before a speaker begins, the possibilities of what he will communicate are practically infinite, or, if his utterances are bound within a discourse, they are at least enormously large. When the first word appears, the possibilities are vastly reduced. (Bolinger, 1965: 219)

With each new word produced within the same utterance, possibilities to continue that utterance are restricted. Linear modification is visualized by two hyperbolic-shaped lines converging into one single point: the 'end' of the utterance. If linear modification indeed takes place, then it can be argued that when possibilities are 'enormously large' there will be a relatively high degree of uncertainty as to how to continue the utterance. Relatively long pauses at such locations are then predicted. On the other hand, if more words are added, possibilities to continue will decrease. That is, uncertainty will decline, hence pause times will gradually decrease. This is called *temporal modification.*

Note that this prediction is crucially related to the unit-issue. The predicted patterns will occur within a particular unit to the extent that such a unit is indeed a 'basic' processing unit as well. This prediction was therefore tested by comparing pause patterns both within sentences and within clauses. If the 'sentence' is the relevant unit of processing, temporal modification will take place, regardless the presence of clause boundaries within that sentence. If, on the other hand, clauses are the relevant 'basic' unit, temporal modification is expected only to occur within clauses. At clause boundaries, possibilities will again be 'enormously large,' resulting in increased pause times at those locations.

To test this hypothesis, the variable pause length X had to be estimated as a function of time $f(t)$, where $X = f(t)$. 'Time' was defined as consecutive between-word positions within the units of interest (clauses *vs.* sentences). Temporal modification was defined in terms of the time function: *a significant decrease of mean pause times.* In addition, if temporal modification indeed occurred, then not only mean pause times will decrease, *but pause time variances as well.* In other words, the mean pause time for a certain position within the unit of interest gradually better predicts the duration as actually observed.

Both statistical hypotheses were confirmed in the case of clauses, but not sentences. That is, clauses do indeed exhibit temporal modification. Mean pause times drop gradually, as well as pause time variances. In addition, this pattern was observed within clauses regardless whether it occupied at the beginning of a sentence. In addition, at clause boundaries, huge increases in mean pause length and variances were observed, indicating that at these locations 'possibilities' to continue are again 'enormously large.' The theoretical explanation presented in Schilperoord (1997) entails that the 'end' of clauses can, in many cases be projected from their onset (this is especially the case for dependent clauses in Dutch which exhibit an SOV-order). In other words: clauses come to an end by obligation. In contrast, sentences can be extended infinitely. Taken together, the results of this study are additional evidence in support for the clause-as-processing-unit hypothesis.

5. CONCLUDING REMARKS

To conclude this chapter, I hope to have shown that, if handled with care, pause analysis is a powerful tool to study cognitive aspects of language production. Obviously, whether or not one likes to make use of this tool depends entirely on the kind of questions one likes to answer. If a researcher is primarily interested in the precise nature and details of the considerations of a writer who is planning some piece of text, or who is revising a text already written, then pauses have little to tell him. If, on the other hand one's interest concerns the intricacies of the word-by-word production process of text, pause analysis presents a non-obtrusive, on-line method to study such processes, and possibilities to put forth and test processing hypotheses. For many years, writing process research has relied on case studies and observational inquiry. Pause analysis, especially when combined with careful text analysis, may raise the scientific discipline of cognitive processes in text production above that level.

6. ACKNOWLEDGEMENTS

I would like to thank three anonymous reviewers for their comments and suggestions.

STUDYING WRITERS' REVISING PATTERNS WITH S-NOTATION ANALYSIS

PY KOLLBERG & KERSTIN SEVERINSON EKLUNDH

Royal Institute of Technology (Sweden)

Abstract. This chapter describes a computer-based technique for analysing revision and text production strategies, called S-notation. On the basis of a keystroke record, a representation is created of all revisions made to a text during a writing session, including their order and internal structure. The resulting representation is embedded in an interactive program, which enables both qualitative and quantitative analyses of revisions made during a writing session. The tools described also support automatic identification of connected episodes of revision, which are relevant for the study of individual and task-specific writing strategies. We present the methodological and theoretical rationale behind the development of the method, and the basic principles for the creation of the S-notation. Subsequently, we describe how the tools can be used to answer particular research questions, including a discussion of the limitations of a purely formal treatment of revision. A multi-level framework is outlined for how to gain knowledge of revision processes using different kinds of data. Finally, we summarize studies made by ourselves as well as other researchers using S-notation analysis.
Keywords: revision, writing, revision trace, revision episode, logging, keystroke methods.

1. INTRODUCTION

The use of computers for writing has profoundly changed the study of revision processes. At present, virtually all writers use a computer, which has opened up new methods of observing and analysing the writer's actions during composing. This is also an important step in order to understand underlying composing processes.

Within the cognitive tradition of writing research, revision is seen as the result of a complex reviewing process, involving the detection and possible diagnosis of a problem in the text (Flower, Hayes, Carey, Schriver, & Stratman, 1986; Flower & Hayes, 1981). By reading and evaluating what has been written, the writer forms a representation of the text, and compares it with his or her intentions. In this process, a problem may be discovered (a *detection*). If the writer can recognize the problem (forming a *diagnosis*), this may lead to finding a strategy for changing the text (i.e., making a *revision*), and thus eliminating the problem. However, this process may be difficult for many reasons, and many writers fail to reach the level of a successful revision. For

P. Kollberg & K. Severinson Eklundh (2001). Studying writer's revising patterns with S-notation analysis. In: G. Rijlaarsdam (Series ed.) & T. Olive & C. M. Levy (Vol. eds.), Studies in Writing: Volume 10: Contemporary Tools and Techniques for Studying Writing, p. 89-104.

example, writers may not have an adequate representation of their texts, or of their own intentions. Moreover, even if they do detect a problem, it is possible that they do not succeed in diagnosing it. Therefore, the strategy decided upon may be to *rewrite* the whole or part of the text rather than to *revise* it. Flower *et al.* (1986) presented this model of revision as a basis for an understanding of writers' cognitive difficulties in revision, and discussed some of its pedagogical implications.

This revision process often starts with the writer's reading the text in order to evaluate it, and it may or may not eventually lead to an actual change in the text. In principle, revision may occur at any time in the writing process, reflecting the recursive nature of writing and the gradual development of the writer's plans. Revisions may affect the text at higher or lower levels, or they may only change the writer's mental representation of the task.

Methodologically, the study of revision involves many challenges. An obvious problem in studying revision is that there is a gap between the cognitive sides of it and the actual changes that the writer makes in the text. In general, it is not possible to relate a change in the text to a certain goal on the part of the writer, without having additional information about the writer's thinking processes. However, the need for a clear distinction between what the writer does and his/her underlying intentions is often ignored, and researchers tend to classify revisions in terms of their assumed purpose rather than just their form.

In this chapter we present a general computer-based method, S-notation[1], for representing and analysing writers' revisions to a text. The method simplifies the study of revision as an online process, by making it possible to follow in detail the continuous shaping and re-shaping of the written text. In contrast to other methods, it gives a complete history of the changes that occur in a text during a writing session, including their order and structure. This representation can be used in combination with other data to provide an understanding of revision at both high and low levels. As we will show, such a computer-based analysis emphasizes the necessity of separating the physical and the cognitive levels of revision. We will outline a multi-level framework, illustrating how different data can be used to reach a successively more advanced understanding of revision processes.

2. THEORETICAL AND METHODOLOGICAL RATIONALES FOR THE S-NOTATION

The work with developing the S-notation grew out of research needs that arose when using keystroke analysis to study revision (Severinson Eklundh, 1990; Severinson Eklundh & Kollberg, 1996b). Keystroke logging is a straightforward way of tracking writers' actions, but when trying to make sense of logging data, the researcher often confronts a number of problems. The records usually represent a writing session as a sequence of keystroke events, including typed characters, pauses, and commands to

1 For convenience, we use the word 'S-notation' both for the notation (representation) of the revisions made to a text, and for the method for generating this representation from a keystroke record. The name 'S-notation' was originally chosen because of the first letter S of the Swedish word for 'write' (skriva). An alternative and simpler term might be just 'revision trace'.

the computer. Because of the variation in the functions and interface of word processors, the language of the keystroke records varies considerably from system to system. And since the actions are represented in a chronological order, it is often quite difficult to identify where the changes made by the writer are located, and how they affect the text. As a result, the researcher must often create meta-level protocols to account for what is really happening in the keystroke session.

The S-notation is an automatic method to generate such a meta-level revision protocol from keystroke data. In contrast to ordinary keystroke logfiles, this notation represents revisions at their place in the text, so that the researcher can directly see the surrounding context including text and other revisions. It also encompasses information about the range, order and structure of revisions, allowing for analyses of more complex patterns of revising activity. The method is intended to be used as an instrument in the study of revision, being complemented by contextual data about the writing session to inform a particular research question.

The design of the S-notation was inspired by a manual notation for revision invented by Matsuhashi (1987). Her concern was the analysis of writing as an ongoing cognitive process, governed at the point of inscription by a set of constraints imposed by characteristics of the writing task. The notation used was applied to handwritten data, and was only partly formalised. However, the application of this framework to a qualitative analysis of a teenage writer's composing sessions embodied some fundamental conceptual distinctions that we found to be useful in the treatment of keystroke data. Matsuhashi's notation transcribed the successive changes made by the writer, the place in the text where a revision was made, and their order. Importantly, this allowed for representation not only of when and how a revision is made, but also its relationship to preceding and following actions.

We developed the S-notation as a formally specified, computer-based representation of revisions, based on some of the principles from Matsuhashi. The following goals were formulated, and eventually realized in the implementation of the method:

1) The S-notation should represent a writing session as a sequence of revisions made to the text – rather than as operations performed in the word processor as in keystroke logfiles – making it possible to investigate revisions in detail.
2) It should be possible for a computer program to generate the S-notation from a keystroke record.
3) The S-notation should be independent of the word processor used during the writing session. Consequently, it should not contain commands made to a computer, but only their effects on the text.
4) It should be possible for a computer to replay a writing session revision by revision, forward or backwards, using only the S-notation as an input.
5) The S-notation should be readable for the user.

Below we summarize the most important principles of the S-notation. For a more detailed account, including the formal rules for the notation and their application, see Kollberg (1998). Aspects of the use of S-notation to analyse online revision processes, and especially the problems of interpreting writers' actions at the computer have been more thoroughly discussed in Severinson Eklundh and Kollberg (1996a).

3. BASIC PRINCIPLES OF THE S-NOTATION

3.1. Definitions and transcription conventions

In S-notation, a revision is either an *insertion* or a *deletion*. Each revision is associated with an *interruption* (or a break in text production) at the position of the last action preceding the revision. The interruptions are numbered according to the sequence of their occurrence in the writing session.

The S-notation uses the following symbols[2]:

`|I`	The interruption with sequential number # i
`{inserted text}`^{i}	An insertion following interruption # i
`[deleted text]`^{i}	A deletion following interruption # i

The following is an example of a short writing session transcribed in S-notation.

Now I am writing a {short }^{1}text.$|_1$ I will[probably]$^2|_3$ change it[somewhat]^3 later.$|_2$ Now I am finished.

The text produced in this example reads as follows:

Now I am writing a short text. I will change it later. Now I am finished.

The above transcription corresponds to the following sequence of actions by the writer:

1) Types *Now I am writing a text*.
2) Inserts *short* between *a* and *text.*
3) Resumes writing at the end of the text: *I will probably change it somewhat later*.
4) Deletes *probably.*
5) Deletes *somewhat.*
6) Resumes writing at the end of the text: *Now I am finished.*

An important requirement on a formal revision notation is that it should be neutral with respect to the writers' intentions, and thus not make any assumptions as to the purpose of a certain change in the text. This was actually a problem with Matsuhashi's notation that has also been present in many previous accounts of revision. For example, if a writer deletes a word, and subsequently inserts another word at the same position in the text, one cannot deduce that the writer intended the second word to replace the first (even if this is often the case). The idea of a computer-generated record requires a strictly formal analysis, only taking account of the overt actions made. As a consequence, S-notation only represents what we call *elementary revisions* (deletions and insertions) made in the word processor, yielding a strictly syntactic repre-

---

2 When needed for the sake of clarity, the index is shown both at the beginning and at the end of a revision.

sentation of the changes made to the text. The deeper, semantic analysis of revisions is left to an interpretation stage, being performed on top of, and with the aid of the S-notation. Depending on the research question, this process may also require access to other data than keystroke logfiles, such as verbal reports. In Severinson Eklundh & Kollberg (1996a), a range of methodological problems in using the S-notation to study revision is discussed.

3.2. Procedure for creating a revision record

The S-notation is generated from a keystroke logfile, by first transforming the logfile to an intermediate format (MID-format). The MID-file consists of a list of elementary operations (moves, insertions and deletions) in their order of occurrence during the writing session. This format is independent of the word processor used, and could in principle be generated by any word processor. Thus, it would be possible to generate a MID file directly rather than using it as an intermediate format.

The following example, which corresponds to the short writing session above, demonstrates the simple syntax of the MID format:

```
1.1 I 23 4.8 Now I am writing a text
8.4 I 1 0.0.
3.8 M -5
1.1 I 6 1.2 short
3.1 M 5
1.7 I 41 8.9  I will probably change it somewhat later
11.0 I 1 0.0.
4.2 M -35
3.4 D 9
1.8 M 10
1.3 D 9
1.1 M 7
0.9 I 19 4.3  Now I am finished.
```

Each line in the MID file contains one elementary operation, preceded by the time elapsed since the previous operation, and followed by the number of characters affected by the operation. For movements, the direction of the movement is indicated in the positive or negative sign before the number of characters. For insertions, the text of the insertion also follows. A more detailed explanation can be found in Kollberg (1998).

The build-up of the MID representation was designed for future inclusion of pauses into the S-notation. Therefore, time information is included, but is presently not used in the interactive program (Trace-it; see below) used for S-notation analysis. This means that in order to study how pauses and other temporal aspects of a writing session relate to revising, one must have access to the original keystroke logfile. This is also necessary to get a more complete account of the writer's activity, including problems in the handling of the word processor.

In our studies using S-notation, we have used the word processor JEdit on the Apple Macintosh, developed for research purposes in our laboratory. JEdit logs a writing session into an easily readable form, and allows the logfile to be translated to MID format with a menu command (see Severinson Eklundh & Kollberg, 1996b).

3.3. Distant and immediate revisions

The S-notation facilitates analysis of the *distance* between a revision and the corresponding interruption (*i.e.*, the place of inscription preceding the revision, or the previous action to the text). This can be an important element in assessing writing strategies, as large distances indicate how the writer moves her attention to new parts of the text. In the present version of the interactive tool Trace-it, revisions can be classified into the two categories of *immediate* and *distant* revisions. Immediate revisions are made directly at the point of inscription (with distance = 0), whereas distant revisions are all other revisions. However, there is reason to assume that intermediate categories are also of interest. For example, Matsuhashi (1987) based her analysis of task-related writing strategies on a three-part classification of revisions: S^i for sentence-immediate revisions (distance = 0 in our terms), S_d for sentence-distal revisions (revisions that are distant but affect only the current sentence) and T (text revision, *i.e.*, revisions ranging across the boundary of the current sentence). In her analysis of the data collected, Matsuhashi eventually collapsed the first two categories, arguing that the sentence was a relevant unit for the distinction between local and distant revisions. Such more elaborated categories can easily be defined in terms of S-notation, and could be included in future versions of Trace-it.

3.4. Analysing episodes of revision

An important idea with the S-notation is that it should help describe individual strategies and personal profiles of writing based on patterns of revision. This has been actualised by studies of computer-supported writing, which often compare the writer's ways of revising during different conditions (see, for example, van Waes, 1991, 1992). Also, previous research has shown that the way in which revisions are grouped into episodes is an important property of a writing strategy, an aspect where experienced and less experienced writers seem to differ in behaviour (Monahan, 1984). On the basis of the S-notation, we have developed computer support for identifying three different types of revision episodes. These types were chosen partly on the basis of our own empirical observations, but their importance is also supported by results from a study by Williamson and Pence (1989). Currently, these types of episodes identify instances of *repetitive revisions*, *embedded revisions*, and *sequences of revisions in previously written text*, respectively[3]:

- *Type 1. Episode with repetitive revisions at one cursor location.* Two or more immediate revisions are performed at one cursor location, where the writer is currently producing text. This episode type occurs for instance when the writer is

---

3 A more detailed explanation of these types of episodes can be found in Kollberg (1998).

trying out different words in one place in the text to find the right way to express something, deleting and inserting repeatedly at the same position.

- *Type 2. Episode with embedded revisions.* This episode type includes all cases when one revision is performed during the course of another revision. It occurs when the writer is making an insertion that is then modified before it is finished, for example, by substituting a word in the sentence being inserted within the text.
- *Type 3. Episode with a sequence of revisions in previously written text.* The writer interrupts the text production to perform a sequence of revisions in the text written previously. After the last revision in the sequence, the writer resumes writing at the position of the interruption. This type of episode occurs, for instance, when the writer goes through a paragraph just written and makes a number of revisions in it.

We have applied this framework in a recent study (Severinson Eklundh & Kollberg, 1999), where analysis of Type 3 episodes was used to explore discourse-level revision in four different writing tasks. The study is summarized in Section 6, below.

4. USING THE TRACE-IT PROGRAM TO ANALYSE A WRITING SESSION

The program Trace-it (Kollberg, Kim, & Severinson Eklundh, 1996; Nilsson & Kollberg, 1996) for the Macintosh was designed to serve as a general-purpose tool for the study of revising and text production strategies, using S-notation as a basis.

Taking a MID file as input, Trace-it presents the writing session in two windows (see Figure 1). One window contains the revision record in S-notation, the other contains the final text, and it also serves as a replay window. Additional windows can be opened to display information about the session, such as a detailed revision analysis with information about each revision, episode analysis and a summary of revisions.

4.1. The S-notation window

Clicking on a revision in the S-notation window highlights the entire range of the revision. By moving from revision to revision with the arrow keys or icons, the analyst gets a view of the order of the writer's movements in the text. It is also helpful to move from a revision to its interruption symbol or vice versa, to visualise where a revision episode started. Character strings can be searched for, both in the text and the S-notation windows. Finally, different options can be selected for the presentation of the revision record.[4]

4.2. The replay window

The type of replay facility usually available in logging systems takes no account of what constitutes one revision, but requires the user to specify the desired interval in seconds. As a contrast, replay in Trace-it is done step by step, *i.e.*, one revision at a

4 For example, deletions can be shown in italics which gives a better visual overview of all revisions. Also, white spaces and tab characters can optionally be made explicit.

time. This is a great advantage when attempting to understand the nature of a certain sequence of revisions, supporting exploration of a writing session. It is also possible to go backwards, and thus to 'undo' the last revision played.

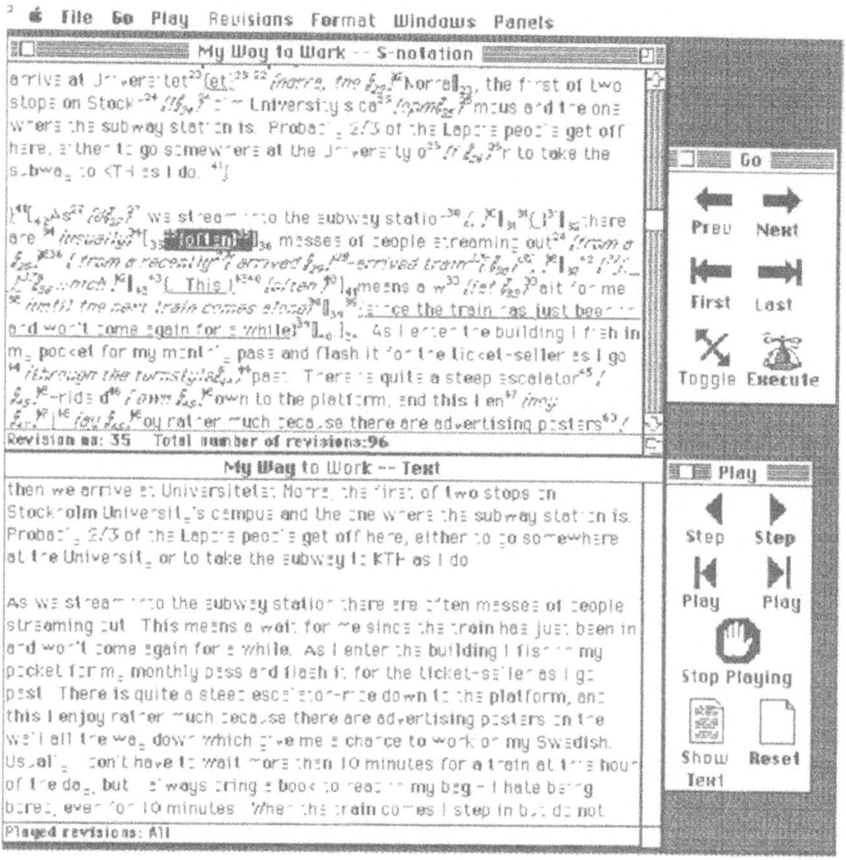

Figure 1. A writing session presented in Trace-it.

4.3. Revision analysis options

A list of all the revisions in a session can be obtained in Trace-it, including their type (insertion or deletion), range and distance from the point of inscription (see Table 1). It is also possible to specify a certain level (paragraph, sentence, phrase, word or character) and have only the revisions on this level listed. A summary of all the revisions (immediate, distant, and total) on various levels can also be obtained.

Table 1. Trace-it's list of revisions.

Revision list File: Pupil6 MID

Rev	Type	Level	Range	Distance	Executed
1	DEL	c	4c	0`	No
2	DEL	w	1w 2c	0	No
3	DEL	c	6c	0`	No
4	DEL	c	3c	0`	No
5	DEL	c	2c	0`	No
6	DEL	c	2c	0`	No
7	DEL	_	1c	0`	No
8	DEL	_	1c	0`	No
9	DEL	c	6c	0`	No
10	DEL	w	1w	0`	No
11	DEL	c	5c	0`	No
12	DEL	c	3c	-22	No
13	INS	c	2c	0	No
...					
126	DEL	w	1w	0`	No
127	DEL	w	1w	0`	No

A separate analysis can be made of the *revision episodes* in the session, divided into the three categories specified earlier. The analysis yields the number of episodes of each type, and the revisions included in each episode.

4.4. Selecting revisions of interest for a certain purpose

For certain types of analysis, only part of the revisions in a writing session may be of interest. Therefore, one may wish to remove some of the revisions from the S-notation, in order to see other revisions more clearly.

4.4.1. Manually removing a revision

There are two distinct ways to remove a revision manually from the S-notation. *Deleting* a revision means that the state-of-affairs before the revision is kept in the S-notation. That is, the writing session will look as though the revision was never performed. *Executing* a revision, on the other hand, means that the S-notation is changed to correspond with the result of the revision. This means that the writing session will appear as though the 'error' repaired by the revision never occurred.

4.4.2. Identification and filtering of typing error corrections

Typing error corrections are low-level revisions that are often of little interest in higher-level revision analyses, because a typing error is never intended by the writer. Trace-it's filtering function automatically diagnoses and executes most typing error corrections, thus removing both the error and its correction from the S-notation records. The function uses a set of rules based on an analysis of common keyboard errors. For instance, one rule looks for errors caused by the writer's pressing an adjacent key to the one intended. In the analysis table, the filtered revisions are listed and categorised into one of eight patterns (*e.g.*, transposition and omission). The filtering function and its application are described in Kim (1996).

5. ADDRESSING DIFFERENT RESEARCH QUESTIONS WITH S-NOTATION ANALYSIS

Since the S-notation describes text-editing actions, it can be used to study all kinds of text editing or word processing activities. So far, it has been used mainly in composition studies, to help analyse text production and revision patterns. The analyses available in Trace-it allow for large data sets to be investigated with respect to patterns of revision activity. However, our own experience is that a purely quantitative analysis of elementary revisions is usually not enough in composition studies, but needs to be supplemented by closer inspection of the writer's actions in their context, in a way targeted to the specific research questions raised. In particular, tracing the gradual growth of the text with the replay function, and investigating details about revisions in the S-notation window, enables an explorative analysis of revision patterns that complements the quantitative measures.

In combination with verbal reports, these methods can be used to study writing processes with an interpretative approach. The detailed revision history together with the writer's own reports lends itself to analyses of, for example, planning and writing strategies. The replay function can *e.g.* be used in *stimulated recall* (DiPardo, 1994) to collect retrospective reports from the writer.

Altogether, the S-notation framework can be used to address a variety of research questions with regard to revision. Such studies will, depending on their claims, rely on other kinds of data in addition to keystroke data and S-notation records. It is essential to be explicit about what conclusions can be drawn from particular data, something that has not always been the case in studies of revision so far. Too often, inferences have been made about the writer's goals and intentions from a superficial analysis of his or her writing activity.

In general, the analysis of revision can be seen as a multi-level process, where the lowest level consists of tracking the writer's physical actions, and the highest level implies gaining an understanding of the writer's overall rhetorical goals. Table 2 illustrates these different levels, in terms of both the type of question addressed, and the type of data relevant for the study[5].

5 This table is a slightly revised version of a similar one presented in Severinson Eklundh & Kollberg (1996b), where we discussed methodological aspects of S-notation in more detail.

Table 2. Data and questions related to the levels of revisions.

Level	Data	Object of analysis	Questions focused
4	Verbal reports; interviews, S-notation & keystroke records	Writer's overall rhetorical goals	How is the writer's view of the task reflected in the revisions?
3	S-notation & keystroke records; verbal reports	Interpreted revisions and revision episodes	Which means of revising are used by the writer to achieve a specific goal?
2	S-notation records	Elementary revisions and revision episodes	In which general patterns does the writer generate and change the text?
1	Keystroke records, video recordings	Text-editing actions and pauses	How does the writer use the computer to shape words and sentences?

Level 1 is the pure text editing level, which describes the writer's keystroke actions at the computer together with temporal information. The input to this level may be an ordinary keystroke logfile or a video recording. The data on this level can be used to draw conclusions about the writer's problems in handling the computer system.

Level 2 is the S-notation analysis, which transforms keystroke records into a sequence of elementary revisions, and also analyses the episodic structure of revisions. This step gives a formal, syntactic description of the writer's changes to the text, including their order and internal structure.

Level 3 is an account of the revisions and episodes in terms of the effect on the text that the writer intended to achieve. In other words, this step gives an interpretative description of the writer's revision activity. Arriving at such a description often requires access to information outside of the computer records, such as verbal reports from the writer.

Level 4 links the revision pattern with the writer's task knowledge and goals, and with his or her global plan for the task. This implies a more comprehensive analysis of the writer's revising strategy in the context of the whole rhetorical situation.

Generally, the analysis in this model is thought to be pursued in a bottom-up fashion, so that data from the lower levels are successively enriched and interpreted in the light of data on higher levels. In practice, most studies have reached only level 2 or level 3 in their analysis, which is not surprising considering the complexity of the issues. In fact, these two levels are sometimes combined in analyses of revision, mixing description and interpretation in, for example, categorizations of changes made to a text. By building upon a formal revision analysis as yielded by S-notation, the researcher's assumptions and claims can more easily be made explicit.

An important methodological agenda is to analyse the relationship between these levels further, to understand what kinds of conclusions can be drawn from particular revision data. Our own work so far suggests that an intermediate level ('level 2.5') is justified, in which S-notation records of a session are built upon to yield preliminary, local interpretations of certain revising patterns. Such an analysis might draw tentative conclusions from sequences of elementary revisions about their purpose in a context, based on statistics, keystroke data or previous research. This would be an alternative to the revision analyses made by many researchers, where interpretations are based on intuition alone. We have plans for extending the Trace-it program with intelligent support for such a local analysis, including annotation and preliminary interpretation of revision patterns.

In the next section, we summarize some studies made using S-notation, to give concrete examples of research problems that the method can help explore. Of course, these studies do not exhaust the possibilities of using the method in writing research. In fact, it is clear that with reference to the multi-level model above, much remains to be done to develop methods for coupling accounts of writers' actions at the computer with their goals in a writing context.

6. EMPIRICAL STUDIES OF WRITING USING S-NOTATION ANALYSIS

The tools described in this chapter have been used extensively by both ourselves and other researchers to study revision processes. These studies have had a broad scope, from theoretical to educational in orientation, and they represent different methodological approaches, from experimental studies to field studies. Below we give a brief overview of some of this work.

6.1. Exploration of text production strategies

We have conducted two laboratory studies with the aim to evaluate and develop the S-notation method, while pursuing an independent research question. Notably, these studies were made at different points in the development of the S-notation method. In the first study, focused on linearity in computer-based writing, we had not yet developed support for the revision episode analysis in Trace-it, which later turned out to be a significant help in the study of revision patterns. Therefore, this study involved much more of explorative work before finding a useful way of operationalising the notion of linearity and exploring it with the S-notation records.

6.1.1. Linear and non-linear writing strategies

Writing with a computer has often been claimed to encourage experimenting with the text, letting the writer compose different parts of the text in any order – in a non-linear fashion – and thus stimulating creativity. However, research has also shown that when using the word-processor, writers work more locally with their texts than when using pen and paper. These different claims about computer-based writing patterns were examined by Severinson Eklundh (1994), in an explorative study of linear and non-linear writing strategies. Linear writing is defined to be the case when the writer produces the text from beginning to end in the order of its final presentation, or with very few and minor revisions.

Linearity as described here can be successfully studied with the S-notation analyses in Trace-it. The program keeps track of the type of revisions, the order in which they are performed, their range, and their distance from the point of inscription. These variables were used to obtain a quantitative assessment of linearity across different tasks. With the measures used, the most non-linear writing sessions were the ones containing repeated insertions of large text portions at a long distance from the current point of inscription.

In the study, five students' writing sessions in four different tasks each (totally 20 sessions) were analysed. The tasks were selected to represent different levels of cognitive complexity, and requiring different amounts of planning and structuring. Initially, replay of the sessions was used extensively for detecting patterns of building up the texts, and making informal assessments of linearity to test the proposed variables. In the next stage, the elementary revisions were charted with respect to their type, level and distance from the point of inscription.

Although only the overt revising records were analysed, it was found that the individual writing styles changed with the task. Writers, who showed a heavily non-linear writing pattern in the most demanding, knowledge-transforming task, applied a linear style in a simple reporting task. The results suggested that the non-linear patterns reflect the recursivity of the writing process:

> by going through cycles of planning, text creation and reviewing on different levels, the writer may gain new insights leading to the development of new goals and a revised high-level plan. (p. 204)

However, in order to provide a more elaborated cognitive explanation for the patterns found, other data than the ones examined should be used. The small number of subjects also prevented us from making generalizations from these results.

6.1.2. Using episode analysis to study discourse-level revision

In a more recent study, we have used episode analysis to study discourse-level revision in twenty writing sessions by university students, carrying out four different composition tasks (Severinson Eklundh & Kollberg, 1999). The study used the same data as the linearity study described above, but went beyond a strictly formal treatment to study how the writers gradually built up the global structure of their texts. An independent purpose was to assess the empirical status and relevance of revision episodes for the study of revision at the level of discourse structure.

The episodes of Type 3 in the twenty writing sessions (in total 283 episodes, each containing a sequence of consecutive revisions in previously written text) were identified, and replayed by the analyst several times in their context. This was done to gain an understanding of the nature of the episode, and the extent to which it affected the text only locally, or if it in some way addressed global text relations. The analysis led to a preliminary classification of discourse-level revisions in the data.[6]

Altogether, the results showed that writers invested significant work trying to build a coherent structure of their texts, while adapting their general writing strategy to the task. To a great extent, their structuring work proceeded on a local basis, making repeated revisions while taking advantage of the word-processor's capacity to re-use text parts. The study revealed substantial individual differences in the way that writers approached the tasks, complementing the linearity study of the same data reported above. This included both the number and nature of the 'global' revision episodes observed.

The experiences from this study show that identifying sequences of elementary revisions through S-notation is a very effective way of finding global revisions in a recorded writing session. Only a small fraction of those revisions were not covered by Trace-it's episode analysis (those consisting of a single, large elementary revision). Moreover, it was found that higher-level revisions tended to occur mainly in those episodes consisting of four elementary revisions or more, whereas episodes of 2 or 3 revisions were mostly small, local changes. This gives a framework for quickly targeting major revisions to a text, which should be further tested in future studies.

6.2.Revision studies within an educational context

In writing education, S-notation analysis can be used in several ways. If students are logged, their writing can be investigated afterwards using the Trace-it program, either by their teachers, by their peers, or by themselves. For the students themselves, this offers an opportunity to reflect upon their own writing. For the teacher, the access to the whole writing history gives another perspective of a particular student's skills and problems compared to a finished draft or essay. A case study using this approach is presented in Lindgren & Sullivan (in press).

The primary objective of the *L2 studies* (Kollberg, Lindgren, & Sullivan, 2000; Sullivan, Lindgren, & Kollberg, 2000; Sullivan, Kollberg, Severinson Eklundh, & Pålsson, 1997) was to examine and compare the writing patterns and revision activities of Swedish learners at different stages of learning English, using a mixed cross-sectional/longitudinal design. The focus of the revision analysis was what and how the pupils revised, how the revisions reflected each pupil's linguistic ability, and to what extent they were concerned with style and content. Writing patterns in the foreign language were compared with those in Swedish, using analyses developed from the S-notation records (Lindgren & Sullivan, 2000).

In the analysis, three main categories of revision were focused upon. In the categories *spelling problem* and *grammar problem* groups of (one or more) elementary revisions related to the same linguistic problem were captured. The third category was other changes at the word or phrase level (*e.g.* changing contents or style). By replaying the writing sessions and examining the S-notation records, these categorisations of

---

6 The categories used were: creating a new global content unit, revising for contrast, revising for consistency, revising for coherence, revising for increased explicitness, revising to eliminate repetition, structuring, and global review.

the students' revision behaviour were carried out. The focus on changes related to linguistic problem areas required tentative interpretations above the level of the S-notation syntax of elementary revisions.

The revising strategies and pausing behaviour of eight pupils from the youngest group of writers, who were aged 13 at the onset of the study, were also analysed in detail over a three-year period. The same categories of analysis as described above were used. In addition, a pause analysis was performed, using JEdit (for examination of the log-files) and Trace-it in combination. In this way, the temporal aspects of writing could be related to the findings about the revision strategies.

In these studies, S-notation and keystroke records were used to support an understanding of pupils' writing ability. Naturally, such studies must be carried out with awareness of the methodological problems involved, and eventually be supported by other information in the classroom context to inform teaching strategies.

6.3. *Field studies of journalistic writing*

Logging can be a suitable method to observe writing in the field, because the writer's actions are silently recorded in such a way that the composing is not disturbed. The revision analysis in Trace-it has been used by Perrin (1997, 1998) to analyse journalists' text production patterns, and how they handle important points of decision in the writing process. The goals were to find the conscious writing strategies applied, to evaluate them, and then discuss alternative strategies with the journalists in order to improve their writing. Perrin's method, ***Progression Analysis*** (Perrin, 1998; Perrin, this volume), analyses writing strategies at three levels:

1) The situation in which the writer is working (*e.g.* social aspects, the writing tool, the task),
2) the text history described by the S-notation and the keystroke logfile,
3) the writer's self-report about conscious writing strategies.

At the third level, Perrin combined the text history with cued retrospective reports: immediately after the deadline of an article, the writer replayed the writing session, and commented on what was done and why. These sessions were tape-recorded. The verbal protocol was encoded and analysed together with the S-notation records in Trace-it, to reveal the writer's repertoire of actual strategies. This procedure is thought to show if the writer has a large repertoire of relevant strategies to apply in a flexible way to the task at hand, or if alternative strategies would enhance her/his writing. With progression analysis, Perrin has also aimed to explore why 'experienced' writers sometimes fail to accomplish their goals.

7. SUMMARY AND CONCLUSIONS

In this chapter, we have described the properties of S-notation as a method, and its application to study writing processes. S-notation goes beyond ordinary keystroke records to provide immediate access to writers' revisions and their structural properties. Furthermore, the automatic identification of revision episodes based on S-notation is a promising way of gaining access to complex revising patterns which may relate to task constraints and individual differences between writers. In general, interactive analysis of a keystroke record with S-notation gives the researcher a set of intelligent tools which both provide an account of the complete text history, and help filter out uninteresting aspects of keystroke data, directing researchers' attention to those aspects relevant to their questions.

We have stressed the fact that S-notation analysis can never explain what goes on in the writer's mind, but needs to be combined with other information sources to lead to an understanding of composing processes. Nevertheless, we feel that the methods described here constitute a fundamentally new way of studying revision, which facilitates both the exploration and description of text production strategies in different contexts. We hope that future use of these tools will help develop them further, and integrate them in everyday research practices as a complement to other ways of studying writing.

PROGRESSION ANALYSIS (PA): INVESTIGATING WRITING STRATEGIES IN THE WORKPLACE

DANIEL PERRIN

University of Berne

Abstract. Progression Analysis (PA) is a computer-based method for research on writing in the workplace. As a multilevel-analysis, PA focuses (1) on the situation of the writing process, (2) on the movement of writing throughout the growing text, and (3) on consciously applied strategies. In this chapter, the innovative procedures of PA are presented on behalf of a pedagogically motivated case study out of a national research project.
Keywords: Writing in the workplace, non-intrusiveness, writing strategies, movement of writing, repertoire of writing strategies, revisions, S-notation, newswriter.

INTRODUCTION

What do journalists do exactly when they write – and copy each other? What do they want to achieve, and what do they really achieve? These are the central questions of a national research project that investigates the working strategies of Swiss journalists under changing technical, economical and institutional conditions. Hundreds of professionals from all around Switzerland have been interviewed (Blum, Bonfadell, Marr, & Wyss, 2001), forty have been observed in case studies (Perrin, 2001c). To establish the relationship among workplace, writing strategies and text product, a non-intrusive methodology had to be developed. We called it Progression Analysis (Perrin, 1999a).

Progression Analysis (PA) is based on S-notation (Kollberg, 1998; Severinson Eklundh & Kollberg, 1996, in this volume) and records the writing process on three levels – *i.e.* as writing situation (in Section 1), as writing progression (in Section 2) and as the application of a repertoire of writing strategies (in Section 3).

1. THE MACRO LEVEL OF PA: STANDARDIZED INTERVIEW AND COOPERATIVE OBSERVATION

The writing process is influenced by the working instrument (Van Waes & Schellens, 2001), as well as by the writer's acculturation and experience, by the aims the writer

D. Perrin (2001). Progression analysis (PA): Investigating writing strategies in the workplace. In: G. Rijlaarsdam (Series ed.) & T. Olive & C. M. Levy (Vol. eds.), Studies in Writing: Volume 10: Contemporary Tools and Techniques for Studying Writing, p. 105-117.

tries to achieve and the constraints she/he submits to, by the people the writer is living and working with and by the texts the writer produces and reads (Hayes, 1996; Perrin, 1997a). PA records such influences with standardized interviews and cooperative observation at work and presents them in the Portrait of the Relational Framework.[1]

To give an example of such a Portrait, we focus on PK, foreign desk editor at the 'Schweizerische Depeschenagentur' SDA (Swiss News Agency). PK gets source texts from other news agencies, processes them and transmits the new text first to the 'desk,' where colleagues check the daily output and send it out to newspapers, radio and TV. There, PK's text serves as basis for new texts again. So what we read, hear or see in the media has been shaped and reshaped in a chain of workplaces. More information can be found on the production chain in Häusermann (2001b), on reproductive writing in journalism in Häusermann (2001a: 49) and on reproductive writing in general in Jakobs (2001)

When PK is writing, time is running against him. He has two hours in the evening to review and summarize the daily events in a crisis area. The writing process presented here starts at 4 p.m. with the cross reading of source texts from other agencies, and it ends at 6:10 p.m., ten minutes after the deadline.[2] At noon, the agency SDA had sent a circular to its customers announcing the availability of the text for 6:00 p.m. PK has overrun the deadline by the same amount of time that one supply agency also overran it. During writing breaks, PK always checks if the last evening summary has arrived. Usually the 'Deutsche Presse-Agentur' DPA (German Press Agency) delivers it to the SDA before 5 p.m..

On the one hand, the time available for writing is given and limited. This also applies to the given text space: The finished article has to contain 450 words. The lead is supposed to consist of exactly five lines.[3] On the other hand, the office is quite spacious: The desk is broad, well illuminated and almost empty. Paper, pens and markers are ready to be used, the laser printer works. Nevertheless, PK who 'has learned to write only by writing on the computer' [4] restricts his workspace to the screen:

PK receives four source texts on the screen right at the beginning of his work. Additionally, his own text and the delayed DPA text are also shown on the screen. Thus,

---

1 This chapter focuses on the innovative aspects of Progression Analysis; the classical implications of interviews and observation are not to be dicussed here. On the discussion of observation and interviews in research into writing processes, see Van der Geest, (1996: 11) or Eigler (1996: 999). On the items investigated in the underlying research project, see Perrin (2001c).

2 The deadline is the last submission date agreed on. The writer who exceeds his own deadline in the chain of journalistic production forces colleagues on the next production level to make up time, because the last date, the transmission to the reader, is unalterable in most cases. On deadlines in journalistic production, see Bell (1991: 152).

3 The lead is the first paragraph of the journalistic text. It is often emphazised by typographical means. In SDA texts, it has to outline the central ideas and raise the reader's desire to read it; standard length is five lines on the screen. PK and some of his colleagues take great pains to write a 'beautiful' lead of exactly *five lines.*

4 After a good decade at university, it took PK one year to write his diploma dissertation and another one to complete his thesis. With the first computer, his writer's block was broken, he says today. Working at the SDA, PK used a computer right from the beginning.

up to six buffers are opened and stacked at the same time. By pressing a button PK moves the buffer he needs to the front, and switches from one window to other, among his own text and the source texts. Due to the small screen, PK is forced to scroll, too, which means that he has to move up and down in the text currently visible (backgrounded area in Figure 1). As soon as these movements lead to changes in PK's new text, they are tracked on the next level of PA.

2. THE MESO LEVEL OF PA: S-NOTATION, LOGGING, AND PROGRESSION DIAGRAM

What happens with the text on the screen during writing? As the very basic structures of what we call writing progression, we can distinguish two actions: insertion and deletion of text. These two actions constitute the revisions. Preceding every revision, there is a break, an interruption in the course of continuous writing.

2.1. S-notation

To depict these steps in a standardized way, S-notation was developed (Severinson Eklundh & Kollberg, in this volume). Everywhere the writer interrupts his flow of writing to delete something in the text or insert something at another place, S-notation puts the break symbol | in the text. Deleted parts stand in [square brackets], later insertions in {pointed brackets}. Indices, small numbers show the order of steps. They are written at the bottom of the break symbol as $|_n$ and on both sides on top of the brackets as $^n[]^n$ or $^n\{\}^n$. In S-notation we can record the order of revisions in PK's writing process in a very compact way:

(a) In Kürze soll ^{4}[en]^4 $|_5$ ^{1}{nun }^{1} $|_2$ das Parlament ^{5}{,}^{5} $|_6$ ^{3}{in dem die Sozialisten die Mehrheit haben, }^{3} $|_4$ aufgelöst ^{2}[und eine Übergangsregierung ernannt werden]^2 $|_3$ ^{6}{ werden}^{6} $|_7$.

Literal translation:

(a') In brief shall ^{4}[-ENDING]^4 $|_5$ ^{1}{now}^{1} $|_2$ the parliament ^{5}{,}^{5} $|_6$ ^{3}{in which the socialists the majority have, }^{3} $|_4$ resolved ^{2}[and a transitional government appointed be]^2 $|_3$ ^{6}{ be}^{6} $|_7$.

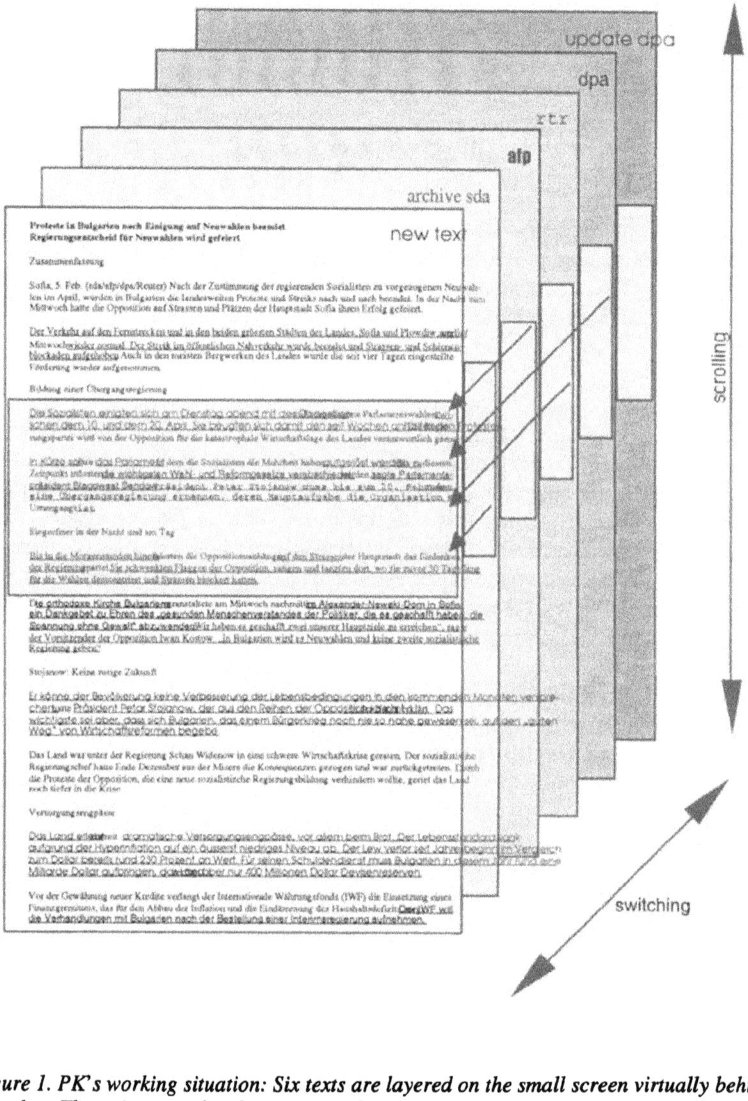

Figure 1. PK's working situation: Six texts are layered on the small screen virtually behind each other. The writer switches from one window to another and scrolls to copy passages from source texts into his text (see below).

Yet what exactly does PK do, step by step? First, he copies an AFP sentence into his own text: 'In Kürze sollen das Parlament aufgelöst und eine Übergangsregierung ernannt werden'. (Soon, the parliament shall be resolved and a transitional government shall be appointed.) After copying, PK puts a nun (now) after 'In Kürze sollen' and turns to other parts of the text for the moment. He revises the sentence much later again, this time more radically. He drops the second part und eine 'Übergangsregierung ernannt werden,' deletes the plural ending 'en after soll' and adds the subordinate clause 'in dem die Sozialisten die Mehrheit haben after Parlament.' As a result, this sentence is shown on his screen: 'In Kürze soll nun das Parlament in dem die Sozialisten die Mehrheit haben, aufgelöst.' (The parliament, in which the socialists have a majority, shall soon [missing: be] resolved now.) Rearranging the text causes grammatical incorrectness for the moment. In a final round, PK corrects it putting a comma after 'Parlament' and adding the missing 'werden' (be).So all the changes a text has undergone during the process of its writing are recorded.[5]

Yet this is still not enough to depict intertextual text production, to describe the writing processes, in which the writer copies passages from sources. Here it is useful to know the origin of the inserted passages. For this reason, copied passages of text are underlined in extended S-notation. When there is more than one source text used, each source is given a different font:[6]

(b) **In Kürze soll** ^{4}[**en**]^{4} $|_{5}$ ^{1}{nun }^{1} $|_{2}$ **das Parlament** ^{5}{,}^{5} $|_{6}$ ^{3}{in dem die Sozialisten die Mehrheit haben, }^{3} $|_{4}$ **aufgelöst** ^{2}[**und eine Übergangsregierung ernannt werden**]^{2} $|_{3}$ ^{6}{ werden}^{6} $|_{7}$.

This way, we are able to describe precisely a whole sequence of revisions without awkwardly showing each intermediate product, step by step.[7]

2.2. Progression diagram

But S-notation requires some reading practice, especially in more complex writing processes, when the writer has made several attempts to revise and rearrange the text.

---

6 The extension of S-Notation to mark the text source is not part of the standard of Severinson Eklundh-Kollberg (ibidem). In the underlying project, sources have been encoded manually after the recording of the writing process. In actual data collections, the tracing software encodes sources of copy-paste-steps automatically.

7 The computer can register and record data for S-Notation and Progression diagrams automatically. To make this happen, the text programs have to be extended by logging modules. We are developing these modules together with the producers of software used for writing and editing by the people investigated. The software for analysing and visualising the steps of the writing processes consists of Excel-modules and of 'Trace-it,' which generates S-Notation from the logfile. Trace-it was developed as a student project at the Royal Institute of Technology, Stockholm. It is based on S-Notation (Nilsson & Kollberg, 1994; Severinson Eklundh &Kollberg, 1996; and Kollberg & Severinson Eklundh, in this volume).

It is easier to show revised writing processes by using graphic illustrations to demonstrate the movement throughout the text. We call it movement progression. Two Progression diagrams are shown in figure 2.

Each point of the Progression diagram represents one revision. The x-axis shows the order of revisions in the writing process; the y-axis shows the order of revisions in the finished text product (including all the parts ever typed). The progression diagram presented here shows ordinal data. It would also be possible to draw the diagram based on metric data, for example to measure the position of a revision in seconds from the beginning of writing. To get the time data, one would have to go back behind the S-Notation to the logfile, where time is encoded automatically. Yet the purpose of the progression diagram is to get an overview of the course of writing, not to provide quantitative representation.

If a writer corrected every typing mistake immediately without jumping back to delete or insert anything in the text above, the Progression diagram would show a straight line pointing from the top left-hand corner to the bottom right-hand corner (see the left portion of Figure 2). Yet PK moves back and forth during the revision of the text, which is very obvious in the small section shown: The first revision, for example, happens in the front part of the text, the second at the end, the third is shortly before it, and the fourth one is made at the beginning of the text.

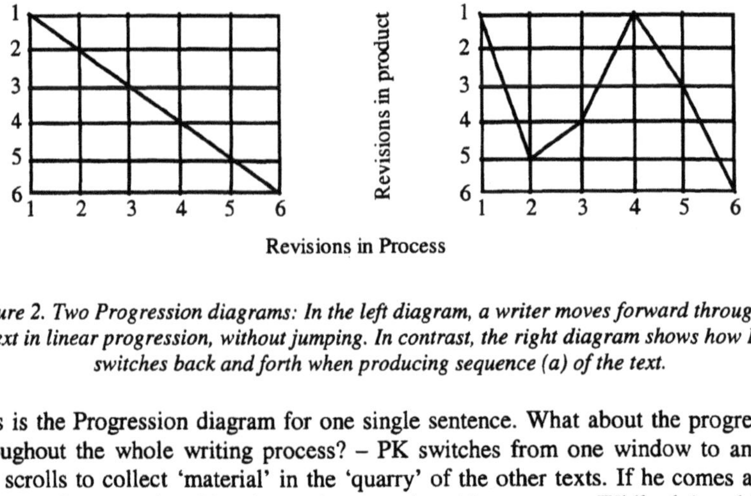

Figure 2. Two Progression diagrams: In the left diagram, a writer moves forward through the text in linear progression, without jumping. In contrast, the right diagram shows how PK switches back and forth when producing sequence (a) of the text.

This is the Progression diagram for one single sentence. What about the progression throughout the whole writing process? – PK switches from one window to another and scrolls to collect 'material' in the 'quarry' of the other texts. If he comes across passages that appeal to him, he copies them into his own text. While doing this, he often loses the overall view, *e.g.* he goes over the same passage twice or he deletes passages by mistake, which forces him to load the source text again into the buffer from time to time as indicates his retrospective verbalisation. This leaves its traces in the text progression.

The Progression leads through the text in three main phases distinguished on the basis of the writer's retrospective verbal protocol: In a first phase, until revision 68,

PK writes the lead, copies passages from source texts into his own text top-down, and formulates short links. In a second phase, moving back and forth considerably, he fills the sense-gaps between the inserted passages with his own text or with direct borrowings from the source texts. In a third phase, starting with revision 143, he revises the text top-down.

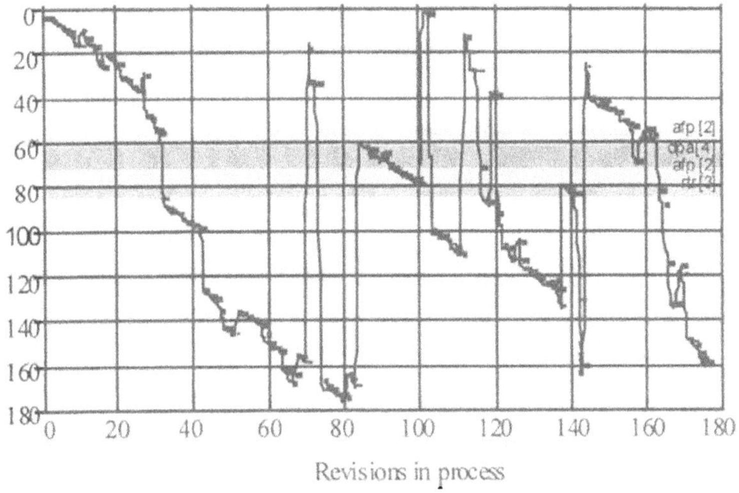

Figure 3. The diagram shows PK's text progression, the 175 revisions, from left to right in chronological order, from bottom to top in their order in the final text (see above, Figure 2). The graph indicates how PK moves up and down in the text to revise most of the passages several times, e.g. the passage painted in grey (see below).

In general, PK revises most of the passages several times, *e.g.* the passage painted in Figure 3:

(c) **In Kürze soll** nun **das Parlament**, in dem die Sozialisten die Mehrheit haben, **aufgelöst werden**. **Bis zu** diesem Zeitpunkt müssten **die wichtigsten Wahl- und Reformgesetze verabschiede**t werden, **sagte Parlamentspräsident Blagowest Sendow**. **Präsident Petar Stojanow muss bis zum 20. Februar** zudem **eine Übergangsregierung ernennen, deren Hauptaufgabe die Organisation de**s Urnengangs **ist**.

(c') General translation: The parliament, in which the socialists have a majority, shall soon be resolved now. Until then, the most important electoral laws should be passed, as the president of the parliament Blagowest Sendow said. Furthermore, president Petar Stojanow has to appoint a transitional government until February 20th, whose main task will be the organisation of the election.

The first sentence of this passage originates in its essential features from the source text of the AFP agency. The second sentence comes from the old DPA text and the third from the Reuters text. The underlined passages are copied electronically. The passages not underlined were added by PK himself. Passages also copied by PK, but rejected and deleted later have become invisible in the final text product. All these processes are shown in the revision protocol in S-notation:

(d) In Kürze soll^{160}[en]^{160} $|_{161}$ ^{31}{nun }^{31} $|_{32}$das Parlament^{161}{,}^{161} $|_{162}$ ^{159}{in dem die Sozialisten die Mehrheit haben, }^{159} $|_{160}$aufgelöst^{158}[und eine Übergangsregierung ernannt werden]^{158} $|_{159}$^{162}{ werden}^{162} $|_{163}$. ^{84}{^{85}{Bis zu ^{86}{diesem Zeitpunkt^{88}{ müss^{91}{t}^{91} $|_{92}$en}^{88} $|_{89}$ }^{86} $|_{87}$^{87}[seiner Auflösung wird die Volksversammlung]^{87} $|_{88}$die wichtigsten Wahl- und Reformgesetze verabschied^{89}[en]^{89} $|_{90}$ ^{90}{et werden}^{90} $|_{91}$, sagte Parlamentspräsident Blagowest Sendow^{157}[^{92}[am Mittwoch]^{92} $|_{93}$nach Angaben der amtlichen Nachrichtenagentur BTA]^{157} $|_{158}$. $|_{86}$}$^{85,\ 93}$[$|_{85}$]^{93} }^{84} $|_{94}$ ^{116}[Der designierte sozialistische Ministerpräsident Nikolai Dobrew ^{94}{hatte am Dienstag darauf }^{94} $|_{95}$verzichtete^{95}[darauf]^{95} $|_{96}$, sein am ^{96}[Montag]^{96} $|_{97}$^{97}{Vortag}^{97} $|_{98}$ gebildetes Kabinett ^{98}[im aktuellen Parlament]^{98} $|_{99}$vereidigen zu lassen, in dem ^{99}[seine BSP]^{99} $|_{100}$ ^{100}{die Sozialisten}^{100} $|_{101}$ die Mehrheit innehat.]^{116} $|_{117}$^{138}{^{139}{Präsident Petar }^{139} $|_{140}$Stojanow muss bis zum 20. Februar ^{163}{zudem }^{163} $|_{164}$eine Übergangsregierung ernennen, deren Hauptaufgabe die Organisation de^{140}[r vorgezogenen Wahlen]^{140} $|_{141}$^{141}{s Urnengangs}^{141} $|_{142}$ ist. $|_{139}$}^{138}

(d') General translation: The parliament, in which the socialists have a majority, shall soon be resolved now. Until then, the most important

> electoral laws should be passed, as the president of the parliament Blagowest Sendow said. On Tuesday, the future Prime Minister Nikolai Dobrew renounced on the swearing of the Cabinet that had been elected the day before and in which the socialists has [!] a majority. Furthermore, president Petar Stojanow has to appoint a transitional government until February 20th, whose main task will be the organisation of the election.

If we compare the revision protocol (d) with the text product (c), deletion 116 at the beginning of the second paragraph in (d) is striking: It is only in the third revision (see above, Figure 3) that PK deletes a passage built up from source texts from Agence France Presse and his own links and additions. Before deletion, this passage reads as follows:

(e) Der designierte sozialistische Ministerpräsident Nikolai Dobrew hatte am Dienstag darauf verzichtete, sein am Vortag gebildetes Kabinett vereidigen zu lassen, in dem die Sozialisten die Mehrheit innehat.

(e') General translation: On Tuesday, the future Prime Minister Nikolai Dobrew renounced on the swearing of the Cabinet that had been elected the day before and in which the socialists has [!] a majority.

Working on the screen, PK inserted a passage (e), revised it (d), but did not finish formulating it and finally cancelled it. Why? What is interesting is not only his behaviour of working on the screen, but mainly those strategies he bears in mind when working on the text.

3. THE MICRO LEVEL OF PA: CUE-BASED RETROSPECTIVE VERBALIZATION

Changing a formulation, rejecting it, trying again – most revisions take place only in the writer's mind, before typing, as revisions of the 'mental pretext' (Wrobel, 1995: 100). And that's not all: The writer often rereads the text already typed and uses it for further planning without even touching the computer (Grabowski, 1996). To record these thoughts at least partially, Progression Analysis tries in a further step to open a window in the mind of the writer.

For this purpose, cue-based retrospective verbalization is used. As soon as possible after writing, the writer has the logfile of the writing process played through; the text emerges once again before his eyes in the same order as during writing, but step by step. While the writer watches this genesis of the text, he continually reads out what has been written, inserted or deleted. Most importantly, he says why he has done so.[8] A tape recorder or the writing computer itself records his verbal protocol. Here is an example of PK's verbal protocol:

(f) The word «nun» is inserted on the screen (see above, example a), and PK comments:[9] 'I'm not paid per line, but still I put in a 'nun'. [...] It's something like, um, to draw attention to what comes now concretely, actually, I, I – I love it, to – I prefer announcements in my texts, concrete announcements that can stress something, right? So when this doesn't happen, then – then the whole thing has gone wrong somehow, hasn't it.' Here, PK expresses what he thinks he has done, and what he thinks were his motivations and feelings – he loves to draw the reader's attention to concrete steps.

This example shows the main weakness of retrospective verbalization: How can we in retrospect remember in detail all the things we did and why we did them? Even the action itself is something we are only partially aware of. For instance, when we save the information in our mind, parts of it are lost, and when we remember it, the overall picture is built up again out of the few remaining parts. Furthermore, when we communicate, verbalize, once again only parts of this new overall picture will be mentioned. We sometimes even invent new things deliberately or unwittingly (for further information on the basic disadvantages of retrospective verbalization, see Levy, Marek & Lea, 1996). Compared with retrospective verbalization, think-aloud protocols recorded while writing would have methodological advantages, but also disadvantages (Stratman & Hamp-Lyons, 1994; Jansen, Van Waes, & Van Bergh, 1996). Disputes about method become unnessecary when the investigation is done with journalists at work: Speaking during writing would make the writers slow down and would irritate the colleagues around them in the open-plan offices.

Nevertheless, with data-based retrospective verbalization, an insight into the mind is offered. Surely, we will not get a full insight of the whole set of reflections the writer really had when he was writing a certain text passage. What becomes apparent are the reflections the writer bears in mind so clearly that he can express them in words spontaneously while looking at the writing process. In short, what is mentioned is not necessarily what the writer really thought, but what he basically could have thought.

So what we can discern is a relevant part of the writer's repertoire of conscious writing strategies (for further information about journalistic writing strategies, see Perrin, 1997b, 2001a, 2001c). Such strategies are action-guiding ideas about how certain aims can be achieved by certain means in a certain social context, *i.e.* aims within

---

8 We do not ask the writers to read and protocol every revision, but 'as many as possible'. For a discussion of these 'cues,' see Greene and Higgins (1994: 123).

9 For all the excerpts of retrospective protocols we will use the following representation: Slips are also shown in the transcription, PK's Swiss dialect is translated into English, keeping breaks and reformulations as true to the original as possible. Protocol statements are given as 'xxx,' text quotations of the speaker during the verbal protocol are given as «xxx.»

or outside the communication; by means of the writing process or the text product; in the social context of the sources, the readers or the writer himself.[10]

Back to the example:

(g) With 'nun' (see above, f) PK adds a structuring particle to 'stress' something in the text. Here, his text-referring strategy consists in marking passages he wants to emphasize with structuring particles. PK wants to call attention to the passage because it contains a concrete 'announcement,' a promise of the source text. So the source-referring strategy is to stress concrete and obligating things. Thereby, PK wants to 'draw attention' to something. The reader-referring strategy consists of pointing out explicitly important things to the reader. PK is doing that because he 'loves' it. So the self-referring strategy consists of doing something because one likes to do it.

The strategy of stressing important things with structuring particles was perhaps developed by PK himself to be able to emphasize something using little space, without apparent judgment. He might have adopted it from his superiors or another example. In any case, he is now so conscious of this strategy that he mentions it several times in his verbal protocol. That is why there are good reasons to suppose that he really uses it when he is writing.

The four strategies PK mentions most frequently in the verbal protocol combine processes of copying with processes of structuring, time adjustment, source adjustment, and actor adjustment. In the passage we have been analysing up to now (see above, a–g), PK verbalizes these strategies in the following way:

Copying and structuring

'Now I'm taking the whole block [«Die Sozialisten einigten sich am Dienstag abend mit der Opposition ...»] in, with the story of the whole thing, then I start a new paragraph to make it a bit clearer, «In Kürze soll das Parlament aufgelöst [...]»' (28).

Copying and time adjustment

'Here we don't need the «Mittwoch» any more, I take it out' (on revision 92). 'Now – that's just – that's true too, time wasn't really correct in my text, this happened earlier, so I put it into the past per-

10 In journalistic text production, possible authorities on the part of the authors are: the media system, the journalistic profession, the media enterprise, the editorial staff, the boss, colleagues – and of course the writer himself, in his role as author, as colleague of the source, as person affected by the subject and so on. On analysis of the author role in journalistic text production, see Van Dijk (1988: 99) or Perrin (1997a: 66).

> fect, here now, because it isn't Wednesday any more, right (94). And because it's on Tuesday, it's enough to say the day before, isn't it, but I think that's not so clear anymore' (97).

> Copying and source adjustment

> 'Now in this second phrase, before the deletion, I'm polishing it a little, so that it fits in better, like that it's still a bit clumsy; «bis zu diesem Zeitpunkt», that means until the dissolution, um, (revision 86) «[...]Reformgesetze verabschiedet werden [...]», «müssten», or, um, reported speech, this one I changed too. Here I still have the source in it' (91).

> Copying and actor adjustment

> 'And now this sentence [...] has been removed, because of the formation of the transitional government, (on revision 136) now we put it in the right place too. Let's look for it, and this one we put here now, that's it, in you go. Now he's – «in Kürze soll nun das Parlament aufgelöst werden» – now he's in this para-, um, in this part, isn't he' (138). 'Now I have to give him a surname too, because he hasn't been mentioned yet over there, so I added this, «Präsident Petar Stonjanow»' (139).

So these strategies determine the repertoire: PK copies passages from the source texts into his own text that he continually restructures. Consequently, he adjusts the references to time, sources and actors according to the changing context.

4. CONCLUSION

After all these details: Where is the difference between PA and experimental methodology?

PA is closer to single cases of reality: It generates data of real writers in their real workplaces. This can help, case by case, to investigate regularities of professional writing – and to establish a sociolinguistic approach in writing research.

In a framework of basic research, such an approach e.g. enables to correlate items of the writing socialisation, the workplace, the writing tool, the writing process and the text producted (Perrin 2001c). As another application. PA enables to describe and to identify phases in writing processes systematically

In a methodological framework, PA enables, e.g., to compare retrospective verbalisation with hard data, to compare the strategies writers talk about with the stuctures, effects and frequencies of their revisions and with their progression data. Based on such correlations, the validity of retrospective verbalisation has to be evaluated for writing research in the field.

In a pedagogical framework finally, PA enables e.g. process-oriented benchmarking of writing coachings (Perrin, 1999b) and validations of suggestions based on experimental data (Britton 1996: 327, who diagnoses coherence problems when text passages are rearranged, or Rijlaarsdam, Van den Bergh, & Couzijn 1996a: 122, who found that texts become better when the writers plan at the beginning and do not just slide into the writing process).

But by getting closer to single cases, PA actually is far away from efficiency in representative samples. Therefore, statistical tools for analysing large corpora on the meso level of PA are being developed.

ON-LINE METHODOLOGIES FOR STUDYING THE WRITTEN PRODUCTION OF ISOLATED WORDS: A BRIEF OVERVIEW

PATRICK BONIN & MICHEL FAYOL

CNRS & Université Blaise Pascal (France)

Abstract. This chapter is aimed at presenting some on-line methodologies dedicated to the investigation of the written production of isolated words. We give specific descriptions and illustrations of three on-line methodologies that can be specifically used to study the nature of the representations and of the processes involved in the written production of isolated words: picture naming tasks, interference paradigm and priming paradigm. We illustrate these methods with some examples taken from various spoken picture naming studies and we briefly show how these methodologies have significantly contributed to improve our knowledge on the nature of the representations involved in spoken language production and their time course of activation. Along with this presentation, we describe how we have adapted these methods to investigate the representations and the processes involved in the written production of isolated words from pictures. Likewise, we present two series of studies that have made use of the interference paradigm. One investigated the obligatory phonological mediation issue in written picture naming. Another study addressed the time course of activation of semantic representations and orthographic/phonological representations. A potential problem associated with the use of the interference paradigm is also briefly addressed. Finally, we report a priming study that addressed the question of whether orthographic codes can be retrieved directly from semantics in the written production of words from pictures.
Keywords: written picture naming, spoken picture naming, latency, inference paradigm, priming paradigm, digitiser pad, orthography, phonology, semantics, lexical access.

1. INTRODUCTION

The objective study of written language production is less far advanced than that of spoken language production (Bock & Levelt, 1994; Fayol, 1997; Levelt, 1989), even though a substantial amount of scientific activity has been directed at this topic during recent years (Levy & Ransdell, 1996a; Piolat & Pélissier, 1998). The reduced level of interest accorded to written language production in cognitive psychology may in part be due to the fact that, in the majority of adults, the written mode of language production is less frequently used than the spoken mode (Ellis, 1988). The fact that studies of written language production are less highly developed may also be partly due to the

P. Bonin & M. Fayol (2001). On-line methodologies for studying the written production of isolated words: A brief overview. In: G. Rijlaarsdam (Series ed.) & T. Olive & C. M. Levy (Vol. eds.), *Studies in Writing: Volume 10: Contemporary Tools and Techniques for Studying Writing*, 119-129.

difficulties involved in the development of theoretical models (for theoretical model in writing, see Hayes & Flower, 1980; Martlew, 1983; Scardamalia & Bereiter, 1986) and the technical and methodological difficulties specific to the investigation of written language production (Ellis, 1984, 1988). For these reasons, research into written language production has long favoured the analysis of linguistic markers of the products. These studies have contributed to the development of the most important of the available models.

In accordance with the aims of this chapter, we will present, in the next two sections, methods we have used to study the written production of *isolated words*. Indeed, consideration of the relatively sophisticated methods and theoretical approaches (*e.g.*, Bock, 1996; Bock & Levelt, 1994; Levelt, Roelofs, & Meyer, 1999; Schriefers, Meyer, & Levelt, 1990) that have been developed to study spoken language production has led us, in recent years, to adapt certain of these methods, specifically to study the written production of isolated words.

2. REAL-TIME METHODS FOR STUDYING THE WRITTEN PRODUCTION OF ISOLATED WORDS

2.1. The picture naming task

If we specifically want to study the processes and representations that are involved in written language production, as those involved in lexical access, *i.e.*, access to the orthographic form of words, it is necessary to focus on extremely well delineated situations that permit the strict, fine-tuned control of the variables. For a number of years, such an approach has been adopted for the study of lexical access in spoken language production and has proved to be extremely fruitful (*e.g.*, Jescheniak & Levelt, 1994; Levelt *et al.*, 1999; Schriefers *et al.*, 1990; Starreveld & La Heij, 1995; Starreveld, 2000). As we will show, this approach has permitted a detailed characterisation of the levels of processing involved in spoken language production and the time course of their access. The theoretical and empirical data relating to the spoken production of isolated words are therefore more numerous and more highly developed than those available for written production (see Bock & Levelt, 1994; Bonin, 1997; Ferrand, 1994, 1997, for reviews).

Frequently used to study spoken language production, the picture naming task is a relatively simple experimental situation during which participants are asked to say the name of a picture as quickly as possible after it is presented on a computer screen. Speech recording equipment is used to measure the spoken naming latencies (that is, the time separating the start of the presentation of the picture and the very first articulation performed by the participant) and to record errors (which may be of various types: 'deviant' articulations, production of non-linguistic sounds ('clicks'), semantic or phonological substitutions, etc.). To some extent, this experimental context operationalises a more 'ecological' production situation in which participants start from an intention to communicate (Bock & Levelt, 1994). Very frequently, researchers try to limit the variability of the names that may be used for certain of the pictures by requiring participants to learn the limited set of labels that they will use later when they engage in the picture naming task (*e.g.*, Bock, 1996; Schriefers *et al.*, 1990; Starreveld & La Heij, 1995). This makes it possible to limit the volume of the latency data that has to be excluded (Bock, 1996). This picture naming task can be combined with other paradigms such as the interference paradigm or the priming paradigm that we shall present in Sections 2.2. and 2.3.

The picture naming task can be used to study the written production of isolated words. However, so far, it has been used very rarely. We used such a task to study lexical access in the written production of isolated words (Bonin, Fayol, & Gombert, 1997, 1998; Bonin, Fayol, & Peereman, 1998; Bonin & Fayol, 2000; Bonin, Peereman, & Fayol, in press; Bonin, Fayol, & Chalard, in press). In order to record the graphic initialisation latencies, we used a digitiser pad such as the WACOM pad (UltraPad A5), equipped with a stylus (UP 401), linked to a Power Macintosh computer. We used the PsyScope software to construct these experiments (PsyScope can be downloaded from the Internet: http://psyscope.psy.cmu.edu/). PsyScope can be used to create interactive psychology experiments. It controls the presentation of the stimuli and makes it possible to record response times with millisecond precision using for instance the Button Box time manager (for a presentation of this software, see Cohen, McWhinney, Flatt, & Provost, 1993). The main results that we have obtained using this technique are presented in Sections 2.2. and 2.3.

The picture naming task can be combined with different paradigms. We consider next two such paradigms: the interference and the priming paradigms that are frequently used to study the nature of the representations activated during the spoken production of isolated words (or groups of words) as well as their time course of activation. These paradigms have been rarely used to study the written production of isolated words.

2.2. The interference paradigm

This paradigm has frequently been used to study the spoken production of isolated words (Schriefers *et al.*, 1990; Meyer & Schriefers, 1991; Jescheniak & Schriefers, 1998) or noun phrases (Schriefers, 1993; Schriefers & Teruel, 1999). Its key interest lies in the possibility of identifying the nature of the representations that are activated at any given moment of processing. For instance, it can be used to determine whether semantic representations are activated only at an early point in time or at both early and late points in time of picture naming. The use of the interference paradigm is based on an elaborate theoretical framework, the three main elements of which are as follows: (1) There are, in memory, representations that possess different activation thresholds (Collins & Loftus, 1975); (2) These representations are interlinked by associations of different types and strengths (Yekovitch & Walker, 1986); (3) The representations that are activated at a given moment transmit activation (spreading activation phenomenon) to the units to which they are connected (Collins & Loftus, 1975). The use of this paradigm makes it possible to determine the types of representation that are activated, the time(s) of their activation as well as the other categories of representations to which they are related.

To use this technique, it is necessary to define a target (for example, the picture of a *CAT*) and a distractor item (for example, the word *DOG* written in the middle of the picture). The participant's task is to name the drawn object or animal as quickly as possible while attempting to ignore the distractor written on the picture. If the distractor item implies a relation – semantic (*e.g.*, *mouse*) or phonological (*e.g.*, *cap*) – with the target item, the processing of the target is different from that performed when the target item is presented alone or with a distractor item that has no evident relationship with the target such as, for example, the case of an unrelated distractor, *e.g.*, *battery* or a neutral distractor, *e.g.*, *xxxx*, because of the existence of a meaningful relationship between the two types of stimuli. This difference in processing can be seen in the initialisation latencies (*i.e.*, the time interval between the onset of the picture presentation and the onset of the naming response) and/or the errors committed. The processing of the target may be slowed down or, in contrast, accelerated. In order to assess the degree to which processing is slowed or accelerated, the initialisation latencies (and the errors) are compared, in particular to those obtained for the processing of the same target when presented in conjunction with an unrelated distractor item. If the difference between the naming latencies in the 'related/unrelated' situations is negative, we speak of a facilitation effect. In contrast, if it is positive, we speak of an interference (or inhibition) effect. It is important to note that when compared to a situation in which the picture is presented without any distractor, the simple presence of a distractor (neutral or unrelated) results in a slowing down of processing (characterised by longer initialisation latencies). This is the reason why this paradigm is known as the *interference paradigm*.

An example may serve to illustrate the above description. We compared the latency resulting from the presentation of a picture (for example the picture of a *CAT*) accompanied by a semantically related distractor word (*dog*) with that resulting from the presentation of the picture presented either alone or with an unrelated item (*train*) or again with a neutral item (*xxxx*). The distractor word can be presented in auditory mode (by means of headphones) or visually (it is written in the middle of, below, above or next to the picture). An interference effect is observed when the latencies obtained with the related items differ statistically from those obtained using unrelated or neutral distractors or in the absence of any distractor. The observation of a reliable semantic interference effect is taken to indicate that semantic representations are activated.

Another important aspect of this paradigm is its ability to manipulate the interval between the presentation of the distractor and that of the target (see Figure 1 for an illustration). This delay is known as SOA: Stimulus Onset Asynchrony. The manipulation makes it possible to obtain information about the representations that are relevant at a given moment in processing and not, or less, relevant at another moment. Thus, the presentation of the distractor can precede that of the target (this is known as a negative SOA), be simultaneous with it (SOA = 0) or can follow it (positive SOA). The use of a negative or simultaneous SOA 'activates' the cognitive system with certain information. A positive SOA is supposed to introduce the information 'later.' The use of this paradigm within the framework of lexical access in spoken language production (Bonin, 1997; Ferrand, 1994, 1997 for reviews) has made it possible to confirm the existence of different levels of representation that had already been strongly hinted at through the analysis of spontaneous production errors (*e.g.*, Garrett, 1975, 1980, 1982; Fay & Cutler, 1977). More precisely, it has made it possible to demonstrate that certain representations that are relevant at a time t appear not to be relevant at time $t+k$. For instance, Schriefers *et al.* (1990) have shown, in spoken picture naming, that semantic representations were activated at an SOA = -150 ms but not at SOA of 0 and +150 ms. Certain examples taken from research into the spoken production of isolated words on the basis of pictures are presented later in this section to illustrate this latter aspect more precisely.

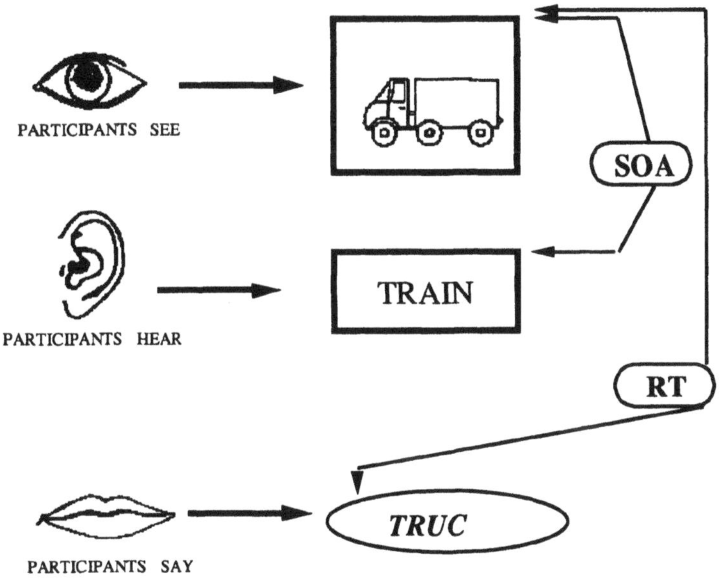

Figure 1. Illustration of an experimental situation in which the distractor is auditorily presented with a positive SOA.

It is generally accepted that spoken language production involves the following four levels of processing:

- Conceptual level (non-linguistic),
- lemma level (*i.e.*, the lemmas are abstract lexical representations, not phonologically specified, which provide syntactic information such as gender, grammatical category; Kempen & Huijbers, 1983),
- lexeme level (the lexemes correspond to the phonological representations in the spoken mode and the orthographic representations in the written mode),
- articulatory level (Schriefers *et al.*, 1990; Levelt *et al.*, 1999; and for an alternative position see Caramazza, 1997; Caramazza & Miozzo, 1998).

Within the framework of studies of lexical access in spoken language production, Schriefers *et al.* (1990) have shown that when participants have to say aloud the names associated with pictures while listening to spoken words via a headset, the spoken onset latencies are longer with distractors that are semantically related to the picture names than with unrelated distractors, but only when these distractors are presented before the target (with an SOA of -150 ms). In contrast, at the same SOA the spoken latencies obtained through the presentation of distractors that are phonologically associated with the verbal label of the pictures do not differ statistically from those obtained through the presentation of unrelated distractors. A facilitation effect of phonological distractors was obtained when these were presented both simultaneously with the picture and also with a positive temporal shift of 150 ms (*i.e.*, SOA = +150 ms). Thus, the authors believe that during lexical access in spoken language production, the semantic level is active before the phonological level and assume that there is no temporal overlap between these levels of processing (For further data in support of a similar interpretation, see Levelt, Schriefers, Vorberg, Meyer, Pechmann & Havinga, 1991). However, these interpretations have been subject to numerous criticisms (*e.g.*, Dell & O'Seaghdha, 1991; Harley, 1993). In brief, these criticisms relate to the likely difficulty of detecting, by means of the available reaction time techniques, a possible phonological co-activation. In other words, the phonological activation of neighbours that are semantically related to the target would be too weak to be statistically detected in experiments in which onset latencies are measured. Nevertheless, while Levelt *et al.* (1991) have obtained results showing that the semantic neighbours of a picture target (*e.g.*, *dog*, *fox*, *sheep*, etc. for a picture of a *cat*) were not phonologically encoded and that therefore, conversely, only one semantically and syntactically specified lexical item (*i.e.*, the lemma) was phonologically encoded, other studies have shown that, in certain special situations, it is possible to observe a phonological co-activation. Thus, using the interference paradigm, Jescheniak and Schriefers (1998) observed phonological co-activation for words having a quasi-synonym (*e.g.*, *couch-sofa*): When participants produced the spoken word '*couch*' when shown a picture of a couch, both '*couch*' and its quasi-synonym '*sofa*' were phonologically encoded (for similar results obtained using a different paradigm see Peterson & Savoy, 1998).

These illustrations make it clear that the interference paradigm has brought about a better understanding of the nature of the representations that are mobilised as well as the time course of access during the spoken production of isolated words in response to pictures. However, this paradigm has also fuelled a debate about whether lexical access during spoken language production operates discretely, in cascade, or functions interactively (Dell & O'Seaghdha, 1991; Harley, 1993; Humphreys, Riddoch, & Quinlan, 1988; Levelt *et al.*, 1991; Schriefers *et al.*, 1990). This debate is still far from a conclusion. Indeed, according to the discrete conception, the stage of the semantic activation of the neighbours of the pictured target is always followed by the phonological activation of the selected lemma unit during the previous stage. In contrast, within the cascaded conception, both the selected lemma unit and its semantic neighbours induce phonological activation. The interactive conception differs from the cascaded conception in that it postulates a feedback from the lexeme level to the lemma level.

We used this paradigm to study the nature of the representations mobilised during lexical access in written language production (Bonin *et al.*, 1997; Bonin & Fayol,

2000). In an initial study (Bonin *et al.*, 1997), we considered the role of the phonological representations in accessing the orthographic codes in picture naming. We attempted to determine whether the phonological representations had to be recovered in order to permit the derivation of the orthography (obligatory phonological mediation hypothesis; Luria, 1970) or whether, in contrast, the retrieval of the orthographic codes could be performed directly on the basis of the semantic codes (orthographic autonomy hypothesis; Rapp, Benzing, & Caramazza, 1997). In effect, one longstanding viewpoint concerning written language production is that it is highly dependent on the spoken mode in that it is thought to make very extensive use of the representations and processes mobilised in spoken language production. In this study, participants produced the names of pictures in spoken or written mode with the corresponding (or non-corresponding) letters or sounds acting as distractors, *i.e.*, the initial letter or initial 'phoneme' respectively (*e.g.*, the sound */b/* for a picture of a *BALLOON*). The main result was that the latencies were shorter, in spoken but not in written picture naming, when the initial sound of the label was simultaneously presented with the picture as compared to an unrelated condition (*i.e.*, the presented sound did not correspond to any of the sounds in the label in question). This facilitation effect, which is specific to spoken language production, was interpreted as supporting the orthographic autonomy hypothesis (for further data in favour of this hypothesis see Bonin, Fayol & Gombert, 1998; Bonin Fayol & Peereman, 1998, and later in this chapter). In effect, if written language production requires the preliminary retrieval of phonological codes, the facilitation effect in spoken mode that is associated with the presentation of the initial sound of the label should also have been observed in connection with performance in written production.

In another study performed using the same paradigm (Bonin & Fayol, 2000), we tried to identify the nature of the mobilised representations and their time course of activation in the written production of isolated words on the basis of pictures. The idea underpinning this study was that the observation of similar effects in written and spoken language production would indicate that similar processes and representations are mobilised. Thus, taking as our starting point the study conducted by Schriefers *et al.* (1990), which has been presented above, we attempted to determine whether access to the semantic representations and the phonological/orthographic representations (*i.e.*, lexemic representations) in written language production followed the same time course of activation as had been identified in the spoken mode. In these experiments, the participants had to produce picture names while listening to distractor words. The distractors could be presented either 150 ms before the start of the pictures (SOA= -150 ms) or at the same time as them (SOA= 0). We recorded the initialisation latencies and the errors. In the first experiment, the pictures were either presented without a distractor or the distractors were semantically related to the pictured targets or were unrelated to them or, finally, were presented with a 'white' noise. The participants produced their response either in spoken or written mode. The results showed that a semantic interference effect was observed in spoken and written production with an SOA of -150 ms but not with an SOA of 0 ms. A second experiment in which different participants performed a picture recognition task (the same pictures as those used in Experiment 1 accompanied by the same distractors, revealed that the semantic interference effect was no longer observed. This experiment allowed us to discard the interpretation according to which the semantic interference effect observed in Experiment 1 resulted from a conceptual and not a linguistic level. In Experiment 3, the distractor words were (1) semantically but not phonologically-orthographically related, (2) phonologically-orthographically but not semantically related, (3) semantically and phonologically-orthographically related, or (4) neither semantically nor phonologically-orthographically related.

Figure 2. Mean written latencies (in ms) as a function of SOA, Semantic relatedness (Related: SEM-REL; Unrelated: SEM-UNR), and Phonological relatedness (Related: PHONO-REL;

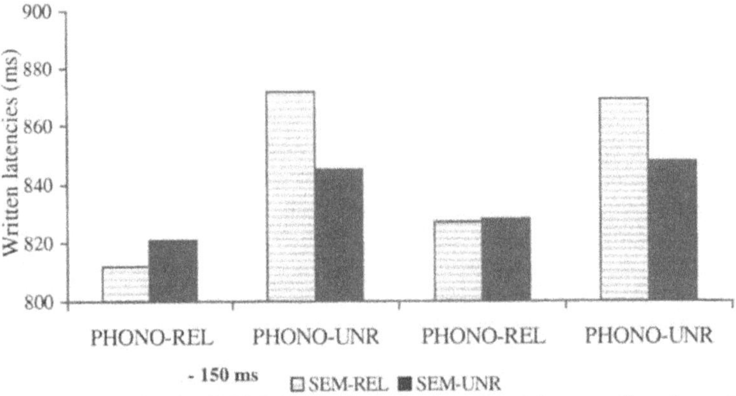

Unrelated: PHONO-UNR) (From Bonin et Fayol, in press, Experiment 3).

The most important result of this experiment (see Figure 2) was that a semantic interference effect was only observed at a statistically significant level when the distractors were not phonologically-orthographically related to the picture names. The presence of a phonological-orthographic similarity for the semantically related distractors cancelled out the semantic interference effect. This pattern of results, when seen in the light of a complex debate relating to discrete versus cascaded access to semantic and lexemic representations (*i.e.*, phonological, orthographic representations), suggests that the discrete conception, which received strong support from the study of lexical access in spoken language production (Schriefers *et al.*, 1990; Roelofs, Meyer & Levelt, 1996; but see also Starreveld & La Heij, 1996), is unable to account for this result pattern. In effect, this view postulates that the stage of semantic activation of the neighbours of a pictured target is followed by the lexemic activation of only the selected semantic candidate. Consequently, the semantically related distractors affect the semantic activation stage and the phonologically/orthographically related distractors affect the lexemic activation stage. The prediction is that the semantic distractors as well as the phonological-orthographic distractors have additive effects. The discrete conception is therefore unable to account for this interaction. Thus, we have interpreted these results as providing a strong suggestion that the alternative account, *i.e.*, that activation is cascaded between the semantic and lexemic processing levels, was more likely in the case of written language production.

One of the criticisms that might be levelled at the interference paradigm is that, given that the distractors are clearly audible or visible in the experiments that have been conducted, the participants may use them strategically. If such an interpretation were proven to be correct, it would severely impair the ability of this paradigm to study fast-acting mechanisms such as those involved during lexical access in production. However, Jescheniak and Schriefers (personal communication) have shown that in a spoken picture naming task involving the interference paradigm, a task in which the participants were strongly encouraged to use the relations between the distractor and the name of the pictured targets through the multiple repetition of the same 'picture/distractor word' pairs, the observed effects (here, phonological facilitation effects) did not vary as a function of the repeated presentations. On the basis of this study it is therefore necessary to discard the interpretation that holds that the effects observed when this paradigm is used are strategic in nature.

2.3. The priming paradigm

This paradigm has certain similarities with the interference paradigm. It is also designed to determine the nature of the representations that are activated at any given moment of processing together with the time course of their activation. In this paradigm, it is necessary to define a target (for example, a picture) and a prime (for example a word). The duration and condition of presentation of the primes can vary. Thus, the prime can be presented for a subliminal period (*e.g.*, 17 ms) or for periods, which permit conscious identification (*e.g.*, 51 ms). Similarly, the prime can be presented in a clearly visible way or, on the contrary, its visibility can be reduced by displaying a mask (#####) before and/or after its presentation. The delay between the prime and the target, *i.e.*, the SOA, can also vary. However, using this technique, the prime always precedes the target.

The priming paradigm has frequently been used to study the visual recognition of words (*e.g.*, Evett & Humphreys, 1981; Forster & Davis, 1984). It has also been used to study lexical access in spoken language production. However, to our knowledge, it has almost never been used to study lexical access in spoken language production. In an earlier study (Bonin, Fayol & Peereman, 1998), we used a variant of this paradigm to study the role of phonology in the written production of isolated words on the basis of pictures. The question, as in Bonin *et al.* (1997), was to determine whether mobilisation of the phonological codes was *obligatory* in order to promote access to the orthographic codes or whether, on the contrary, the orthographic codes could be directly retrieved on the basis of semantic specifications. We used the variant of the priming paradigm known as the masked priming paradigm. Using this technique, the visibility of the prime is drastically reduced through the use of short presentation durations and masks that either precede and/or follow the prime. When the primes are presented under such conditions, we can be certain that the observed effects are due to obligatory, rapid and non-intentional mechanisms. This technique had already been used by Ferrand, Grainger and Segui (1994) to study spoken production in response to pictures. The primes were non-words that were (1) phonologically identical and orthographically similar to the picture labels, *i.e.*, 'pseudohomophone' condition (*e.g.*, *lanpe* for the picture of a lamp (French *LAMPE*)); or (2) phonologically and orthographically similar to the pictured targets. Although the orthographic overlap between primes and labels was the same as for conditions (1) and (2), the phonological overlap was not as great as in condition (1) as it was in (2), *i.e.*, 'orthographic' condition (*e.g.*, *larpe*). An additional priming condition (3) was also used, orthographically and phonologically related to the labels, but only insofar as the initial letters or phonemes were concerned, *i.e.*, 'control' condition (*e.g.*, *lourm*). The articulatory initialisation latencies were shorter when the pseudohomophone primes were presented alone, with primes (2) and (3) giving rise to similar performances. In consequence, spoken language production is influenced by the preactivation of phonological codes, but not by that of orthographic codes. In the study conducted by Bonin *et al.* (1998), participants were asked to write down picture labels under three different priming conditions. The same non-words as those used in the Ferrand *et al.* study (1994) were used as primes (Figure 3).

We have shown (Figure 3) that the orthographically related primes (conditions (1) and (2)) (*e.g.*, *lanpe* and *larpe* for a pictured target corresponding to *LAMPE*) facilitated written initialisation at prime durations of 34 ms and 51 ms. In contrast, no improvement on written performance was specifically observed with primes with a homophone relationship (*lanpe*) with the picture labels compared to the 'orthographic' (*larpe*) and 'control' (*lourm*) conditions. It is therefore clear that the written production of isolated words from pictures does not require the *preliminary and systematic* activation of phonological codes.

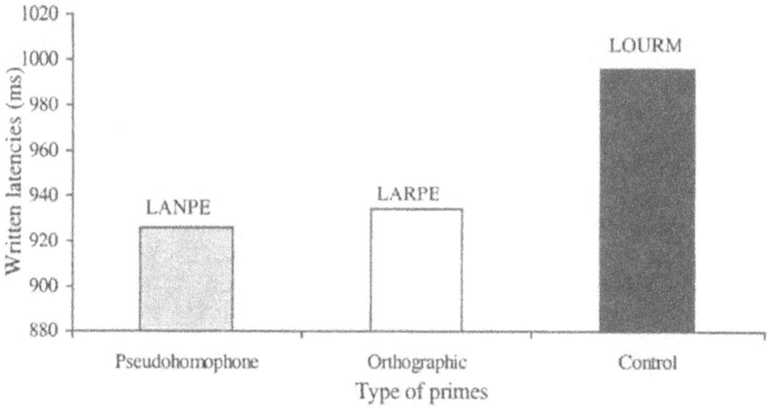

Figure 3. Effect of the type of prime when presented during 34 ms (Bonin, Fayol, & Peereman, 1998).

We have decided to focus our presentation of the methods used for the real-time study of the written production of isolated words on the picture naming task. However, the methodologies that we have described in presenting this task can also be used to study the written production of isolated words on the basis of their visual presentation (copying task) or auditory presentation (dictation task). Similarly, the interference and priming paradigms can be used in combination with these tasks. Here again, there are very few real-time studies that have made use of word dictation or word copying production tasks (see Bonin, Peereman, & Fayol, in press; Lambert, 1999, for examples).

3. CONCLUSION

The methods used for the real-time study of written language production are designed to identify the processes and representations that are involved in language production and the time of their activation. They also investigate the cost of implementing these processes either in isolation or when co-ordinated with others. We have shown that, within the framework of studies of the written production of isolated words, the use of naming tasks performed under conditions which permit a fine-tuned control of the variables, and undertaken in combination with the interference or priming paradigm, make it possible to gain an insight into the nature of the information mobilised in the written mode together with the associated time course of activation. It is self-evident that the necessary assembly of empirical data must be complemented by theoretical work that, although already underway in connection with lexical access in written language production (see Bonin, Peereman, & Fayol, in press), is still lacking in most of the research devoted to written language production. Our position is that this theoretical investigation of lexical access in written language production can be made simpler, and doubtlessly more fruitful, if it also takes into account of the theoretical and empirical data drawn from the fields of cognitive neuropsychology, spoken language production and, to a lesser degree, word recognition (Bonin, Pacton, & Fayol, in press).

POTENTIAL APPLICATIONS OF LATENT SEMANTIC ANALYSIS TO WRITING ANALYSIS

PETER W. FOLTZ* & THOMAS K. LANDAUER**

**New Mexico State University (USA), **University of Colorado at Boulder (USA)*

Abstract. Manually analysing and evaluating writing can be a time consuming, difficult, subjective and sometimes error-prone task. Latent Semantic Analysis (LSA) provides a new technique for performing a variety of useful semantic analyses. LSA serves both as an approximate psychological theory of aspects of human word and passage meaning and as a practical tool for research and applications. It can evaluate the conceptual content of writing, including, the kind, quality and quantity of semantic information expressed and the conceptual coherence of arguments presented. In this chapter we provide an overview of LSA and then discuss four techniques for performing automatic analysis of the content of written information using LSA, both from the standpoint of teaching expository writing and from the standpoint of its analysis.
Keywords. Latent Semantic Analysis, Content Analysis, Text Coherence, Essay scoring, Cognitive model, Knowledge Acquisition, Tutoring systems, Summarization

1. INTRODUCTION

Manually analysing and evaluating writing can be a time consuming, difficult, subjective and sometimes error-prone task. Although technology would seem to have the potential to automate writing analysis, few fully automatic techniques have been developed. Most have relied on non-semantic characteristics such as parts of speech, spelling, punctuation or literal word and word overlap counts. Typical rule-based or word matching systems can provide feedback about the frequency and distribution of countable features, but they do not address well the most important aspect of writing, its conceptual content, that is, the kind, quality and quantity of semantic information expressed or the conceptual coherence of arguments presented, nor do they provide complementary automated procedures for evaluating effects on readers.

Latent Semantic Analysis (LSA) (Landauer & Dumais, 1997; Landauer, Foltz, & Laham, 1998) provides a new technique for performing a variety of useful semantic analyses. LSA serves both as an approximate psychological theory of aspects of human word and passage meaning and as a practical tool for research and applications. In this chapter we provide an overview of LSA and then discuss four techniques for analysing the content of written information using LSA, both from the standpoint of teaching expository writing and from the standpoint of its analysis.

P. W. Foltz & T. K. Landauer (2001). Potential applications of latent semantic analysis to writing analysis. In G. Rijlaarsdam (Series ed.) & T. Olive & C. M. Levy (Vol. eds.), *Studies in Writing: Volume 10: Contemporary Tools and Techniques for Studying Writing*, 131-144.

2. OVERVIEW OF LATENT SEMANTIC ANALYSIS

2.1. What is Latent Semantic Analysis?

Latent Semantic Analysis is a fully automatic mathematical/statistical technique for extracting and inferring relations among the meanings of words and passages of discourse. It is not a traditional natural language processing or artificial intelligence program; it uses no humanly constructed dictionaries, knowledge bases, semantic networks, grammars, syntactic parsers, morphologies, or the like, and takes as its input only raw text parsed into words defined as unique character strings and separated into meaningful passages or samples, such as sentences or paragraphs.

The problem faced by a natural language learner can be represented as follows. The meaning conveyed by a spoken or printed passage must be a function of the meaning of the words it contains, and the meaning of a word must be a function of the meanings of the contexts (*e.g.* paragraphs) in which it has occurred. Thus, the natural language learner is presented with equations of the form

$$m(psg_i) = f\{m(wd_{i1}), \ldots, m(wd_{in}), m[X_i]\} \quad (1)$$

where m(psg), m(wd), m[X] are the meanings of passages, words, and accompanying non-linguistic context. To induce the meaning of words and passages, the language learner, whether human or machine, must solve a very large set of such equations. To make a solution feasible, LSA makes strong simplifying assumptions. It uses only text as input, and assumes that the meaning of a passage is a just the sum of the meaning of its words, *i.e.*

$$m(psg_i) = m(wd_{i1}) +, \ldots, + m(wd_{in}) \quad (2)$$

These simplifications obviously make the model far from complete as a theory of language, most importantly because merely adding words ignores their order, so that syntactic and grammatical functions that depend on word order are ignored. However, LSA's empirical successes in simulating language phenomena, as reviewed below, show that this first order approximation to word and passage meaning is surprisingly good. Indeed, we have found it to be so effective in emulating human meaning of text that we believe the traditionally dominant emphasis of linguistic analysis on syntax and grammar may be misplaced.

The mathematics of LSA. LSA solves such systems of equations by Singular Value Decomposition (SVD), a powerful matrix algebra technique used widely in engineering and science. Here, for those who wish to know, is a sketch of the mathematical procedure. LSA starts with a large collection of representative text, divides it into meaningful passages such as paragraphs, and forms these into a matrix, A_{wxp}, of unique word types, **w**, by passages, **p**. The initial cell values are given by a transform of the frequencies of word types in passages that is related to the mammalian learning function giving the likelihood of a particular response occurring in a given context (Rescorla & Wagner, 1972). The matrix A_{wxp} is then decomposed by SVD (Eckart &

Young, 1936; Berry, 1992), into the linear product of three matrices, $A_{wxp} = T_{wxn}S_{nxn}(P_{pxn})^T$. This yields a representation in which the value of any word or paragraph is a vector of coefficients on a large number of orthogonal basis vectors, or dimensions, **n**. Typically, retaining only the largest 100–500 dimensions produces the best results in simulating semantic phenomena, presumably because fewer dimensions cannot capture all the underlying components of word meaning that are reflected in the way words are used in context, and more dimensions reflect unique or unrepresentative differences in usage or differences that do not affect meaning, such as unsystematic alternation between synonyms. The solution defines a continuous value for the relation of every word to every other word, including the >98% of word-word pairs never used in the same paragraph of a 12M word corpus, thus going far beyond the pair-wise co-occurrence counts that appear to have been assumed in some arguments against the possibility of a machine learning to understand human language (*e.g.* Chomsky, 1957, 1965).

The measure used to represent the similarity between two words is one that estimates the degree to which a passage would have the same meaning if one word were substituted for the other. The cosine of the angle between two words in the high dimensional space gives the best empirical results. Similarities between passages, and between passages and words are measured analogously. The vector for a new passage is computed, as in equation **2**, by the sum of the vectors of the words in it.

Additional technical details may be found in Berry (1992), Berry, Dumais, and O'Brien (1995), Deerwester, Dumais, Furnas, Landauer, and Harshman (1990), Landauer and Dumais (1997), Landauer, Foltz, and Laham (1998).

2.2. Some demonstrations and tests of LSA's performance

LSA has been compared with human language and knowledge in many ways. For some initial intuitive grasp, here are some qualitative examples of relations between words and passages as derived by LSA. When trained on a large representative corpus of English, LSA infers appropriate degrees of relations between synonyms (e. g. *tiny-small* cos = .54), antonyms (*left-right*, .72), singulars and plural forms of nouns (*house-houses*, .54; *child-children*, .62) and present and past tenses of verbs (*talk-talked*, .67; *run-ran*, .57) whether regular or irregular, and various other related forms (*think-thinking*. -.67; *quick-quickly*, .62; *thankful-thankless*, .22; *birdcage-bird*, .13; *birdcage-cage*, .23). Cosine measures of similarity for such pairs range from about three to twenty-five standard deviations above that for randomly chosen words, *i.e.* they are highly significant. Similarities between passages are also fairly well represented when of moderate lengths – from around 50 to 500 words – and complexity[1]. Recall from equation **2** that a passage is represented as the sum of its word vectors (*e.g.* [1042...] + [2031...] = [3073...].

Here is an example.

1 The actual computation is somewhat more complex, weighting words by their communicative importance. See Deerwester et al.(1990) for technical details.

Text 1 — Fearing that her pony might have strayed into a neighbour's pasture, Sarah went in search of it. After half an hour of fruitless looking in nearby pastures, she began to worry that the animal had been stolen by a band of thieves or hit by lightening. Then she thought, 'Maybe the kid next door has borrowed her again without asking.'

Text 2 — At first Tom was afraid that his horse had wandered into the next field. After failing to locate it in thirty minutes of searching, he imagined the delinquent child from the next farm had taken it once more – or a theft by rustlers, or maybe a highway accident.

Text 3 — There were deep motorcycle tracks and skid marks in the driveway, the gate was hanging from one hinge, in the garage signs of a struggle, a heavy wrench on the floor, and a trail of blood led...'Oh my God', to a mangled body.

Between the intuitively similar story pairs (Text 1 and 2) the cosine is .32, between unrelated pairs only .08 and .14, a difference of about two standard deviations[2]. Note that there is very little overlap in literal word forms between the stories, and remember that no human input has been used to lemmatise or classify words by part-of-speech, or in any other way relate them.

In controlled quantitative tests, LSA has yielded good simulations of human verbal meaning across a wide spectrum of verbal phenomena and test applications: (1) In text-retrieval applications, LSA's knowledge of word-word similarities produces significant improvements in query-to-document matching (Dumais, 1994). (2) LSA correctly mimics human judgments of word-word semantic relations and category membership and accurately simulates hierarchical clusterings based on human pair-wise semantic similarity ratings (Landauer, Foltz, & Laham, 1998; Laham, 2000). (3) LSA accurately measures the conceptual coherence of text and resulting comprehensibility (Foltz, Kintsch, & Landauer, 1998). (4) It correctly predicts word-word and passage-word priming of word recognition in psycholinguistic experiments (Landauer & Dumais, 1997). (5) It accurately matches the conceptual content of student essays to the textbook sections from which the knowledge was gained (Foltz, 1996; Landauer, Foltz, & Laham, 1998; Landauer & Psotka, 2000). (6) It optimally matches instructional texts to a learner's prior knowledge as displayed in an essay (Wolfe, *et al.*, 1998). (8) It represents word ambiguity and polysemy, the apparent expression of two or more distinct senses or meanings by the same word in different contexts. It also offers a new interpretation of ambiguity in which *words* are not disambiguated by context; rather combining words produces a merged total meaning that is usually unambiguous. (9) LSA provides significant improvement for language modelling in

2 The population of random stories that would be required to establish chance variability is impossible to define quantitatively, so these values are only rough descriptions.

automatic speech recognition (*e.g.* Belagarda, 1999). (10) It can effectively match textual descriptions of disparate sorts, for example personnel work histories to discursive job and task descriptions (Laham, Bennett, & Landauer, 2000). (11) It can estimate the conceptual overlap among large numbers of training courses on the basis of the text of their multiple-choice certification exams (Laham, *et al.* 2000). (12) It accurately simulates the phenomenal rate of growth of human vocabulary during K-12 school years (Landauer & Dumais, 1997).

All this is not to imply that LSA always produces intuitively or quantitatively correct representations of meaning. For example, similarities and differences in short phrases are often not well represented. Nor are differences that depend strongly on word order, such those between metaphors such as '*My surgeon is a butcher*' and '*My butcher is a surgeon,*' or where predication is especially important, as in '*The hunter killed the bear*' *vs.* '*The bear killed the hunter.*' Kintsch (1998) has shown that LSA can be extended to capture some such phenomena, but so far human help has been required to specify subject and object, and additional computation is needed to resolve their mutual constraints in meaning. In addition, certain phenomena that might appear to be good targets for LSA simulation, notably free-association norms, have not succumbed (in this case, possibly because the disambiguating context is only implicit in the subject's mind). Moreover, LSA analyses are statistical and subject to random error, as well as unexpected behaviour due to the crudeness of its approximations. Researchers who wish to use LSA for writing analysis need to be mindful of these limitations and subtleties, and apply it judiciously and with some ingenuity.

To better exhibit the kinds of writing analysis of which LSA is capable, we next we elaborate in more detail on a few of these quantitative tests.

2.3. LSA's knowledge of word meanings: Multiple-choice vocabulary and domain knowledge tests

In these evaluations, LSA was first trained on text corpora intended to be representative in size and content of the text from which humans gained most of the semantic knowledge to be simulated. In one set of tests, LSA was trained on 5–11 million words of text sampled from either a high-school level encyclopaedia, the Associated Press newswire, or the TASA[3] systematic sampling of text read by American schoolchildren, then tested on multiple choice items from the Educational Testing Service Test of English as a Foreign Language (TOEFL) (Landauer & Dumais, 1997; Landauer, Foltz, & Laham, 1998.). These test questions present a target word or short phrase and ask the student to choose the one of four alternative words or phrases that is most similar in meaning. LSA's answer was determined by computing the cosine between the derived vector for the question word or phrase and that for each of the alternatives and choosing the largest. LSA was correct on 64% of the 80 items, identical to the average of a large sample of students from non-English speaking countries that had applied for admission to U.S. colleges. When in error, LSA's choices showed the same pattern as students'.

3 We thank Touchtone Applied Science, who developed this corpus as the basis of their Educator's Word Frequency Guide, for sharing it with us at considerable effort.

In a second set of tests, LSA was trained on a popular introductory psychology textbook and tested with the same four-alternative multiple choice tests used on final exams for students in two large classes (Landauer, Foltz, & Laham, 1998). In these experiments, LSA's score was about 60% – slightly lower than class averages but well above passing level and far above the guessing probability of .25. Its errors again closely resembled those of students. LSA generally had most difficulty with the same kinds of items that college students do.

2.4. Passage meaning similarity: Essay tests

In these tests, students wrote 50–500 word essays to answer a posed question. In various experiments, the topics included anatomy and function of the heart, basic phenomena in neuroscience, neuropsychology, the experimental psychology of learning and development, the history of the Panama Canal and of the great depression, a discussion of diversity in America, evaluation of a proposed advertising campaign, and open-ended narrative stories constrained only by a scene-setting sentence fragment. Each essay was represented as the average of the vectors for the words it contained. Cosines were computed between each unscored student essay and every essay in a set of fifty or more previously scored by experts. A small set of the most similar previously scored essays was identified, and the unscored essay assigned a score based on the scores of those weighted by their similarity (see Landauer, Laham, & Foltz, 2000, or at http://LSA.colorado.EDU for psychometric detail and discussion). Two or more human experts independently rated the overall quality of the essays that were scored by LSA in this way.

Overall the LSA-based measure correlated as highly with single human scores as one human score correlated with another. On over 15 topics and a total of over 3,200 individual student essays, the LSA scores were correlated .81 with an average human expert, while two independent human expert scores were correlated .83. Thus there was very little difference between the reliability of the LSA-based evaluation, based on its simulation of human passage meaning similarities, and that of human judges. Indeed, the larger the number and variety of essay grades there were to mimic, the larger the number of expert humans graders for each essay, and the better they agreed with each other, the better LSA simulated the humans. Thus, LSA and human scores in these applications must reflect very nearly the same qualities and quantities. In the heart topic case, each student had also taken a short answer test with near perfect human scoring agreement on the same material. Its correlation with the LSA essay score was .81, that between expert human essay scores and the objective test only .74.

3. APPLICATIONS OF LSA TO WRITING ANALYSIS

Relatively little work has been done applying LSA to the typical problems of writing analysis, and we believe that its potential is far greater than its accomplishments to date. We think workers in this field will soon find many ingenious ways to use its powers. Kintsch's application of LSA word-word and passage similarities for modelling literary devices such as metaphor is just one harbinger of what we hope will come (Kintsch, 2000). However, there have already been a small handful of relevant applications of sufficient interest to present as possible stimuli for other ideas.

3.1. Sources and gaps in conveyed knowledge

In the process of writing and revision, students often focus on the task of improving the quality of the writing as such while not improving the quantity or quality of conceptual information expressed. In addition, students are often unaware of what additional information should be expressed in their expository essays. LSA can be used not only to provide overall scores of essays, but to analyse what individual pieces of information are missing. This analysis can be used to inform students where to look for additional information in their texts or notes, or to get them to think more completely about the missing concepts before writing revisions. It could also be used by researchers to study what characteristics of writing lead to notice and absorption of its content by readers.

At an abstract level, one can distinguish three properties of expository writing that are desirable to assess: The correctness and completeness of its contained conceptual knowledge, the soundness of arguments that it presents in discussion of issues, and the fluency, elegance, and comprehensibility of its writing. Evaluation of superficial mechanical and syntactical features is fairly easy to separate from other factors, but the rest – content, argument, comprehensibility, and aesthetic style – are likely to be difficult to pull apart because each influences the other, if only because each depends on the choice of words.

3.2. Experiences in the classroom: Content analysis, grading, and tutorial feedback

Over the past two years, the Intelligent Essay Assessor has been used in a course in Psycholinguistics at New Mexico State University. Designed as a web-based application, it permits students to submit essays on a particular topic from their web browsers. Within about 20 s, students receive feedback with an estimated grade for their essay and a set of questions and statements of additional subtopics that are missing from their essays. Students can revise their essays immediately and resubmit. A demonstration is currently available at: http://psych.nmsu.edu/essay.

To create this system, LSA was trained on portions (four chapters) of the psycholinguistics textbook used in the class. The holistic grading method was used to provide an overall grade for any essay. The average correlation among the three human graders was .73 while the average of the individual correlation of LSA's holistic grade to a human grader was .80. To identify missing information, every individual sentence in an essay was compared against the sentences in the textbook that conveyed information on a desired subtopic. If no essay sentence was found that matched a particular subtopic, it was concluded that the student's process of acquiring and transmitting that information was faulty; the information was either missed, not digested, or not expressed. The same kind of analysis could easily be used to study what variants in expression in text – perhaps best experimentally manipulated – would cause a reader to miss or inadequately understand or remember its content.

In the educational experiment, students were permitted to use the system independently to write their essays and were encouraged to revise and resubmit as many times as they wanted until they were satisfied with their grades. The average grade for the students' first essays was 85 (out of 100). By the last revision, the average grade was 92. Students' essays improved from revision to revision, with the improvements in scores ranging from 0 to 33 points over an average of 3 revisions (Foltz, Gilliam, & Kendall, 2000).

In both undergraduate and middle school trials, students and teachers have enjoyed and valued using the system. All but one of the students said they would definitely or probably use such a system if it were available for their other classes. Overall, the results show that the LSA-based system is successful at helping students improve the quality of their essays through targeted feedback. It follows that the inverse process of using reader's success as measured by LSA to analyse the effectiveness of text should also succeed.

3.3. *Teaching summarization skills*

In one series of field experiments in an elementary school setting, a variant of the LSA-based essay scoring technique was used as an intelligent tutor for twelve-year old students learning to write short summaries of substantive articles (E. Kintsch, Steinhart, Stahl, Matthews, Lamb, & the LSA Research Group, 2000). Summary writing is widely believed to be an effective learning activity for both reading and writing skills. It forces students to read for understanding so that they can then select, capture and rephrase the important ideas and facts in their own words. The need to be succinct imposes a requirement for carefully considered wording and structure. The opportunity for repeated private revision afforded by the system gave students greatly expanded practice in this important aspect of the writing art.

In the experimental trial, students read two and a half to three page articles about a variety of topics, ranging from heart function to alternative energy sources and ancient American civilizations. After reading an article, the students entered a 200–300 word essay into the computer system. The system displayed the current length of the summary, indicated irrelevant, extraneous, and redundant sentences, marked misspellings, told the writer how well the information in each subsection of the reading had been covered in the summary, and gave an overall quality score.

Students revised their summaries until satisfied with them, then turned them in to the teacher. In the most recent experiment, students either used the full system or a minimal counterpart text-editor that showed length but none of the other feedback variables. Blind scores on content and style quality variables were made independently by two teachers. Students who used the system wrote significantly better (by greater than one standard deviation) summaries both in content and style than did those using the plain text-editor version. And not only did they write better summaries while using the system as an aid, when switched to the minimal system after a week, they wrote better essays without tutorial help. In addition, when using the system, students voluntarily (and by their report, happily) spent more than twice as much time writing.

Again, we point out that the results of this study can be inverted to show the promise of the method for studying effects of text characteristics. The fact that the feedback was effective in producing better quality of summaries, ones that were at once shorter, conveyed more information, and were judged better written, suggests strongly that LSA's ability to identify extraneous and redundant sentences was reasonably accurate. One can easily imagine useful applications in the analysis of other kinds of writing.

3.4. Determining the influence of texts on writers

The process of writing often involves integrating prior knowledge acquired from texts and then expressing that knowledge in new writing. However, it is not easy to determine where a writer has acquired knowledge or how well that knowledge has been integrated into written expression. LSA provides an automatic computational technique for determining how readers are influenced by the texts they have read through an analysis of the content of sources and essays. By comparing sentences in student essays to the original texts presumably read by the students, LSA is able to determine where in the source texts the readers have acquired their knowledge and what pieces of information are having the greatest influence on the written output. In one study (Foltz, 1996), students read 24 short texts on the history of the Panama Canal and then wrote an essay on the topic. LSA was able to determine which texts where having the greatest influence on the content almost as accurately as human judges. In another study, LSA was able to accurately predict which texts students had and had not read (Foltz, Britt, & Perfetti, 1996). The results indicate that LSA can be used for assessing what knowledge was acquired from texts, and, therefore, also for measuring the amount of influence different texts have on a reader's writing.

3.5. Text coherence and segmentation

LSA-based techniques have also been developed to estimate the conceptual coherence of texts. Kintsch and his colleagues (*e.g.*, van Dijk & Kintsch, 1983; Kintsch & Vipond, 1979) have developed methods for representing text in a propositional language and have used it to analyse the coherence of discourse. They have shown that the comprehension of text depends heavily on its coherence, as measured by the overlap between the arguments in propositions (Kintsch & Vipond, 1979; McNamara, Kintsch, Songer, & Kintsch, 1996). However, in order to perform such an analysis, a text must first be propositionalized by hand. This process can be very time consuming, often limiting the size of texts analysed.

By computing the cosine between one sentence (or larger text unit) and the following one, LSA can automatically estimate their degree of semantic relatedness. The cosines for all adjoining text units can be averaged in order to derive an overall measure of coherence for a text. This approach is similar to a propositional analysis in that it measures conceptual similarity between adjoining sections of text. The concept of coherence derived by LSA captures primarily referential coherence, the overlap of related concepts between text units. While LSA does not measure all of the additional features found in coherence, for example, syntactic and temporal markers, it still manages to successfully measure the flow of semantic content across a text. As illustrated below, this approach can provide accurate measures of text comprehensibility, readability and indications of places where coherence breaks down in a text.

In analyses of a series of texts that systematically varied the coherence of the texts, Foltz (1996) and Foltz, Kintsch, and Landauer (1998) found that the LSA measure of coherence texts predicted their comprehension by readers very well (r = .93). In addition, they found that applying this analysis to different textbooks could provide indications of the difficulty of the textbooks. For example, textbooks that professors thought were more difficult tended to have lower overall coherence.

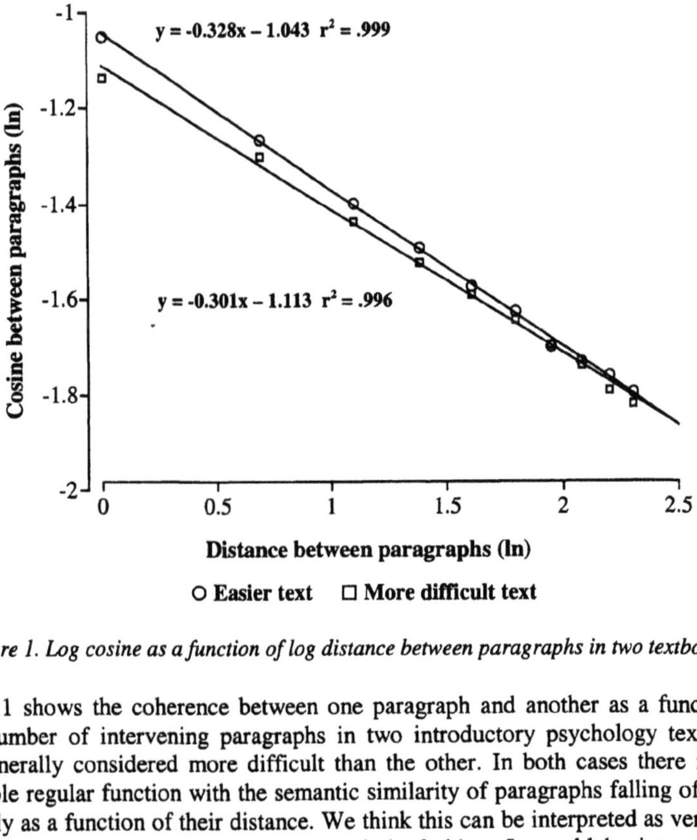

Figure 1. Log cosine as a function of log distance between paragraphs in two textbooks.

Figure 1 shows the coherence between one paragraph and another as a function of their number of intervening paragraphs in two introductory psychology textbooks, one generally considered more difficult than the other. In both cases there is a remarkable regular function with the semantic similarity of paragraphs falling off exponentially as a function of their distance. We think this can be interpreted as very close attention to introducing concepts in an orderly fashion. It would be interesting to compare a wider variety of texts with same and different authors, same and different genres, eras, formats, etc. using this metric.

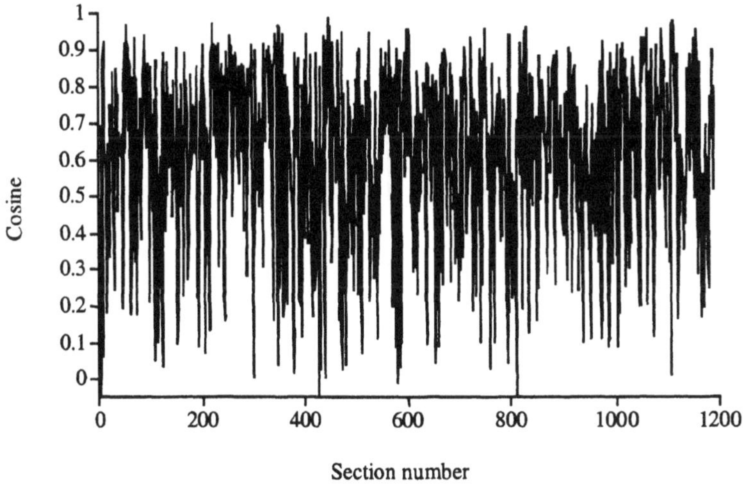

Figure 2. Coherence between each section of text to the next in a large book.

The general approach of using LSA for computing textual coherence also permits more detailed examination of conceptual coherence; for example, detection of places in a text where coherence breaks down because the author has purposely changed topics or subtopics, voice or diction, written poorly or oddly, etc. Two examples of such analyses are given in Figures 2 and 3. Figure 2 illustrates how the method can reveal erratic changes in topic between short sections of text across a very large book by computing the similarity of each section to the next. Figure 3 zooms in on the first 130 sections of the book. The arrows on the figure indicate the places in the text that represent breaks between chapters. Note that the how it can show systematicity of changes between chapters as one might expect. At the end of chapters there tends to be a general drop in coherence between one chapter and the next. With more development, such methods might also be used to characterize and assess more global organizational issues such as the optimal order for introducing ideas or sequencing sections or chapters.

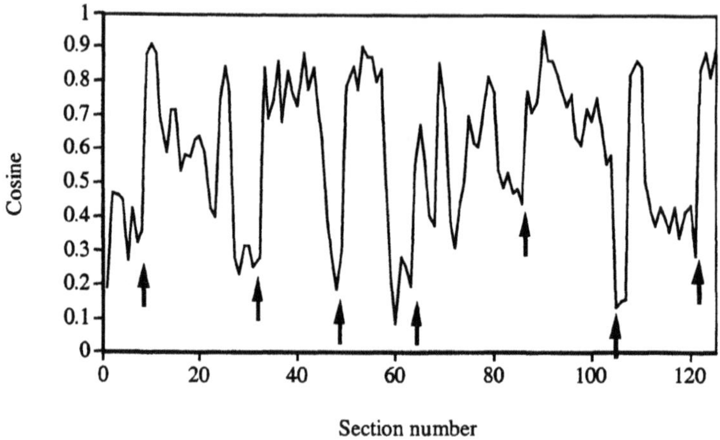

Figure 3. Coherence between sections of text with breaks between chapters indicated with arrows.

Computing coherence by LSA can be applied to a wide variety of problems beyond those tasks for which it has so far been employed. For example, it could be used as a research tool for comparing genres, authors, historical periods, languages, writing styles, effects of context, settings, experimental instructions, or discourse variables.

3.6. Content analysis

LSA has not yet, to our knowledge been applied to content analysis of the traditional sort. However its success in retrieving documents on a particular topic whether or not they share identical word types suggests that it could be quite useful. If, for example, a researcher wanted to know how often the concept of love was used in writings of different authors, eras, or genres, LSA could be put to work in several ways. A crude way would be simply to compute the cosine between the word 'love' in each paragraph of the work and average. This would tend to give paragraphs actually containing the word relatively high cosines (although others could sometimes be higher), but more importantly it would also estimate the amount of love related conceptual content in all the paragraphs not containing 'love'. A more sophisticated procedure would be to first find a small set of paragraphs that are intuitively highly devoted to love, then use each such paragraph as a whole query to match against all the others, and average over all the comparisons.

4. TECHNICAL CONSIDERATIONS FOR USING LSA

A web site is available (http://lsa.colorado.edu) on which investigators can enter words or passages and obtain LSA-based word or passage vectors, similarities between words and words, words and passages, and passages and passages, and do a few other related operations. The site offers results based on several different training corpora, including ones based on an encyclopaedia, a grade and topic partitioned collection of schoolchild reading, newspaper and other text in several languages, introductory psychology textbooks, and a small domain-specific corpus of text about the heart.

To carry out LSA research based on their own training corpora, investigators will need to consult the more detailed sources, (see Berry, 1992; Landauer & Dumais, 1997; Landauer, Foltz, & Laham, 1998). The hardware to perform LSA research typically requires a UNIX-based system with large amounts of memory. For example, analyses on large corpora, such as encyclopaedia are typically run on computers with at least 1GB of RAM. As of this writing, research licenses for code for using LSA may be obtained from Telcordia Technologies and additional code for performing sparse matrix SVDs and parsing texts and files into matrices and vectors may be obtained from Mike Berry's University of Tennessee web set (www.cs.utk.edu/~lsi/).

5. CONCLUSIONS

We have found the LSA technique quite accurate both in focused research investigations of its validity in simulating human judgments and behaviour with respect to the meaning of words and text, and for a variety of applications. The latter fall into two main classes, practical methods for writing and content education, and current and potential tools for research on writing.

5.1. Educational applications

Educational applications include scoring essays, providing feedback to writers on the quality of content, and mapping the source of knowledge to original texts. For scoring essays, at a minimal level, LSA can be used as a consistency checker, in which the teacher scores the essays and then LSA re-grades them and indicates discrepancies. Because the technique is not influenced by fatigue, deadlines, or biases, it can provide a consistent and objective view of the quality of the essays. The technique can further be used in large scale standardized testing or large classes, by either providing consistency checks or serving as an automatic grader. The importance of these capabilities for the teaching of writing lies in the opportunity to give students much more evaluated practice.

At a more interactive level, LSA can help students learn both to write better expository text and to learn content better. LSA can be integrated with other software tools for education. For example, in most software for distance education, tools for administering writing assignments are often neglected in favour of tools for creating and grading multiple-choice exams. Incorporating LSA permits writing to be a more central focus in online education. For example, in web-based training systems, LSA can be incorporated as an additional module to permit many more writing assignments and practice opportunities. Textbook supplements can similarly use LSA to enhance automated study guides. At the end of chapters, students can be asked to write essay questions addressing topics covered in the chapter. Based on an analysis of their essays, the software can suggest sections of the textbook that the students need to review before they take their exams. An application of this approach that we view as especially useful is practice in writing summaries. In experiments with twelve-year-old students, the LSA-based automatic practice had significant positive effects on their writing abilities.

5.2. Research tools

We believe that there are many potentially useful applications of LSA in research on writing. For example, many kinds of analysis that have employed propositional coding to capture meaning relations can now be done more easily and extensively. Changes in topic and theme could be automatically tracked, redundancy and irrelevance could be automatically detected and measured, and semantic structures of both small and large texts could be objectively mapped. Content analyses could be performed at concept level instead of by word matching. Indeed, we think the opportunities have only been scratched, and hope that readers of this monograph will find new fruitful uses.

6. ACKNOWLEDGEMENTS

This chapter has benefited from collaborative research with a number of people including: Darrell Laham, Eileen Kintsch, Walter Kintsch, Susan Dumais, Adrienne Lee, and David Steinhart

REFERENCES

Baddeley, A. D., & Hitch, G. (1974). Working memory. In G. Bower (Ed.), *The psychology of learning and motivation, Vol. 8* (pp. 281–301). London: Academic Press.

Barbier, M.-L. (1998). Rédaction en langue première et en langue seconde: comparaison de la gestion des processus et des ressources cognitives [Writing in L1 and in L2: comparison of management of processes and of cognitive resources]. *Psychologie Française, special number on Bilinguism, 43* (4), 361-370.

Barbier, M.-L., Piolat, A., & Roussey, J.-Y. (1998). Effet du traitement de texte et des correcteurs sur la maîtrise de l'orthographe et de la grammaire en langue seconde [Effect of word processor on mastering of spelling and of grammar in L2]. *Revue Française de Pédagogie, 122*, 83-98.

Beaugrande, R. de (1984). *Text production*. Norwood, NJ: Ablex.

Bell, A. (1991). *The language of news media*. Oxford: Blackwell.

Bellegarda, J. R. (1999). Speech recognition experiments using multi-span statistical language models. *IEEE Intl. Conf. on Acoustics, Speech, and Signal Processing*, 717-720.

Berninger, V. W., & Sanson, H. L. (1994). Modifying Hayes and Flower's model of skillled writing to explain beginning and developing writing. In J. S. Carlson (Series ed.) & C. Butterfield (ed.), *Advances in cognition and educational practices, Vol. 2: Children's writing: Toward a process theory of the development of skilled writing* (pp. 57-81). Greenwich, CT: JAI Press.

Berry, M. W. (1992). Large scale singular value computations. *International Journal of Supercomputer Applications, 6*, 13-49.

Blum, R., Bonfadelli, H., Marr, M., & Wyss, V. (2001). *Journalisten in der Schweiz. Eigenschaften, Einstellungen, Einflüsse [Journalists in Switzerland. Characteristics, attitudes, influences]*. Konstanz: UVK.

Bock, J. K. (1996). Language production: Methods and methodologies. *Psychonomic Bulletin & Review, 3*, 395-421.

Bock, J. K., & Levelt, W. J. M. (1994). Language production: Grammatical encoding. In M. A. Gernsbacher (Ed.), *Handbook of Psycholinguistics* (pp. 945-984). New York: Academic Press.

Bolinger, D. (1965). *Forms of English: Accent, morpheme, order*. Cambridge, MA: MIT Press.

Bonin, P. (1997). Produire des mots oralement et par écrit [Producing words in the speaking and writing mode]. *Revue de Neuropsychologie, 7*, 29-70.

Bonin, P., & Fayol, M. (2000). Writing words from pictures: What representations are activated and when? *Memory & Cognition, 28*, 677-689.

Bonin, P., Fayol, M., & Chalard, M. (in press). Age of acquisition in written picture naming. *The Quarterly Journal of Experimental Psychology*.

Bonin, P., Fayol, M., & Gombert, J.-E. (1997). Role of phonological and orthographic codes in picture naming and writing: An interference paradigm. *Current Psychology of Cognition, 16*, 259-324.

Bonin, P., Fayol, M., & Gombert, J.-E. (1998). An experimental study of lexical access in the writing and naming of isolated words. *International Journal of Psychology, 33*, 269-286.

Bonin, P., Fayol, M., & Peereman, R. (1998). Masked form priming in writing words from pictures: Evidence for direct retrieval of orthographic codes. *Acta Psychologica, 99*, 311-328.

Bonin, P., Pacton, S., & Fayol, M. (in press). La production verbale écrite de mots isolés: Evidences en faveur d'une (relative) autonomie de l'écrit [The written production of isolated words: Evidence for a (relative) autonomy of writing]. *Pyschologie Française*.

Bonin, P., Peereman, R., & Fayol, M. (in press). Do phonological codes constrain the selection of orthographic codes in written picture naming? *Journal of Memory and Language*.

Boomer, D. (1965). Hestitation and grammatical encoding. *Language and Speech, 8*, 148-158.

Breetvelt, I., van den Bergh, H., & Rijlaarsdam, G. (1994). Relations between writing processes and text quality: When and how? *Cognition and Instruction, 12,* 103-123.

Britton, B. K. (1996). Rewriting the arts and sciences of improving expository instructional text. In C. M. Levy & S. E. Ransdell (Eds.), *The science of writing. Theories, methods, individual differences, and applications* (pp. 323-346). Mahwah, NJ: Lawrence Erlbaum Associates.

Britton, J., Burgess, T., Martin, N., McLeod, A., & Rosen, H. (1975). *The development of writing abilities.* London: Macmillan.

Broadbent, D. (1958). *Perception and communication.* Oxford: Permagon.

Brown, J. L., McDonald, J. S., Brown, T. L., & Carr, T. H. (1988).Adapting to processing demands in discourse production. *Journal of Experimental Psychology: Human perception and performance, 14, 45-59.*

Burtis, P. J., Bereiter, C., Scardamalia, M., & Tetroe, J. (1983). The development of planning in writing. In G. Wells & B. M. Kroll (Eds.), *Explorations in the development of writing* (pp. 153-174). New York: Wiley.

Butterworth, B. (1975). Hesitation and semantic planning in speech. *Journal of Psycholinguistic Research 4,* 75-87.

Butterworth, B. (1980). Evidence from pauses in speech. In B. Butterworth (Ed.), *Language production: Volume 1. Speech and talk.* London: Academic Press.

Caramazza, A. (1997). How many levels of processing are there in lexical access? *Cognitive Neuropsychology, 14,* 177-208.

Caramazza, A., & Miozzo, M. (1998). More is not always better: A response to Roelofs, Meyer, and Levelt. *Cognition, 69,* 231-241.

Chanquoy, L., Foulin, J.-N., & Fayol, M. (1995). Writing in adults. A real time approach. In G. Rijlaarsdam, H. van den Bergh, & M. Couzijn (Eds.), *Theories, models and methodology: Current trends in research on writing.* Amsterdam: Amsterdam University Press, pp. 36-44.

Chanquoy, L., & Negro, I. (1996). Subject-verb agreement errors in written productions: A study of French children and adults. *Journal of Psycholinguistic Research, 25,* 553-570.

Cherry, C. (1953). Some experiments on the recognition of speech with one and two ears. *Journal of the Acoustical Society of America, 23,* 915-919.

Chomsky, N. (1957). *Syntactic structures.* The Hague, Netherlands: Mouton.

Chomsky, N. (1965). *Aspects of the theory of syntax.* Cambridge, MA: MIT Press.

Clark, H. (1995). *Using language.* Cambridge: Cambridge University Press.

Cohen, J., McWhinney, B., Flatt, M., & Provost, J. (1993). PsyScope: An interactive graphic system for designing and controlling experiments in the psychology laboratory using Macintosh computers. *Behavior Research Methods, Instruments, & Computers, 25,* 257-271.

Collins, A. M., & Loftus, E. F. (1975). A spreading activation theory of semantic processing. *Psychological Review, 82,* 407-428.

Cooper, M., & Holzman, M. (1983). Talking about protocols. *College Composition and Communication, 34,* 284-293.

Cumming, A. (1994). Writing expertise and second language proficiency. In A. Cumming (Ed.). *Bilingual performance in reading and writing* (pp. 173-221). Amsterdam: Johns Benjamins.

Daneman, M., & Green, I. (1986). Individual differences in comprehending and producing words in context. *Journal of Memory and Language, 25,* 1-18.

Dechert, H. W., & Raupauch, M. (1980). *Temporal variables in speech. Studies in honour of Frieda Goldman-Eisler.* The Hague: Mouton.

Deerwester, S., Dumais, S. T., Furnas, G. W., Landauer, T. K., & Harshman, R. (1990). Indexing by Latent Semantic Analysis. *Journal of the American Society For Information Science, 41,* 391-407.

Dell, G. S., & O'Seaghdha, P. G. (1991). Mediated and convergent lexical priming in language production: A comment on Levelt *et al. Psychological Review, 4,* 604-614.

DiPardo, A. (1994). Stimulated recall in research on writing: an antidote to 'I don't know, it was fine.' In P. Smagorinsky (Ed.), *Speaking about writing: Reflections on research methodology* (pp. 163-181). Thousand Oaks, CA: Sage Publications.

Eckart, C., & Young, G. (1936). The approximation of one matrix by another of lower rank. *Psychometrika, 1,* 211-218.

Eigler, G. (1996). Methoden der Textproduktionsforschung [Methods in text production research]. In H. Günther & O. Ludwig (Eds.), *Schrift und Schriftlichkeit. Ein interdisziplinäres Handbuch internationa-*

ler Forschung [Writing and written language. An interdisciplinary handbook of international research] (pp. 992-1004). Berlin: de Gruyter.

Ellis, A. W. (1984). Spelling and writing. In A. W. Ellis (Ed.), *Reading, writing and dyslexia: A cognitive analysis* (pp. 60-85). Hillsdale, NJ: Lawrence Erlbaum Associates.

Ellis, A. W. (1988). Normal writing processes and peripherical acquired dysgraphias. *Language and Cognitive Processes, 3*, 99-127.

Emig, J. (1971). *The composing processes of twelfth graders*. Urbana, IL: NTCE.

Ericsson, K. A., & Simon, H. A. (1993). *Protocol analysis: Verbal reports as data*. Revised edition. Cambridge: MIT Press.

Evett, L. J., & Humphreys, G. W. (1981). The use of abstract graphemic information in lexical access. *Quarterly Journal of Experimental Psychology, 33A*, 283-321.

Faigley, L. (1986). Competing theories of process: A critique and a proposal. *College English, 48* (6), 527-542.

Farioli, F., & Piolat, A. (May, 1999). *Mobilisation et coût des processus rédactionnels en fonction de la hiérarchie des buts assignés aux rédacteurs [Activation and cost of writing processes as a function of hierarchy of goals assigned to writers]*. Graphic presentation at the biennial congress of the Société Française de Psychologie, Aix-en-Provence, France.

Fay, D., & Cutler, A. (1977). Malaproprisms and the structure of the mental lexicon. *Linguistic Inquiry, 8*, 505-520.

Fayol, M. (1991). From sentence production to text production: Investigating fundamental processes. *European Journal of Psychology of Education, 6* (2), 99-117.

Fayol, M. (1997). *Des idées au texte, Psychologie cognitive de la production verbale, orale et écrite [From ideas to text; Cognitive psychology of spoken and written verbal production]*. Paris: Presses Universitaires de France.

Ferrand, L. (1994). Accès au lexique et production de la parole: Un survol [Lexical access in speech production: A brief review]. *L'Année Psychologique, 94*, 295-312.

Ferrand, L. (1997). La dénomination d'objets: Théories et données [Picture naming: Theories and data]. *L'Année Psychologique, 97*, 113-146.

Ferrand, L., Grainger, J. & Segui, J. (1994). A study of masked form priming in picture and word naming. *Memory & Cognition, 22*, 431-441.

Fisk, A. D., Denick, W. L., & Schneider, W. (1986). A methodological assessment and evaluation of dual-task paradigms. *Current Psychological Research & Reviews, 5*, 315-327.

Flower, L. S., & Hayes, J. R. (1980). The dynamics of composing: Making plans and juggling constraints. In L. Gregg & E. Steinberg (Eds.), *Cognitive processes in writing* (pp. 31-50). Hillsdale, NJ: Lawrence Erlbaum Associates.

Flower, L. S., & Hayes, J. R. (1981). A cognitive process theory of writing. *College Composition and Communication, 32*, 365-387.

Flower, L. S., & Hayes, J. R. (1984). Images, plans, and prose: The representation of meaning in writing. *Written Communication, 1*, 120-160.

Flower, L. S., Hayes, J. R., Carey, L., Schriver, K., & Stratman, J. (1986). Detection, diagnosis, and the strategies of revision. *College Composition and Communication, 37* (1), 16-55.

Foltz, P. W. (1996). Latent Semantic Analysis for text-based research. *Behavior Research Methods, Instruments and Computers, 28*, 197-202.

Foltz, P. W., Britt, M. A., & Perfetti, C. A. (1996). Reasoning from multiple texts: An automatic analysis of readers' situation models. In G. Cottrell (Ed.), *Proceedings of the 18th Annual Cognitive Science Conference* (pp. 110-115). Hillsdale, NJ: Lawrence Erlbaum Associates.

Foltz, P. W., Gilliam, S., & Kendall, S. A. (2000). Supporting content-based feedback in online writing evaluation with LSA. *Interactive Learning Environments, 8* (2), 111-129.

Foltz, P. W., Kintsch, W., & Landauer, T. K. (1998). The measurement of textual coherence with Latent Semantic Analysis. *Discourse Processes, 25* (2&3), 285-307.

Ford, M. (1982). Sentence planning units: implications for the speaker's representation of meaningful relations underlying sentences. In J. Bresnan (Ed.), *The mental representation of grammatical relations* (pp. 797-827). Cambridge, MA: MIT Press.

Ford, M., & Holmes, V. M. (1978). Planning units and syntax in sentence production. *Cognition, 6*, 35-53.

Forster, K. I., & Davis, C. (1984). Repetition priming and frequency attenuation in lexical access. *Journal of Experimental Psychology: Learning, Memory, and Cognition, 10*, 680-698.

Foulin, J.-N., (1995). Pauses et débits: les indicateurs temporels de la production écrite [Pauses and Fluency: Temporal indexes of written production], *L'Année Psychologique, 95*, 483-504.

Garrett, M. F. (1975). The analysis of sentence production. In G. Bower (Ed.), *Psychology of learning and motivation, Vol. 9* (pp. 133-175). New York: Academic Press.

Garrett, M. F. (1980). Levels of processing in sentence production. In B. Butterworth (Ed.), *Language production, Vol. 1* (pp. 177-220). New York: Academic Press.

Garrett, M. F. (1982). Production of speech: Observations from normal and pathological use. In A. Ellis (Ed.), *Normality and pathology in cognitive functions* (pp. 19-76). London: Academic Press.

Glynn, S. M., Britton, B. K., Muth, D., & Dogan, N. (1982). Writing and revising persuasive documents: Cognitive demands. *Journal of Educational Psychology, 74*, 557-567.

Goldman-Eisler, F. (1972). Pauses, clauses, sentences. *Communication and Speech, 15*, 103-113.

Grabowski, J. (1996). Writing and speaking. Common grounds and differences toward a regulation theory of written language production. In C. M. Levy & S. E. Ransdell (Eds.), *The science of writing. Theories, methods, individual differences, and applications* (pp. 73-92). Mahwah, NJ: Lawrence Erlbaum Associates.

Green, D., & Swets, J. (1966). *Signal detection theory and psychophysics*. New York: Wiley.

Greene, S., & Higgins, L. (1994). 'Once upon a time.' The use of retrospective accounts in building theory in composition. In P. Smagorinsky (Ed.), *Speaking about writing. Reflections on research methodology* (pp. 115-140). Thousand Oaks, CA: Sage Publications.

Gregg, L. W., & Steinberg, E. R. (1980). *Cognitive processes in writing: An interdisciplinary approach.* Hillsdale, NJ: Lawrence Erlbaum Associates.

Gufoni, V. (1996). Les protocoles verbaux comme méthode d'étude de la production écrite: approche critique [Verbal protocols as a method for studying written production]. *Etudes de Linguistique Appliquée, 101*, 20-32.

Harley, T. (1993). Phonological activation of semantic competitors during lexical access in speech production. *Language and Cognitive processes, 8*, 291-309.

Häusermann, J. (2001a). Der Text als Ort der öffentlichen Kommunikation. Zur sprachlichen Aus- und Fortbildung im Journalismus [The text as a place of public communication. Linguistic education and training in journalism]. In U. Breuer & J. Korhonen (Eds.), *Mediensprache, Medienkritik [Media language, media criticism]* (pp 45-54). Frankfurt a. M.: Lang.

Häusermann, J. (2001b). *Journalistisches Texten. Sprachliche Grundlagen für professionelles Informieren [Journalistic text composition. Linguistic foundations of professional information]*. Konstanz: UVK.

Hayes, J. R. (1996). A new framework for understanding cognition and affect in writing. In C.M. Levy & S. Ransdell (Eds.), *The science of writing. Theories, methods, individual differences and applications* (pp. 1- 27). Mahwah, NJ: Lawrence Erlbaum Associates.

Hayes, J. R., & Flower, L. S. (1980). Identifying the organization of writing process. In L.W. Gregg & E.R. Steinberg (Eds.), *Cognitive processes in writing: An interdisciplinary approach* (pp. 3-30). Hillsdale, NJ: Lawrence Erlbaum Associates.

Hayes, J. R., & Flower, L. S. (1983). Uncovering cognitive process in writing: An introduction to protocol analysis. In P. Rosenthal, L. Tamor, & S. A. Walmsley (Eds.), *Research of writing, principles and methods* (pp. 207-221. New York: Longman.

Henderson, A. I. (1974). Time patterns in spontaneous speech – cognitive stride or random walk? A reply to Jaffe *et al.* 1972. *Language and Speech, 17*, 119-125.

Henderson, A. I., Goldman-Eisler, F., & Skarbek, A. (1966). Sequential temporal patterns in spontaneous speech. *Language and Speech, 9*, 207-216.

Henderson, R. W. (1989). *EventLog*. Iowa City, IO: Conduit.

Holmes, V. M. (1988). Hesitation and sentence planning. *Language and Cognitive Processes, 3*, 323-361.

Howe, M. L., & Rabinowitz, F. M. (1989). On the uninterpretability of dual-task performance. *Journal of Experimental Child Psychology, 47*, 32-38.

Humphreys, G. W., Riddoch, M. J., & Quinlan, P. T. (1988). Cascade processes in picture identification. *Cognitive Neuropsychology, 5*, 67-103.

Jaffe, J., Breskin, S., & Gerstman, L. J. (1972). Random generation of apparent speech rythms. *Language and Speech, 15*, 68-71.

Jakobs, E. M. (2001, in preparation). Reproductive writing – Writing from sources. In D. Perrin (Ed.), The pragmatics of writing. *Journal of Pragmatics. Special issue.*

Janssen, D., Schilperoord, J., van den Bergh, H., van Waes, L., & Wassenaar, W. (1994). Effecten van hardop denken op het schrijfproces [Effects of thinking out loud on the writing process]. In A. Maes, P.

Van Hauwermeieren, & L. van Waes (Eds.), *Perspectieven in taalbeheersingsonderzoek [Perspectives in functional linguistic research]* (pp. 177-191). Dordrecht: Foris Publications,.

Janssen, D., van Waes, L., & van den Berg, H. (1996). Effects of thinking aloud on writing processes. In C. M. Levy & S. E. Ransdell (Eds.), *The science of writing. Theories, methods, individual differences, and applications* (pp 233-250). Mahwah, NJ: Lawrence Erlbaum Associates.

Jescheniak, J. D., & Levelt, W. J. M. (1994). Word frequency effects in speech production: Retrieval of syntactic information and of phonological forms. *Journal of Experimental Psychology: Learning, Memory, and Cognition, 20,* 824-843.

Jescheniak, J. D., & Schriefers, H. (1998). Discrete serial versus cascaded processing in lexical access in speech production: Further evidence from the coactivation of near-synonyms. *Journal of Experimental Psychology: Learning, Memory, and Cognition, 24,* 1256-1274.

Jones, D. M., Miles, C., & Page, J. (1990). Disruption of proofreading by irrelevant speech: Effects of attention, arousal, or memory? *Applied Cognitive Psychology, 4,* 89-108.

Kahneman, D. (1973). *Attention and effort.* Englewood Cliffs, NJ: Prentice-Hall.

Kaufer, D. S., Hayes, J. R., & Flower, L. S. (1986). Composing written sentences. *Research in the Teaching of English, 20,* 121-140.

Kellogg, R. T. (1987a). Effects of topic knowledge on the allocation of processing time and cognitive effort to writing processes. *Memory and Cognition, 15* (3), 256-266.

Kellogg, R. T. (1987b). Writing performance: Effect of cognitive strategies. *Written Communication, 4,* 269-298.

Kellogg, R. T. (1988). Attentional overload and writing performance: Effects of rough draft and outline strategies. *Journal of Experimental Psychology: Learning, Memory and Cognition, 14* (2), 355-365.

Kellogg, R. T. (1990). Effectiveness of prewriting strategies as a function of task demands. *American Journal of Psychology, 103* (3), 327-342.

Kellogg, R. T. (1993). Observations on the psychology of thinking and writing. *Composition Studies, 21,* 3-41.

Kellogg, R. T. (1994). *The psychology of writing.* New York: Oxford University Press.

Kellogg, R. T. (1996). A model of working memory in writing. In C. M. Levy & S. E. Ransdell (Eds.), *The science of writing. Theories, methods,individual differences and applications* (pp. 57-71). Hillsdale, NJ: Laurence Erlbaum Associates.

Kellogg, R. T. (1998, May). *Long-term working memory in text production.* Paper presented at the meeting of American Psychological Society, Washington, D.C.

Kellogg, R. T. (1999). Components of working memory in writing. In M. Torrance & G. Jeffery (Eds.), *Cognitive demands of writing* (pp. 43-61). Amsterdam: Amsterdam University Press.

Kellogg, R. T. (2001). Competition for working memory among writing processes. *American Journal of Psychology, 114,* 175-191

Kellogg, R. T., & Mueller, S. (1993). Performance amplification and process restructuring in computer-based writing. *International Journal of Man-Machine Studies, 39,* 33-49.

Kempen, G., & Huijbers, P. (1983). The lexicalization process in sentence production and naming: Indirect election of words. *Cognition, 14,* 185-209.

Kerr, B. (1973). Processing demands during mental operations. *Memory and Cognition, 1,* 401-412.

Kim, H.-C. (1996). *Diagnosing and filtering typing error corrections in text revision history.* Report TRITA-NA-P9633, IPLab-113, Department of Numerical Analysis and Computing Science, Royal Institute of Technology, Stockholm.

Kintsch, E., Steinhart, D., Stahl, G., Matthews, C., Lamb, R., & LSA Research Group (2000). Developing summarization skills through the use of LSA-based feedback. *Interactive Learning Environments, 8* (2), 87-109.

Kintsch, W. (1998). *Comprehension: A paradigm for cognition.* New York: Cambridge University Press.

Kintsch, W. (2000). Metaphor comprehension: A computational theory. *Psychonomic Bulletin & Review, 7* (2), 257-266.

Kintsch, W., & Vipond, D. (1979). Reading comprehension and readability in educational practice and psychological theory. In L. G. Nilsson (Eds.), *Perspectives on memory research.* Hillsdale, NJ: Lawrence Erlbaum Associates.

Kollberg, P. (1998). *S-notation – a computer-based method for studying and representing text composition.* Licentiate thesis, TRITA-NA-P9808, IPLab-145, Department of Numerical Analysis and Computing Science, Royal Institute of Technology, Stockholm.

Kollberg, P., Kim, H.-C., & Severinson Eklundh, K. (October 1996). *Trace-it: An interactive tool for revision analysis.* Paper presented at the 1996 European Writing Conference, Barcelona, Universitat de Barcelona.

Kollberg, P., Lindgren, E., & Sullivan, K. P. H. (September, 2000). *Coupling progression analysis with revision details to study foreign language writing.* Abstracts of Eurosla-10, Krakow, Poland.

Kowal, S. & O'Connell, D. C. (1987). Writing as language behaviour: myths, models, methods. In A. Matsuhashi (Ed.), *Writing in real time. Modelling production processes* (pp. 108-133). Norwood, NJ: Ablex.

Laham, D. (2000). *Automated content assessment of text using Latent Semantic Analysis to simulate human cognition.* Doctoral Dissertation, University of Colorado, Boulder.

Laham, D., Bennett, W. & Landauer, T. (2000). An LSA-based software tool for matching jobs, people, and instruction, *Interactive Learning Environments, 8* (3), 171-185.

Lambert, E. (1999). *Ecrire des mots: La syllabe comme unité de traitement [Writing words: The syllable as a processing unit].* Unpublished doctorale dissertation. Université de Poitiers, France.

Landauer, T. K., & Dumais, S. T. (1997). A solution to Plato's problem: The Latent Semanctic Analysis theory of the acquisition, induction, and representation of knowledge. *Psychological Review, 104,* 11-140.

Landauer, T. K, Foltz, P. W., & Laham, D. (1998). An introduction to Latent Semantic Analysis. *Discourse Processes, 25 (2&3),* 259-284.

Landauer, T. K., Laham, D., & Foltz, P. W. (2000). The Intelligent Essay Assessor. *IEEE Transactions in AI, Issues and Controversies. November,* 27-31.

Landauer, T. K., & Psotka, J. (2000). Simulating text understanding for educational applications with Latent Semantic Analysis: Introduction to LSA. *Interactive Learning Environments, 8* (2), 73-86.

Lea, J. D. (1998). *Verbal and visuo-spatial processing demands in writing.* Unpublished doctoral dissertation. University of Florida.

Levelt, W. J. M. (1983). Monitoring and self-repairs in speech. *Cognition, 14,* 41-104.

Levelt, W. J. M. (1989). *Speaking: From intention to articulation.* Cambridge: MIT Press.

Levelt, W. J. M., Roelofs, A., & Meyer, A. S. (1999). A theory of lexical access in speech production. *Behavioral and Brain Sciences, 22,* 1-75.

Levelt, W. J. M., Schriefers, H., Vorberg, D., Meyer, A. S., Pechmann, T., & Havinga, J. (1991). The time course of lexical access in speech production: A study of picture naming. *Psychological Review, 98,* 122-142.

Levy, C. M. (1997). The 'R' that psychology forgot: Research on writing processes. *Behavior Research Methods, Instruments, and Computers, 29,* 137-145.

Levy, C. M., Marek, J. P., & Lea, J. (1995). *The reliability and validity of retrospective protocols in writing research.* Unpublished manuscript.

Levy, C. M., Marek, J. P., & Lea, J. (1996). Concurrent and retrospective protocols in writing research. In G. Rijlaarsdam, H. van den Bergh, & M. Couzijn (Eds.), *Writing research: Theories, models and methodology* (pp. 542-556). Amsterdam: Amsterdam University Press.

Levy, C. M., Ragosta, J., White, K., Lee, J., & Ransdell, S. E. (July, 1998). Testing Kellogg's multicomponent model of working memory and writing automaticity in the execution process. Paper presented at the 1998 European Writing Conference, Poitiers, France.

Levy, C. M., & Ransdell, S. E. (1994). Computer-aided protocol analysis of writing processes. *Behavior Research Methods, Instruments, & Computers, 26,* 219-223.

Levy, C. M., & Ransdell, S. E. (1995). Is writing as difficult as it seems? *Memory and Cognition, 23,* 767-779.

Levy, C. M., & Ransdell, S. E. (Eds.) (1996a). *The science of writing: Theories, methods, individual differences and applications.* Mahwah, NJ: Lawrence Erlbaum Associates.

Levy, C. M., & Ransdell, S. E. (1996b). Writing signatures. In C. M. Levy & S. Ransdell (Eds.), *The science of writing. Theories, methods, individual differences and applications* (pp. 149-161). Mahwah, NJ: Lawrence Erlbaum Associates.

Levy, C. M., White, K., Lea, J., & Ransdell, S. E. (July, 1998). *The role of the visuo-spatial scratchpad in writing: Testing Kellogg's multicomponent model.* Paper presented at the 1998 Writing Conference, Poitiers, France.

Lindgren, E., & Sullivan, K. P. H. (September, 2000). *The Lindgren-Sullivan graph: A methodology to present L2 writing revision.* Paper presented at the Second Language Research: Past, Present and Future, Madison, Wisconsin, USA.

Lindgren, E., & Sullivan, K. P. H. (in press). Self-assessment in autonomous computer aided L2 writing. *The English Language Teaching Journal.*

Lounsbury, F. G. (1954). Transitional probability, linguistic structure and systems of habit-family hierarchies. In C. E. Osgood & T. Sebeok (Eds.), *Psycholinguistics: a survey of theory and research problems* (pp. 88-126). Bloomington: Indiana University Press.

Luria, A. R. (1970). *Traumatic aphasia.* The Hague: Mouton.

Marek, P., & Levy, C. M. (October, 1996). *The role of working memory in writing processes and performance: II. Evaluation of formulating, monitoring and execution processes.* Paper presented at the 1996 European Conference on Writing and Computers, Barcelona, Spain.

Martin, R. C., Wogalter, M. S., & Forlano, J. G. (1988). Reading comprehension in the presence of unattended speech and music. *Journal of Memory & Language, 27,* 382-398.

Martlew, M. (1983). Problems and difficulties: Cognitive and communicative aspects of writing. In M. Martlew (Ed.), *The psychology of written language* (pp. 295-333). New York: John Wiley & Sons.

Matsuhashi, A. (1981). Pausing and planning: The tempo of written discourse production. *Research in the Teaching of English, 15,* 113-134.

Matsuhashi, A. (1987). Revising the plan and altering the text. In A. Matsuhashi (Ed.), *Writing in real time - Modelling production processes* (pp. 197-223). Norwood, NJ: Ablex Publishing Company.

McCutchen, D. (1996). A capacity theory of writing: Working memory in composition. *Educational Psychology Review, 8* (3), 299-325.

McCutchen, D., Covil, A., Hoyne, S.H., & Midles, K. (1994). Individual differences in writing: Implications of translating fluency. *Journal of Educational Psychology, 86,* 256-266.

McNamara, D. S., Kintsch, E., Songer B. N., & Kintsch, W. (1996). Are good texts always better? Interactions of text coherence, background knowledge, and levels of understanding in learning from text. *Cognition and Instruction, 14* (1), 1-44.

Meyer, A. S., & Schriefers, H. (1991). Phonological facilitation in picture-word interference experiments: Effect of stimulus onset asynchrony and types of interfering stimuli. *Journal of Experimental Psychology: Learning, Memory, and Cognition, 17,* 1146-1160.

Monahan, B. D. (1984). Revision strategies of basic and competent writers as they write for different audiences. *Research in the Teaching of English, 18,* 289-304.

Moray, N. (1959). Attention in dichotic listening. *Quarterly Journal of Experimental Psychology, 11,* 56-60.

Navon, D. (1984). Resources: A theoretical soup stone? *Psychological Review, 91,* 216-234.

Navon, D., & Gopher, D. (1979). On the economy of the human-information processing system. *Psychological Review, 86,* 214-255.

Negro, I., Levy, C. M., & Chanquoy, L. (September, 2000). *Subject-verb agreement errors: Effect of working memory load in English.* Paper presented at the EARLI SIG Writing Conference 2000, Verona, Italy.

Newell, A., & Simon, A, (1972). *Human problem solving.* Englewood Cliffs, NJ: Prentice-Hall.

Nilsson, M., & Kollberg, P. (1994). *Trace-it 2.0 user's manual,* IPLab, Department of Numerical Analysis and Computing Science, Royal Institute of Technology (KTH), Stockholm.

O'Connell, D. C., & Kowal, S. (1983). Pausology. In W. A. Sedelow & S.Y. Sedelow (Eds.), *Computers in language research: Part I. Formalization in literary and discourse analysis* (pp. 221-301). Berlin: Mouton.

Olive, T. (1997). Validité de la méthode de temps de réaction et de rétrospection dirigée pour étudier la production de texte [Validity of the method of reaction time and directed retrospection for studying text production]. *Informations in Cognito, 9,* 19-30.

Olive, T., Piolat, A., & Polge, M. (August, 1997). *An evaluation of mental effort of professional and experienced writers during the use of a word processor.* Graphic presentation at the 7th European Conference for Research on Learning and Instruction, Athens, Greece.

Olive, T., Piolat, A., & Roussey, J.-Y. (1997a). Effort cognitif et mobilisation des processus: Effet de l'habileté rédactionnelle et du niveau de connaissances [Cognitive effort and mobilisation of the writing processes: Effect of writing skill and of the level of knowledge]. In D. Mellier & A. Vom Hofe (Eds.), *Attention et contrôle cognitif: Mécanismes, développement des habiletés et pathologies [Attention and cognitive control: mechanisms, skill development and pathologies]* (pp. 71-85). Rouen: Presses Universitaires de Rouen.

Olive, T., Piolat, A., & Roussey, J.Y. (1997b). The effect of expertise and knowledge on cognitive effort associated to writing processes. In J.L. Rodriguez Illera & L. Tolchinsky (Eds.), CD-Rom *Proceedings of the 1996 European Writing Conferences*. Barcelona: ICE Universitat of Barcelona.

Olive, T., Roussey, J., Piolat, A., & Amada, M. (September, 2000). *Text revision and cognitive demands.* Paper presented at the Writing Conference 2000, Verona, Italy.

Pélissier, A., & Piolat, A. (July, 1998). *Are writing processes activated sequentially or in parallel? The appropriate way to use Kellogg's triple task method.* Paper presented at the 1998 European Writing Conferences, Poitiers, France.

Penningroth, S. L., & Rosenberg S. (1995). Effects of a high information processing load on the writing process and the story written. *Applied Psycholinguistics, 16,* 189-210.

Perrin, D. (1997a). *Journalistische Schreibstrategien optimieren [Optimizing strategies in journalistic writing].* Doctoral dissertation of the University of Bern. [Online: www.cx.unibe.ch/imw/strate.pdf].

Perrin, D. (1997b). Kompressionsfaktor 100. Strategien journalistischer Textproduktion optimieren. [Compression factor 100. Optimizing the strategies of journalistic text production]. In K. Adamzik, G.Antos & E.M. Jakobs, (Eds), *Domänen- und kulturspezifisches Schreiben. [Domain and culture specific writing]* (pp. 167-202). Frankfurt: Lang.

Perrin, D. (1999a). Warum es plötzlich 'läuft'. Schreibprozessdiagnostik im journalistischen Schreiben [Why it suddenly 'works.' Diagnostics in the writing process of journalistic writing]. In O. Kruse, E.M. Jakobs & G. Ruhmann (Eds.), *Schlüsselkompetenz Schreiben: Konzepte, Methoden, Projekte für Schreibberatung und Schreibdidaktik an der Hochschule [Key competence writing. Plans, methods, projects for writing advice and writing didactics at university]* (pp 73-93). Neuwied: Luchterhand.

Perrin, D. (1999b). Woher die Textbrüche kommen. Der Einfluss des Schreibprozesses auf die Sprache im Gebrauchstext [Where the breaks in the text come from. The influence of the writing process on the language in the utility text]. *Zeitschrift für Deutsche Sprache, 2/99,* 134-155.

Perrin, D. (2001a). 'Mit etwas Lustigem anfangen.' Prozedurale Grundmuster der Nachrichten-Dramaturgie ['Start with something funny'. Basic process patterns in news dramaturgy]. In U. Breuer & J. Korhonen (Eds.). *Mediensprache, Medienkritik [Media language, media criticism]* (pp. 55-68). Frankfurt: Lang.

Perrin, D. (2001b). *Schreiben ohne Reibungsverlust. Schreibcoaching für Profis. [Writing without friction. Coaching for professional writers].* Zürich: Werd. [http://www.schreibcoaching.com].

Perrin, D. (2001c, in press). *Wie Journalisten schreiben. [How journalists write].* Konstanz: UVK.

Peterson, R. R., & Savoy, P. (1998). Lexical selection and phonological encoding during language production: Evidence for cascade processing. *Journal of Experimental Psychology: Learning, Memory, and Cognition, 24,* 539-557.

Piolat, A., & Blaye, A. (1991). Effects of word processing and writing aids on revision processes. In M. Carretero, M. Pope, R. Simons & J.I. Pozo (Eds.). *Learning and instruction. European research in an international context. Vol. III* (pp. 379-399). Oxford: Pergamon Press.

Piolat, A., & Fruttero, L. (July, 1998). *Effects of memory span on cognitive load and composing strategies related to writing processes.* Graphic presentation at the meeting of the 1998 European Writing Conferences, Poitiers, France.

Piolat, A., & Olive, T. (2000). Comment étudier le coût et le déroulement de la rédaction de textes? La méthode de la triple tâche: Un bilan méthodologique [How to study the cost and unfolding of writing? A methodological assesment]. *L'Année Psychologique, 100,* 465-502.

Piolat, A., & Pélissier, A. (1998). Approche cognitive de la rédaction de textes: contraintes théoriques et méthodes de recherches [Cognitive approach of text composition: theoretical constraints and research methods]. In A. Piolat & A. Pélissier (Eds.). *La rédaction de texte. Approche cognitive [Text composition. Cognitive approach].* Neuchatel: Delachaux & Niestlé.

Piolat, A., & Pélissier, A. (Eds.) (1998). *La rédaction de textes: Approche cognitive [Text production: A cognitive approach].* Lausanne: Delachaux et Niestlé.

Piolat, A., Isnard, N., & Della Valle, V. (1993). Traitement de texte et stratégies rédactionnelles [Word processors and writing strategies]. *Le travail Humain, 56* (3), 79-99.

Piolat, A., Olive, T., Roussey, J.-Y., Thunin, O., & Ziegler, J. C. (1999). ScriptKell: A tool for measuring cognitive effort and time processing in writing and other complex cognitive activities. *Behavior Research Methods, Instruments, & Computers, 31* (1), 113-121.

Piolat, A., Roussey, J.-Y., Olive, T., & Farioli, F. (1996). Charge mentale et mobilisation des processus rédactionnels: examen de la procédure de Kellogg [Mental load and mobilisation of the writing processes: test of Kellogg's procedure]. *Psychologie Française, 41,* 339-354.

Piolat, A., Roussey, J.-Y., & Rous, P. (October, 1996). *Effects of attention directed to different texts on the mental effort related to writing processes*. Graphic presentation at the 1996 European Writing Conferences, Barcelone, Spain.

Power, M. J. (1986). A technique for measuring processing load during speech production. *Journal of Psycholinguistic Research, 15*, 371-382.

Ransdell, S. E. (1990). Using a real-time replay of students' word processing to understand and promote better writing. *Behavior Research Methods, Instruments, & Computers, 22*, 142-144.

Ransdell, S. E. (1995). Generating thinking-aloud protocols: Impact on the narrative writing of college students. *American Journal of Psychology, 108*, 89-98.

Ransdell, S. E., & Levy, C. M. (1996). Working memory constraints on writing quality and fluency. In C. M. Levy & S. E. Ransdell (Eds.). *The science of writing: Theories, methods, individual differences and applications* (pp. 93-105). Mahwah, NJ: Lawrence Erlbaum Associates.

Ransdell, S. E., & Levy, C. M. (1998). Writing, reading, and speaking memory spans and the importance of resource flexibility. In G. Rijlaarsdam (Series ed.) & G. C. Jeffery & M. Torrance (Vol. eds.), *Studies in Writing: Volume 3. Cognitive demands on writing* (pp. 99-133). Amsterdam: Amsterdam University Press.

Rapp, B., Benzing, L., & Caramazza, A. (1997). The autonomy of lexical orthography. *Cognitive Neuropsychology, 14*, 71-104.

Rescorla, R. A. & Wagner, A. R. (1972). A theory of Pavlovian conditioning: Variations in the effectiveness of reinforcement and non-reinforcement. In A. H. Black & W. F. Prokasy (Eds.), *Classical conditioning II* (pp. 64-99). New York: Appleton-Century-Crofts.

Rijlaarsdam, G., & van den Bergh, H.(1996a). The dynamics of composing – An agenda for research into an interactiv compensatory model of writing. Many questions, some anwers. In M. Levy & S. Ransdell (Eds.), *The science of writing*. (pp 107-125). Mahwah (NJ): Lawrence Erlbaum Associates.

Rijlaarsdam, G., van den Bergh, H., & Couzijn, M. (Eds.) (1996b). *Theories, models and methodology in Writing Research*. Amsterdam: Amsterdam University press.

Roediger, H. L., & McDermott, K. B. (1995). Creating false memories: Remembering words not presented in lists. *Journal of Experimental Psychology: Learning, Memory, and Cognition, 21*, 803-814.

Roelofs, A., Meyer, A. S., & Levelt, W. J. M. (1996). Interaction between semantic and orthographic factors in conceptually driven naming: Comment on Starreveld and La Heij (1995). *Journal of Experimental Psychology: Learning, Memory, and Cognition, 22*, 246-251.

Roussey, J.-Y. (1999). *Le contrôle de la rédaction de textes. Perspective cognitive [The control of text composition: Cognitive perspective]*. Habilitation à Diriger des Recherches. Université de Provence, France.

Russo, J. E., Johnson, E. J. & Stephens, D. L. (1989). The validity of verbal protocols. *Memory and Cognition, 17*, 759-769.

Salame, P., & Baddeley, A. D. (1982). Disruptions of short-term memory by unattended speech: Implications for the structure of working memory. *Journal of Verbal Learning and Verbal Behavior, 21*, 150-165.

Scardamalia, M., & Bereiter, C. (1986). Research on written composition. In M. Wittrock (Ed.), *Handbook of research on teaching* (pp. 778-803). New York: Mac Millan.

Schilperoord, J. (1996a). The distribution of pause time in written text production. In G. Rijlaarsdam, H. van den Bergh, & M. Couzijn (Eds.), *Theories, models and methodology: Current trends in research on writing* (pp. 21-37). Amsterdam: Amsterdam University Press.

Schilperoord, J. (1996b). *It's about time: Temporal aspects of cognitive processes in text production*. Amsterdam/Atlanta: Rodopi.

Schilperoord, J. (1997). Temporele modificatie in clauses; een pauze-analytische studie naar tekstproductie [Temporal modification in clauses; a pause-analytical study of text production]. In H. van den Bergh, D. Janssen, N. Bertens, & M. Damen (Eds.), *Taalgebruik ontrafeld [Unraveling language use]* (pp. 263-276). Dordrecht: Foris Publications.

Schilperoord, J. (2000). Pauses and hierarchical text structure: A study of discourse production processes. In T. Virtanen & I. Maricic (Eds.), *Perspectives on discourse* (pp. 37-60). Vaxjo: Vaxjo University Press.

Schilperoord, J. (2001). Linguistic and conceptual processes in text production: Integretative or autonomous? In T. Sanders, J. Schilperoord & W. Spooren (Eds.), *Text representation, linguistic and psycholinguistic aspects* (pp. 309-336). Amsterdam: Benjamins.

Schilperoord, J., & Janssen, D. (1993). De 'text produced so far' in het schrijfproces [The text produced so far in the writing process]. *Tijdschrift voor Taalbeheersing, 15*, 266-288.

Schilperoord, J., & Sanders, T. (1997). Pauses, cognitive rhythms and discourse structure; An empirical study of discourse production. In A. Liebert, G. Redeker & L. Waugh (Eds.), *Discourse and perspective in cognitive linguistics* (pp. 247-269). Amsterdam/Philadelphia: Benjamins,.

Schilperoord, J., & Sanders, T. (1999). How hierarchical text structure affects retrieval processes: Implications of pause and text analysis. In G. Rijlaarsdam (Series ed.) & M. Torrance & D. Galbraith (Vol. eds.), *Studies in Writing: Volume 4. Knowing what to write: Conceptual processes in text production* (pp. 13-31). Amsterdam: Amsterdam University Press.

Schilperoord, J., & Verhagen, A. (2001, in press). Grammar and language production: Where do function words come from? In J. Luchjenbroers (ed.).

Schriefers, H. (1993). Syntactic processes in the production of noun phrases. *Journal of Experimental Psychology: Learning, Memory, and Cognition, 19*, 841-850.

Schriefers, H., Meyer, A. S., & Levelt, W. J. M. (1990). Exploring the time-course of lexical access in language production: Picture-word interference studies. *Journal of Memory and Language, 29*, 86-102.

Schriefers, H., & Teruel, E. (1999). Phonological facilitation in the production of two-word utterances. *European Journal of Cognitive Psychology, 11*, 17-50.

Schumacher, G. M., Klare, G. K., Cronin, F. C., & Moses, J. D. (1984). Cognitive activities of beginning and advanced college writers: A pausal analysis. *Research in the Teaching of English, 18* (2), 169-187.

Severinson Eklundh, K. (1990). Global strategies in computer based writing: the use of logging data. In Ö. Dahl & K. Fraurud (Eds.), *Papers from the Second Nordic Conference on Text Comprehension in Man and Machine* (pp. 15-29). Stockholm: Stockholm University.

Severinson Eklundh, K. (1994). Linear and nonlinear strategies in computer-based writing. *Computers and Composition, 11*, 203-216.

Severinson Eklund, K., & Kollberg, P. (October, 1994). *Computer tools for tracing the writing process: From keystroke records to S-notation*. Paper presented at the EARLI/ECWC SIG-conference, Utrecht, The Netherlands.

Severinson Eklundh, K., & Kollberg, P. (1996a). A computer tool and framework for analysing on-line revisions. In C. M. Levy & S. Ransdell (Eds.), *The science of writing: Theories, methods, individual differences and applications* (pp. 163-188). Mahwah, NJ: Lawrence Erlbaum Associates.

Severinson Eklundh, K., & Kollberg, P. (1996b). Computer tools for tracing the writing process: from keystroke records to S-notation. In G. Rijlaarsdam, H. van den Bergh, & M. Couzijn (Eds.), *Current Research in Writing: Theories, models and methodology, Vol. 1* (pp. 526-541). Amsterdam: Amsterdam University Press,.

Severinson Eklundh, K., & Kollberg, P. (1999, in press). Emerging discourse structure: Computer-assisted episode analysis as a window to global revision in university students' writing. To appear in *Journal of Pragmatics*, Special issue edited by Daniel Perrin. Also available as Technical report TRITA-NA-P9904, IPLab-159, Department of Numerical Analysis and Computing Science, Royal Institute of Technology, Stockholm.

Smagorinsky, P. (Ed.) (1994). *Speaking about writing. Reflections on research methodology*. Thousand Oaks, CA: Sage Publications.

Starreveld, P. A. (2000). On the interpretation of onsets of auditory context effects in word production. *Journal of Memory and Language, 42*, 497-525.

Starreveld, P. A., & La Heij, W. (1995). Semantic interference, orthographic facilitation and their interaction in naming tasks. *Journal of Experimental Psychology: Learning, Memory and Cognition, 21*, 686-698.

Starreveld, P. A., & La Heij, W. (1996). The locus of orthographic-phonological facilitation: Reply to Roelofs, Meyer, and Levelt (1996). *Journal of Experimental Psychology: Learning, Memory, and Cognition, 22*, 1-4.

Stratman, J. F., & Hamps-Lyon, L. (1994). Reactivity in think-aloud protocols: Issues for research. In P. Smagorinsky, (Ed.), *Speaking about writing: Reflections of research methodology* (pp. 89-112). Thousand Oaks, CA: Sage Publications.

Sullivan, K. P. H., Kollberg, P., Severinson Eklundh, K., & Pålsson, E. (1997). L2 writing: A pilot investigation using key-stroke logging. In L. Díaz & C. Pérez (Eds.), *Views on the acquisition and use of a second language* (pp. 553-566). Barcelona, Spain: Universitat Pompeu Fabra.

Sullivan, K. P. H., Lindgren, E., & Kollberg, P. (September, 2000). *Writing FL at High-school: A comparison with L1 Swedish*. Paper presented at the Symposium on Second Language Writing, Purdue University, West Lafayette, Indiana, USA.

Swarts, H., Flower, L. S., & Hayes, J. R. (1984). Designing protocol studies of the writing process: An introduction. In R. Beach & L.S. Bridwell (Eds.), *New direction in composition research* (pp. 53-71). New York: The Guilford Press.

Vallar, G., & Baddeley, A. D. (1984). Fractionation of working memory: Neuropsychological evidence for a phonological short-term store. *Journal of Verbal Learning and Verbal Behavior, 23*, 151-161.

van Dijk, T. A. (1988). *News as discourse*. Hillsdale: Lawrence Erlbaum Associates.

van der Geest, T. (1996). Professional writing studied. Authors' accounts of planning in document production processes. In M. Sharples & T. van der Geest (Eds.), *The new writing environment. Writers at work in a world of technology* (pp. 7-24). London: Springer.

van der Pool, E. (1995). *Writing as a conceptual process. A text-analytical study of developmental aspects*. Doctoral dissertation, Tilburg University.

van Dijk, T. A., & Kintsch, W. (1983). *Strategies of discourse comprehension*. New York: Academic Press.

van Waes, L. (1991). *De computer en het schrijfproces. De invloed van de tekstverwerker op het pauze- en revisiegedrag van schrijvers [The computer in the writing process. The influence of the word processor on the pause and revision patterns of writers]*. Doctoral dissertation, Universiteit Twente, Netherlands.

van Waes, L. (1992). The influence of the computer on writing profiles. In H. P. Maat & M. Steehouder (Eds.), *Studies of functional text quality. Utrecht Studies in Language and Communication 1* (pp. pp.173-186). Amsterdam: Rodopi Publishers,

van Waes, L. & Schellens, P. J. (2001, in preparation). Writing profiles. The effect of the writing mode on pausing and revision patterns of experienced writers. In D. Perrin (Ed.), *The pragmatics of writing. Journal of Pragmatics. Special issue*.

Varnahagen, C. K. (1995). Children's spelling strategies. In V.W. Berninger (Ed.), *The varieties of orthographic knowledge II: Relationships to phonology, reading, and writing* (pp. 251-290). Dordrecht, The Netherlands: Kluwer Academic Publishers.

Voss, J. F., Vesonder, G. T., & Spilich, G. J. (1980). Text generation and recall by high-knowledge and low-knowledge individuals. *Journal of Verbal Learning & Verbal Behavior, 17*, 651-667.

Williamson, M. M., & Pence, P. (1989). Word processing and student writers. In B. K. Britton & S. M. Glynn (Eds.), *Computer writing environments: Theory, research, and design* (pp. 93-127). Hillsdale, NJ: Lawrence Erlbaum Associates.

Wilson, T. D. (1994). The proper protocol: Validity and completeness of verbal reports. *Psychological Science, 5* (5), 249-252.

Wolfe, M. B., Schreiner, M. E., Rehder, B., Laham, D., Foltz, P. W., Kintsch, W., & Landauer, T. K. (1998). *Learning from text: Matching readers and text by Latent Semantic Analysis*. Discourse Processes, *25* (2&3), 309-338.

Wrobel, A. (1995). *Schreiben als Handlung. Überlegungen und Untersuchungen zur Theorie der Textproduktion [Writing as action. Reflections and investigations in the text production theory]*. Tübingen: Niemeyer.

Yekovich, F. R., & Walker, C. H. (1986). Retrieval of scripted concepts. *Journal of Memory and Language, 25*, 627-644.

AUTHOR INDEX

SUBJECT INDEX

Studies in Writing

7. P. Tynjälä et al. (eds.): *Writing as a Learning Tool.* 2001
   ISBN HB 0-7923-6877-0; PB 0-7923-6914-9
8. L. Tolchinsky (ed.): *Developmental Aspects in Learning to Write.* 2001
   ISBN HB 0-7923-6979-3; PB 0-7923-7063-5
9. D. Alamargot and L. Chanquoy: *Through the Models of Writing.* 2001
   ISBN HB 0-7923-6980-7; PB 0-7923-7159-3
10. T. Olive and C.M. Levy (eds.): *Contemporary Tools and Techniques for Studying Writing.* 2001
    ISBN HB 1-4020-0035-9: PB 1-4020-0106-1

For Volumes 1 – 6 please contact Amsterdam University Press, at www.aup.nl

KLUWER ACADEMIC PUBLISHERS – DORDRECHT / BOSTON / LONDON

www.ingramcontent.com/pod-product-compliance
Ingram Content Group UK Ltd.
Pitfield, Milton Keynes, MK11 3LW, UK
UKHW020628120926
15112UKWH00034B/125
* 9 7 8 9 4 0 1 0 0 4 6 9 5 *